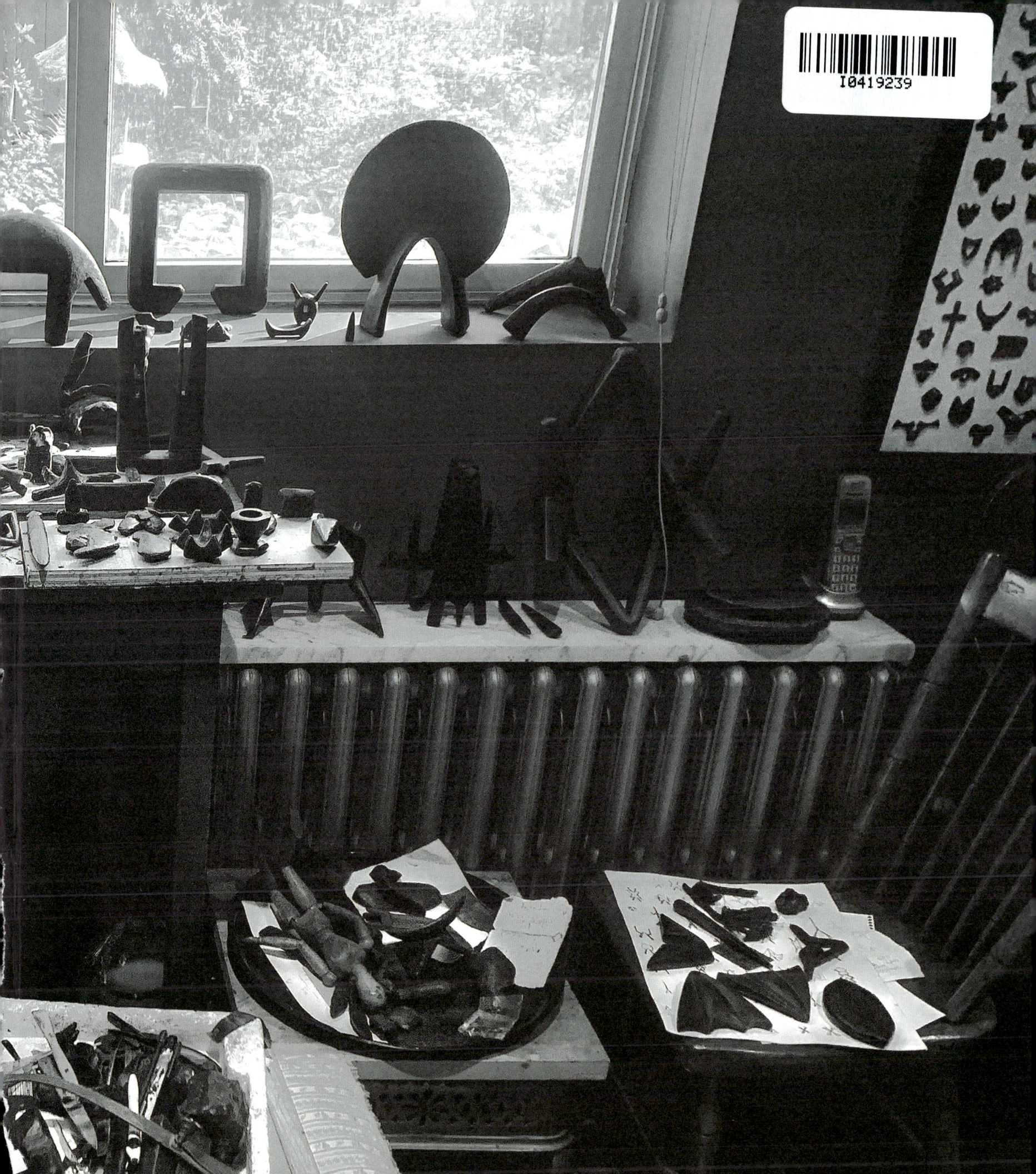

PETER DECAMP HAINES

PETER DECAMP HAINES

Sculpture, 1975–2024

Foreword by Murray Whyte

Essay by Belinda Rathbone

THE ARTIST BOOK FOUNDATION

North Adams, Massachusetts

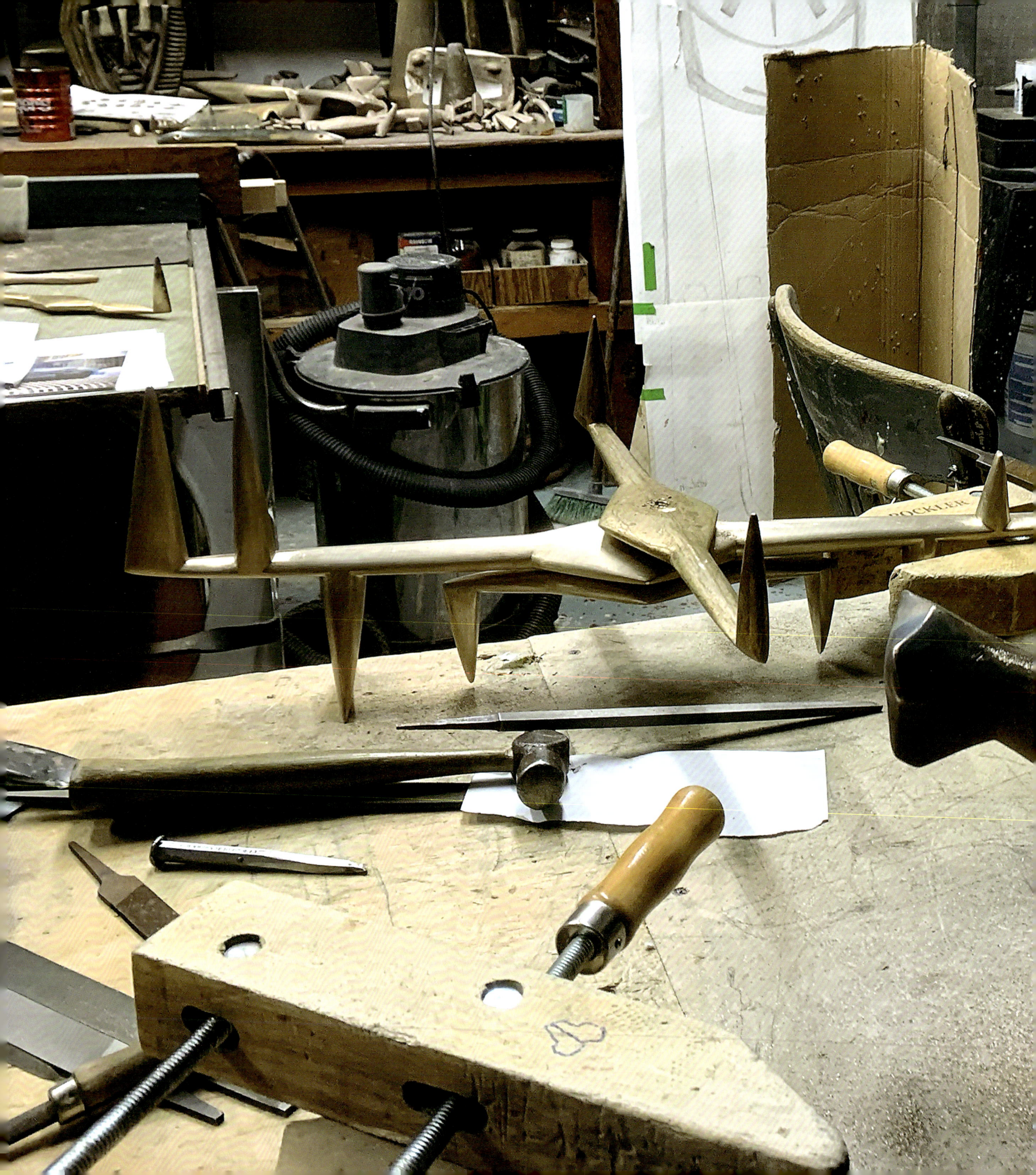

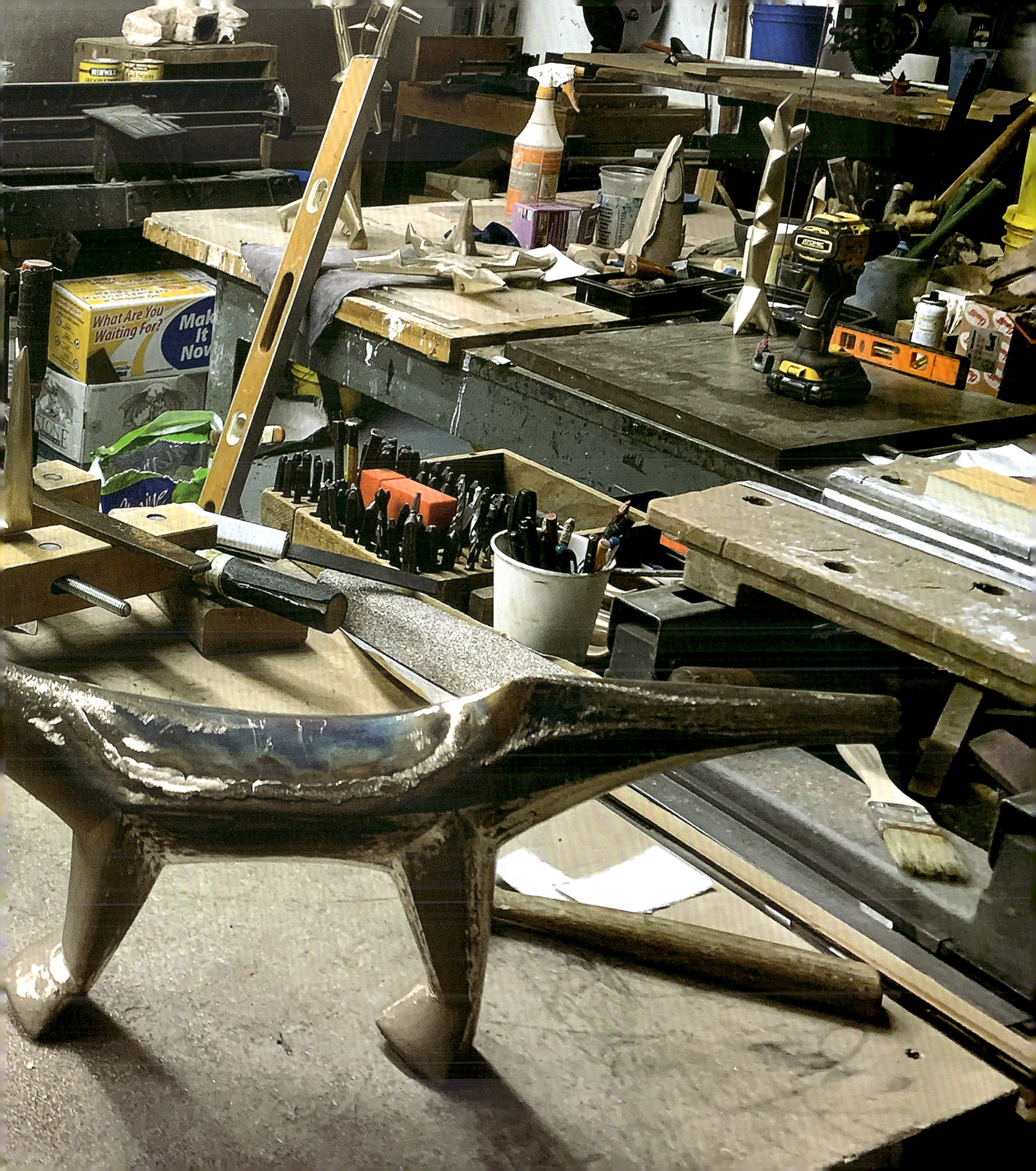

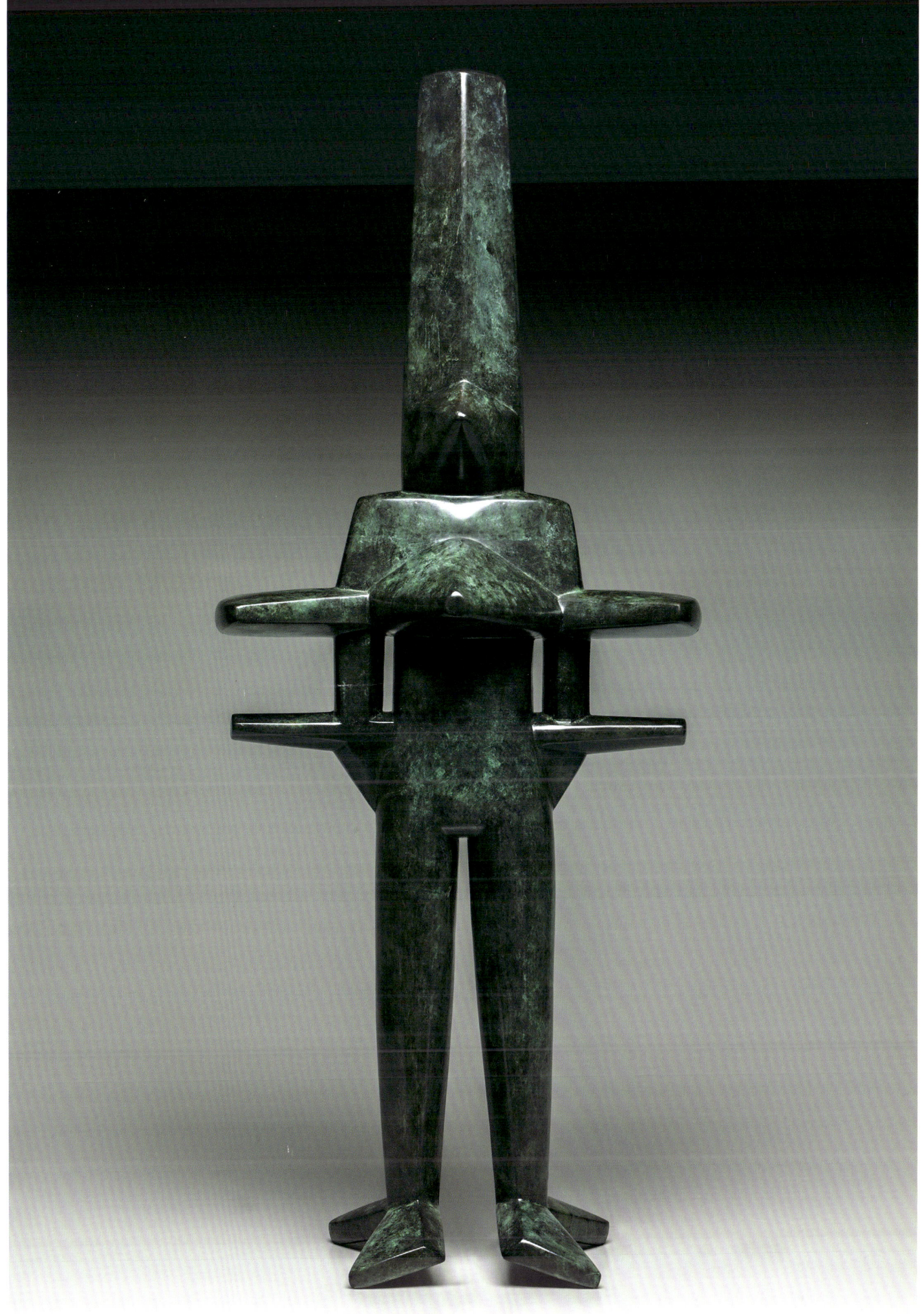

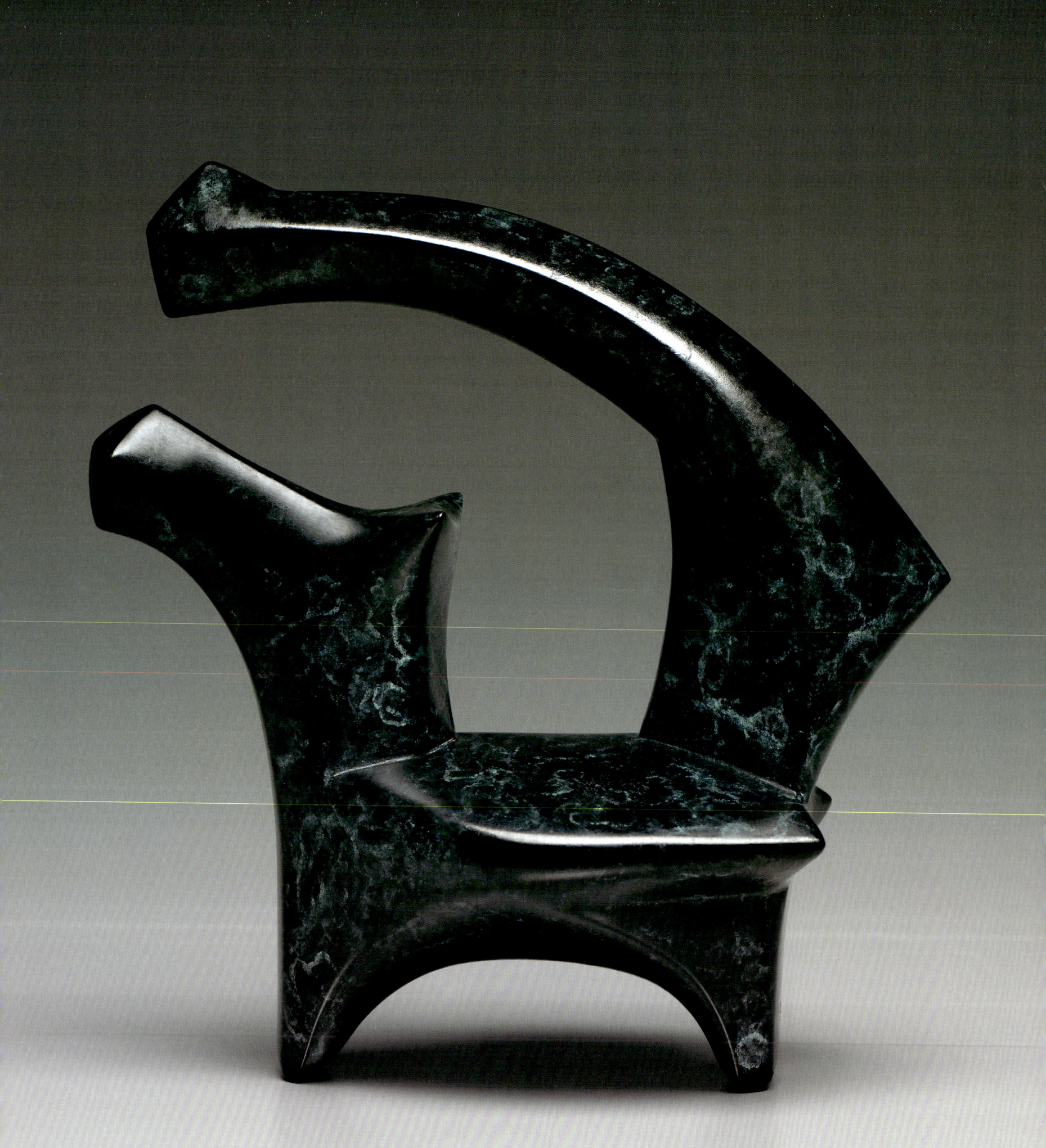

TABLE OF
CONTENTS

Abstraction

is a way to convey

the relationship

between man

and ancient

universal sources.

Isamu Noguchi

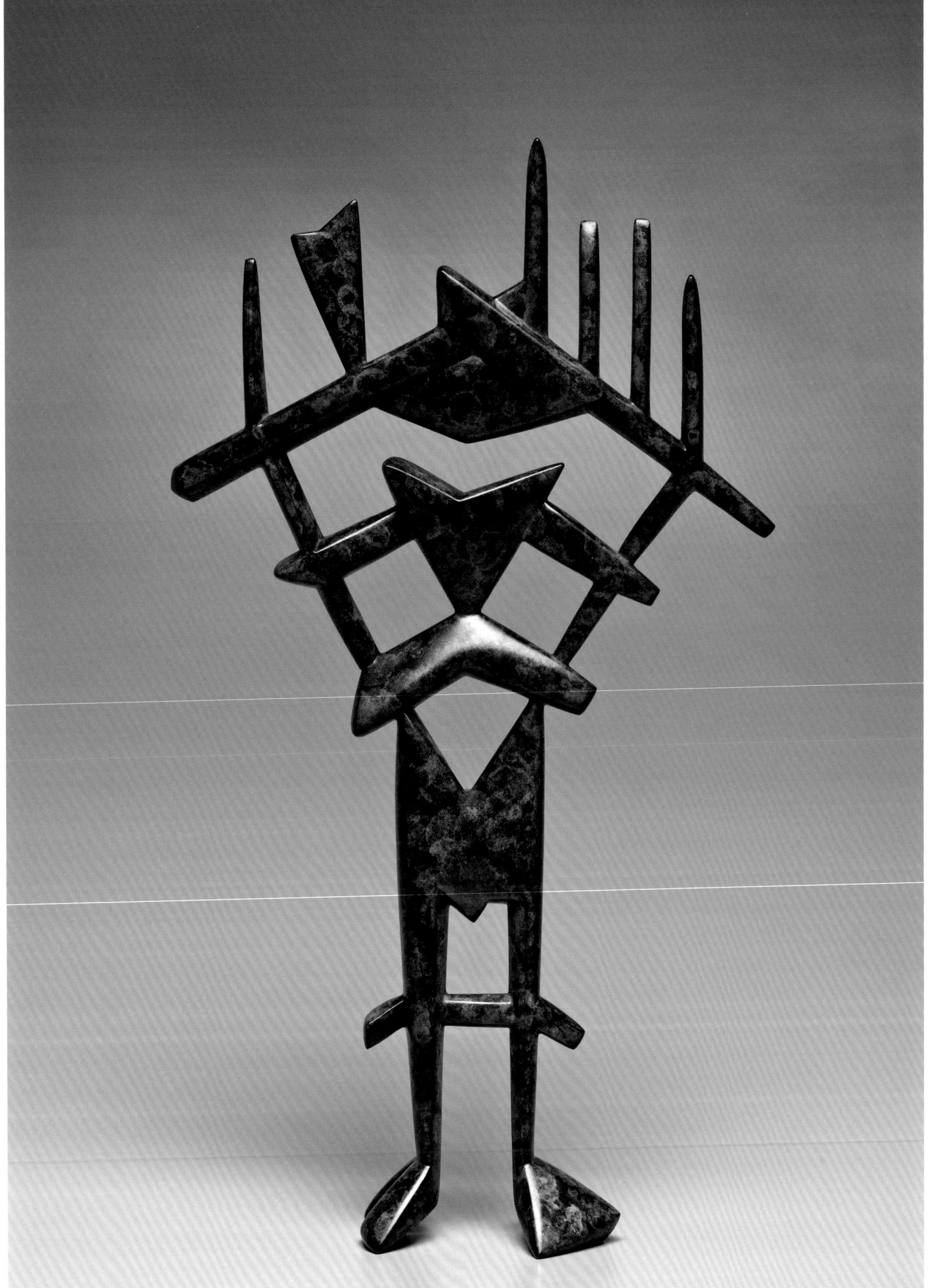

ARTIST
STATEMENT

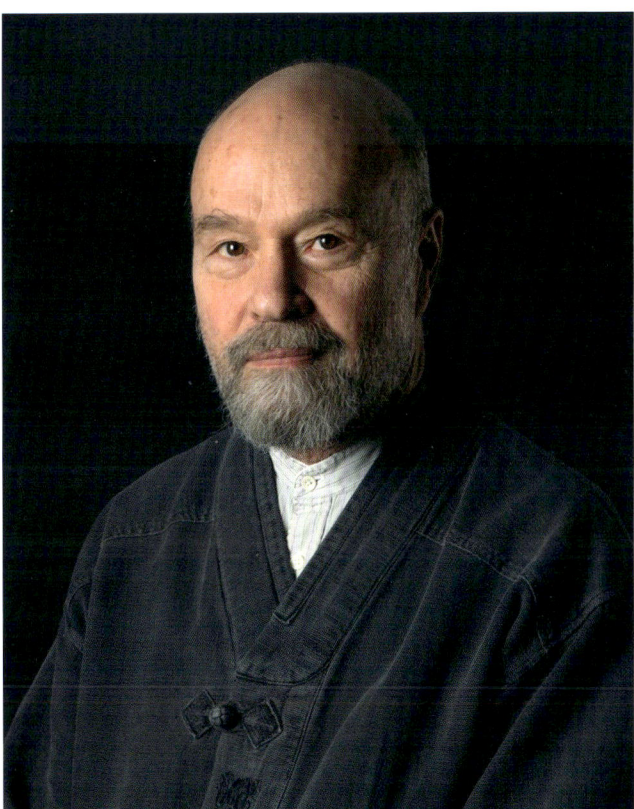

I am a maker of objects, and the object itself is the main idea in my sculpture.

Simple shapes elaborate into complexity. Images (humans, animals, architecture, tools) inevitably appear. I believe this is the projection of the warm subconscious onto the cool geometry of elemental forms. Since Marcel Duchamp introduced his Readymades in the 1910s, ideas about sculpture have proliferated in countless directions, from Andy Warhol to Nam June Paik. My own pursuit has been a continuing exploration of the formal attributes of Modernist sculpture: form, scale, negative space, composition. An advantage of sculpture is that ideas such as wholeness, timelessness, and beauty can be expressed without words. One of the elements of this wordless expression is negative space. A doughnut is defined by its hole. If one accepts space as part of the doughnut, where does the doughnut end? Thus, the doorways, windows, silhouettes of my sculptures can suggest an area larger than the sculpture itself.

For me, the process of sculpting is not the execution of a design. Rather, it is a search for shapes and images that appeal to my taste. From the miasma of a lump of wax, objects emerge as if seen in an inkblot or in the night sky. I refine and essentialize the sculptures with an eye to true form, negative space, and composition.

Imaginary Friend, 2020
Bronze
19⅝ x 10¹³/₁₆ x 3 in. (49.8 x 27.4 x 7.6 cm)
Collection of the artist

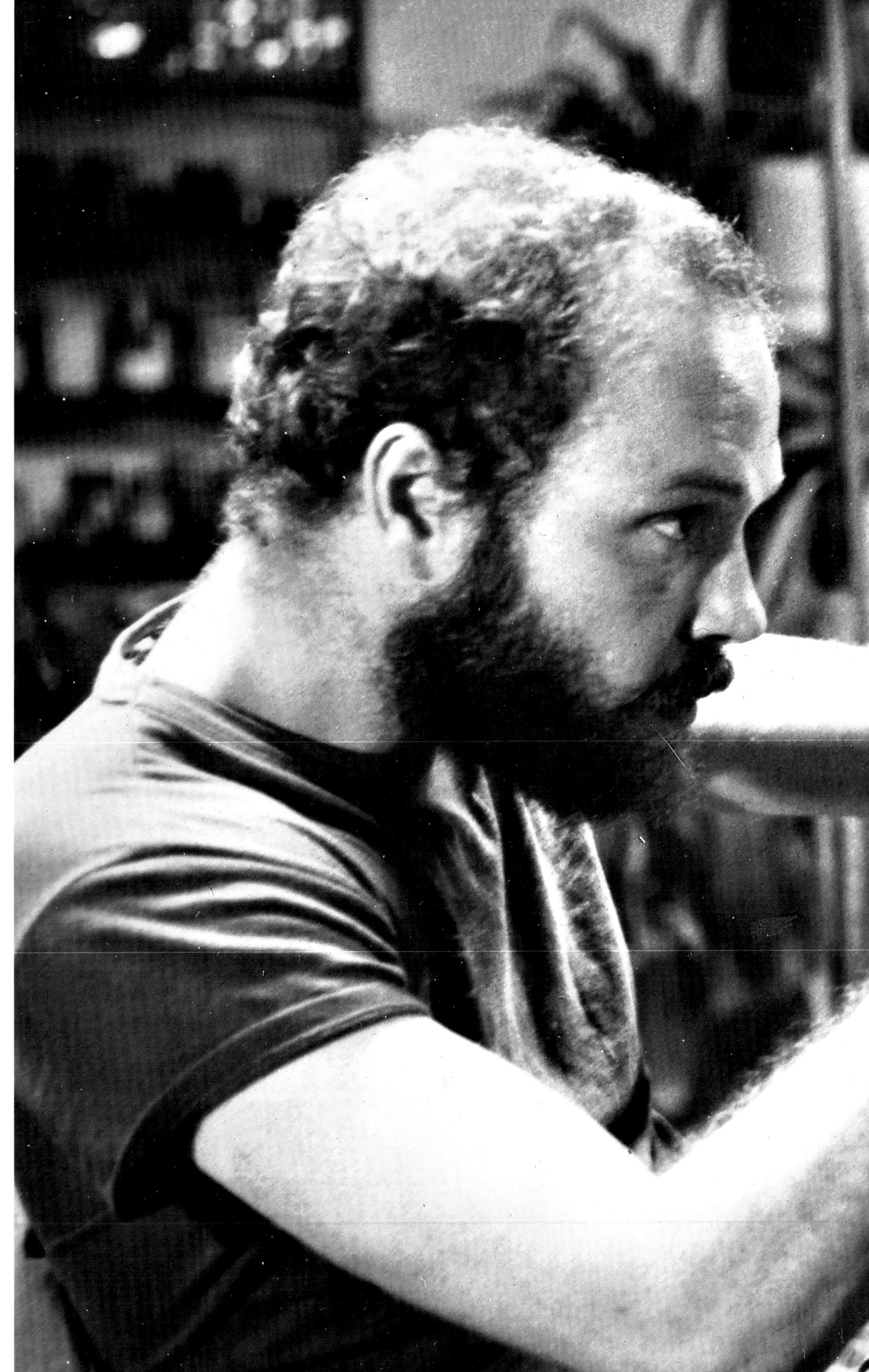

Peter in his studio, 1980

NEXT SPREAD
Snake Handlers, 1996
Bronze
10½ x 18⅜ x 5½ in. (26.7 x 46.5 x 14 cm)
Private collection

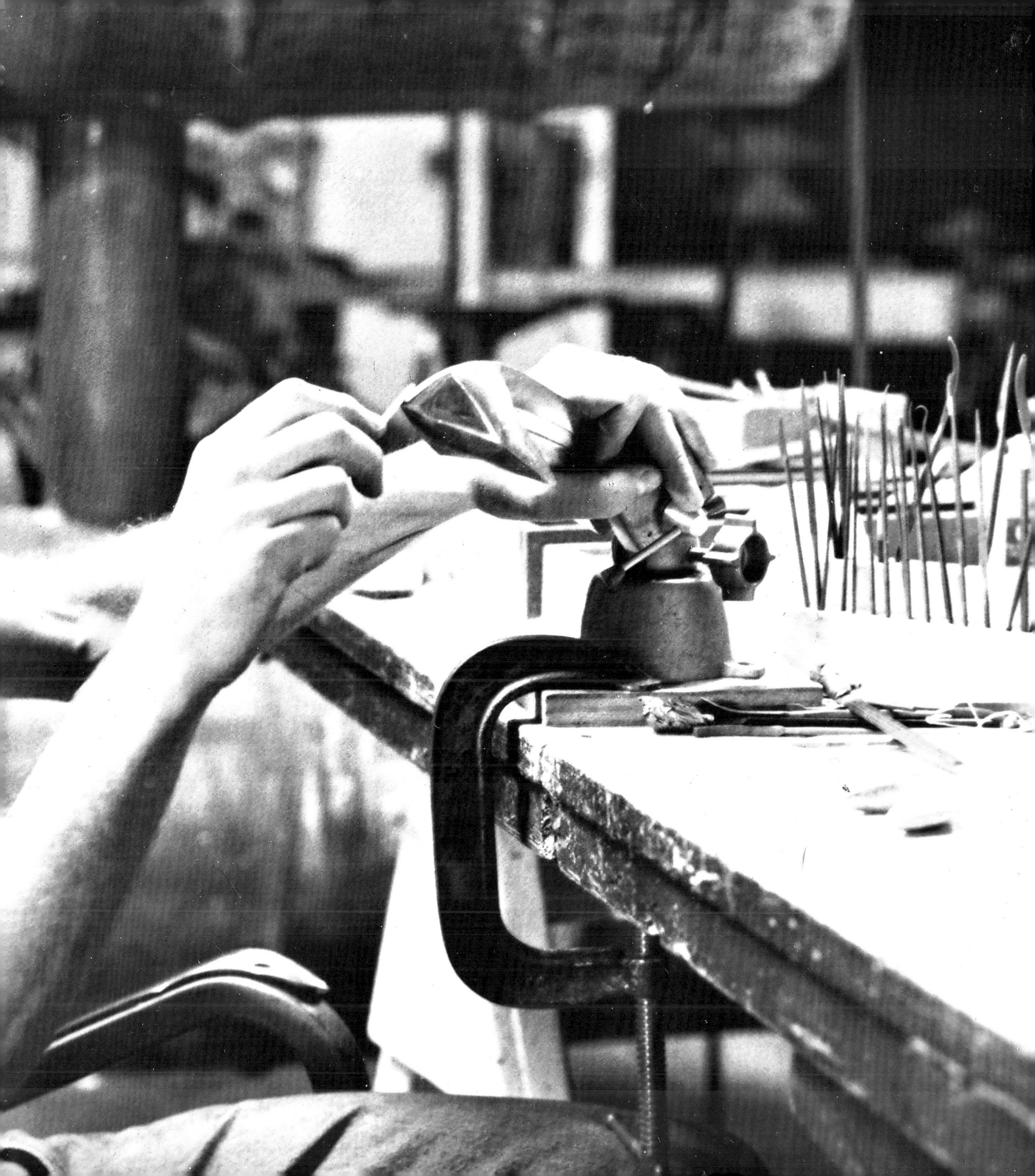

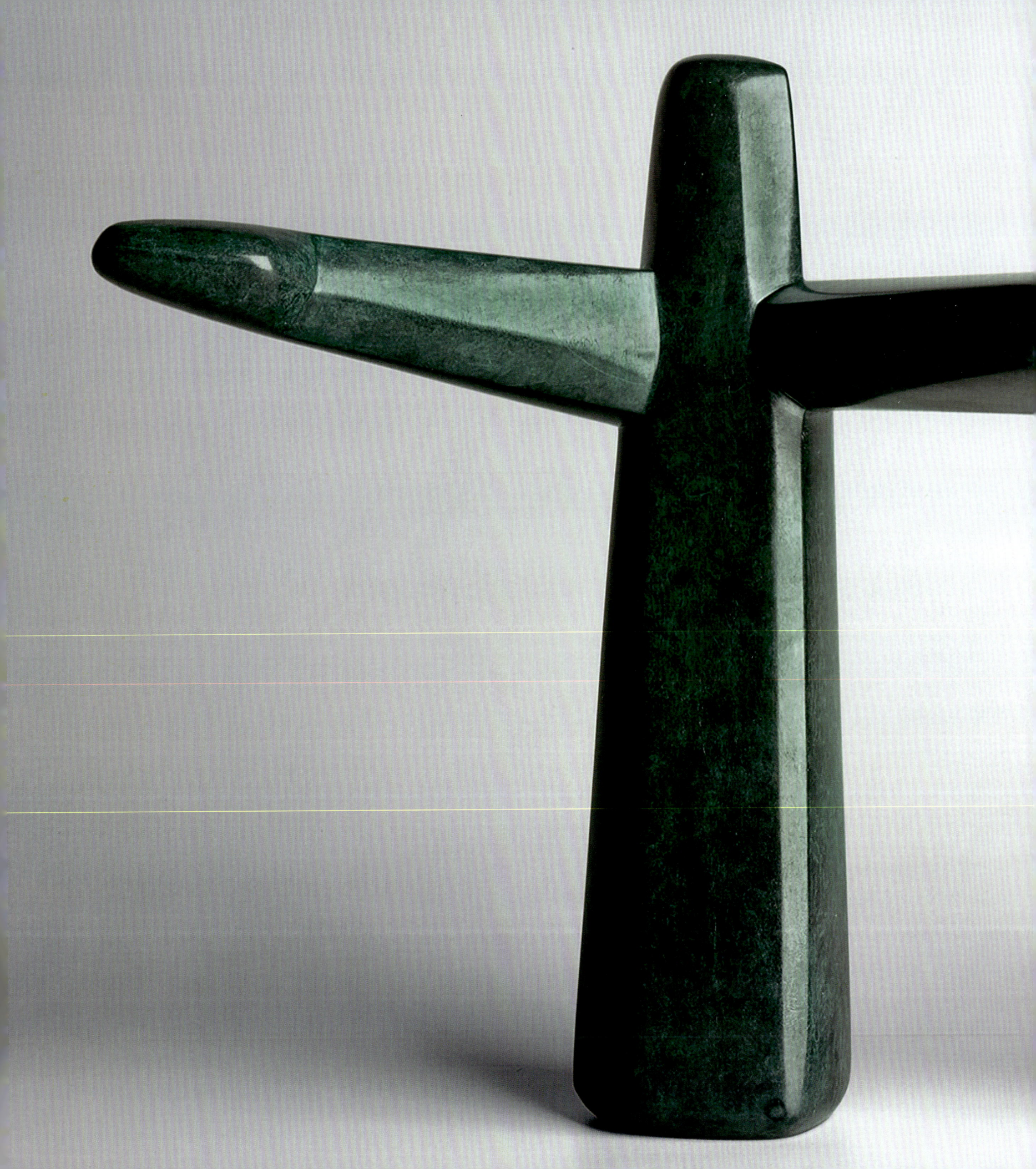

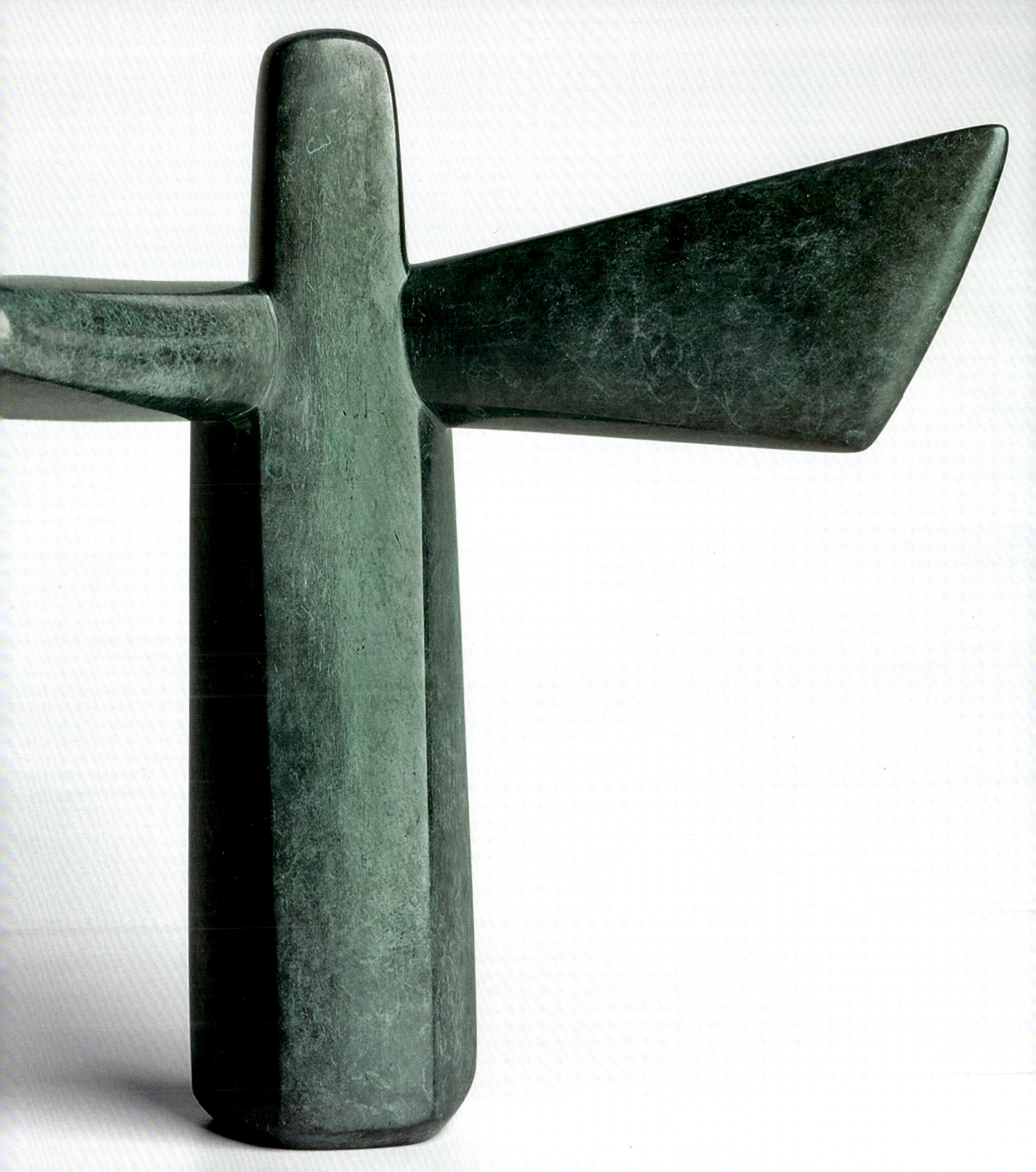

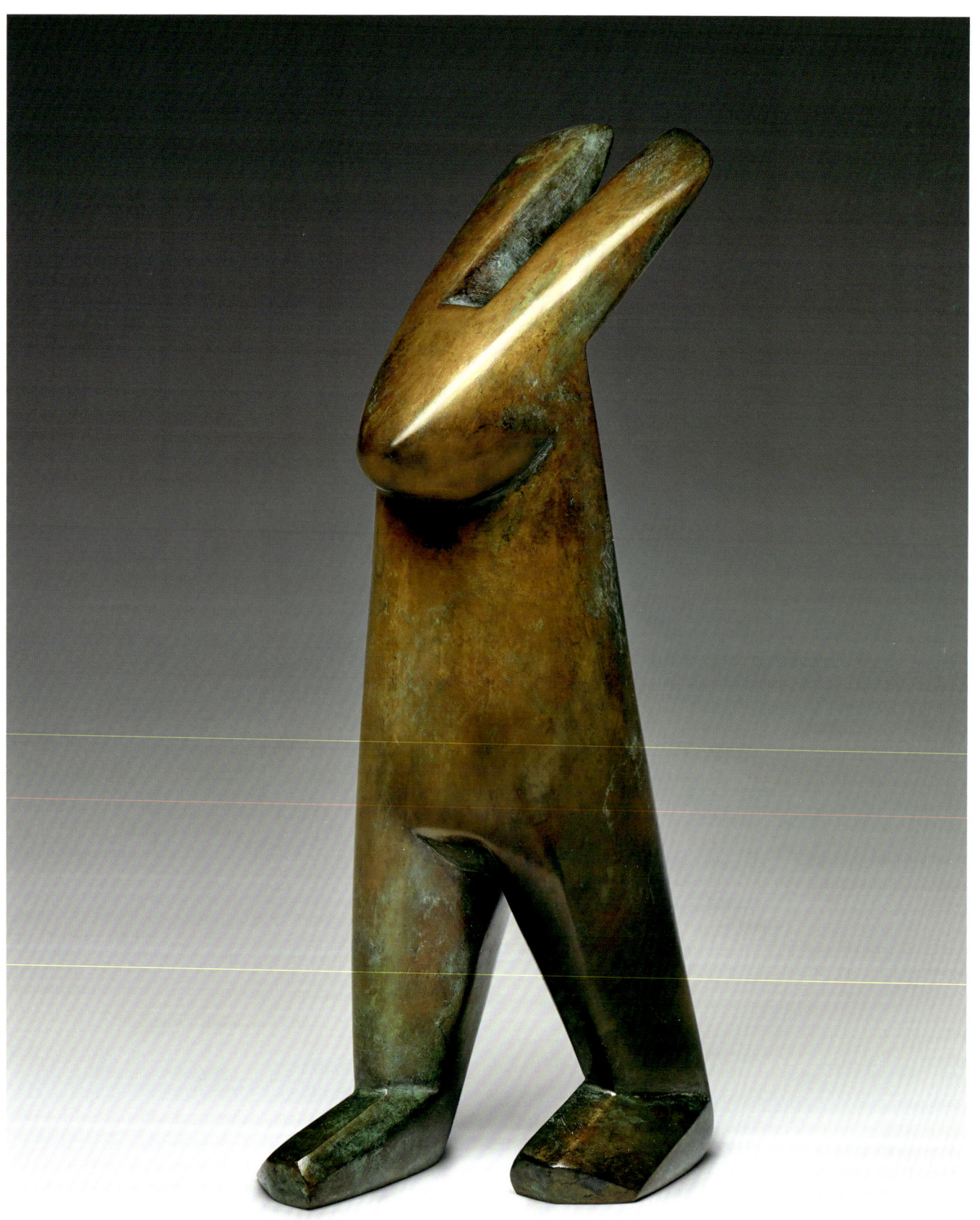

FOREWORD

Murray Whyte

In a scrubbed-up corner of Cambridgeport, tucked next to a commercial complex full of multibillion-dollar biotech firms, Peter DeCamp Haines's home and studio feels like a vestige of another time. That's at least partly because it is: when Haines first moved here, decades ago, the neighborhood was a down-on-its-luck post-industrial husk. Now, it's an evolving hub of an emergent economy that pivots on the monetization of the building blocks of life itself.

Haines's home is a powerful instrument by which to measure the change. With its capacious courtyard and generous interiors, here his children grew up and his sculptural practice evolved, side by side. It's where Haines's creative and emotional life grew and flourished as the city around him transformed, and a refuge where his art, and his life, could thrive safely insulated from those external upheavals. What happened out there is, in many ways, the counterpoint of what happened in here: time permitted to unfold as it should and not in the hurry-up mode that boomtowns increasingly demand.

Where an artist works—where an artist can work—matters. The relationship between artist and studio is an intimate one, almost familial, where ease and trust become the foundation of a creative practice. That's even more accurate in Haines's case, where home and work life blend seamlessly into one.

In the courtyard, broad and generously treed, his works in bronze and stone popu-late a rock garden; some, he told me, were an experiment begun but abandoned, left as a marker of an incomplete thought—the luxury of that space, that time, to allow a remarkable continuum of creative enterprise to exist side by side, all in constant conversation with one another.

Inside, Haines's soaring living space is a museum of the work of some of his favorite contemporaries amid the homey comforts of sofa, study, and kitchen; and an

Flaneur, 2017
Bronze
7⅜ x 3³⁄₁₆ x 2½ in. (18.8 x 8.1 x 6.3 cm)
Collection of the artist

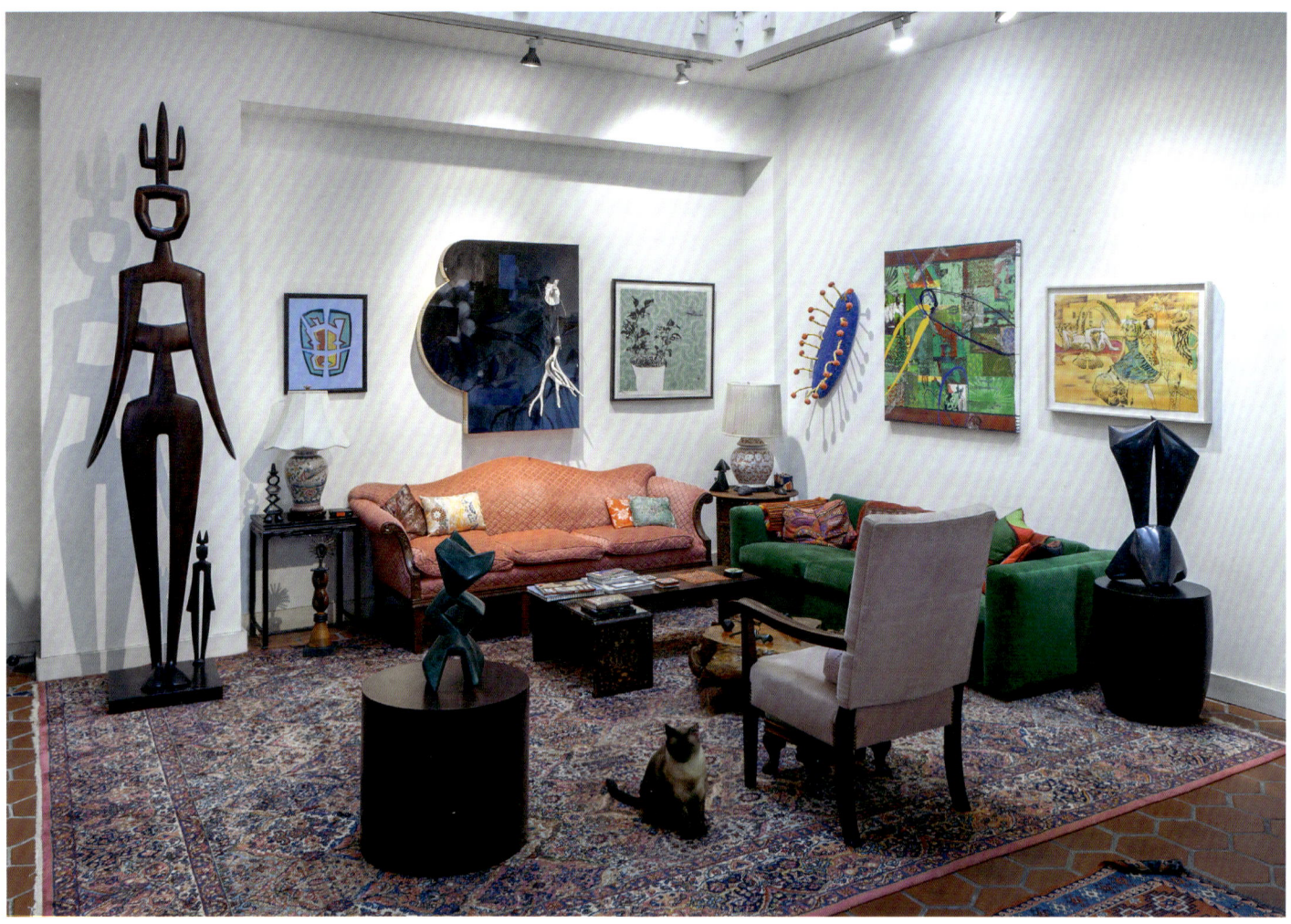

FIG. 1
Peter and Sekyo's home in Cambridge.
On the far left is Peter's carved mahogany
statue, *Princess*; Peter's beloved cat, Juno,
sits in the middle.

emblem not of clichéd artistic solitude but a convivial, creative life lived among a richness of community and intellectual exchange (fig. 1).

Haines's work is here, too, of course, host to the party, in all shapes and sizes—figures tall and spindly, made of wood; or tabletop pieces in bronze or stone, smoothed to a shine. They are all characters in the long-running drama of Haines's creative life, ever-present reminders of art not as the product of a moment, but a life in progress, ever-changing, each connected to the last.

These are the things that an artist's space can tell you about intention and process—things, perhaps, the artist himself feels more than knows. You can look at Haines's work, in so many scales and materials, and divine clear inspirational markers: the early Modernist abstract impulses of Constantin Brâncuşi; the amorphous figurative works of Henry Moore. Haines, though, departs from both more

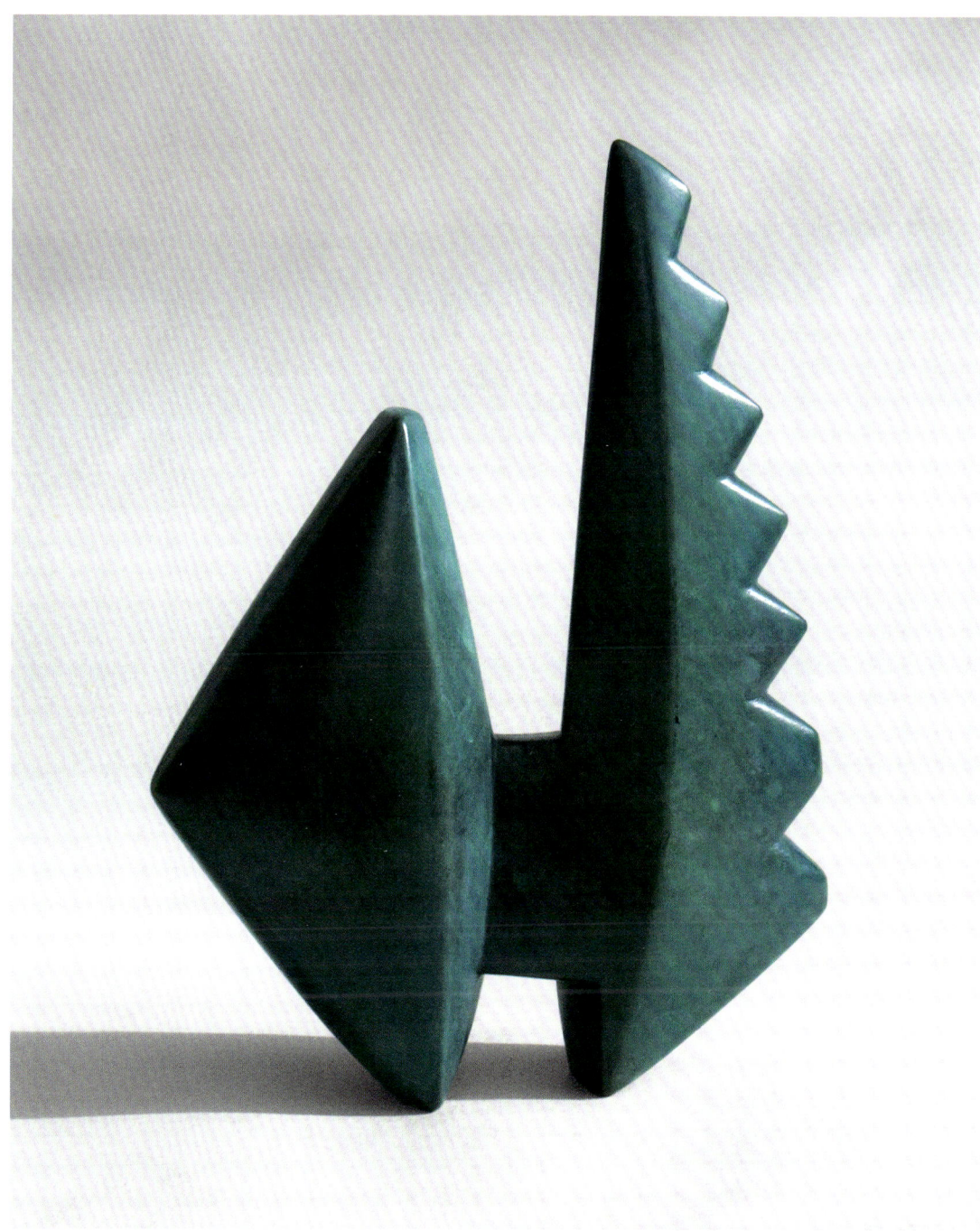

than derives from either. The inscrutable quest for formal purity that underpinned Brâncuşi's work is, in Haines's hands, a riddle to scrutinize and question (fig. 2); Moore's somber, tortured figuration, born of the artist's ghastly experiences in the London bombing raids of World War II, are replaced with what I can only describe as manifest joy.

FIG. 2

Brâncuşi Bird, 2009
Bronze
7 3/16 x 4 1/2 x 2 in. (18.3 x 11.4 x 5.1 cm)
Collection of the artist

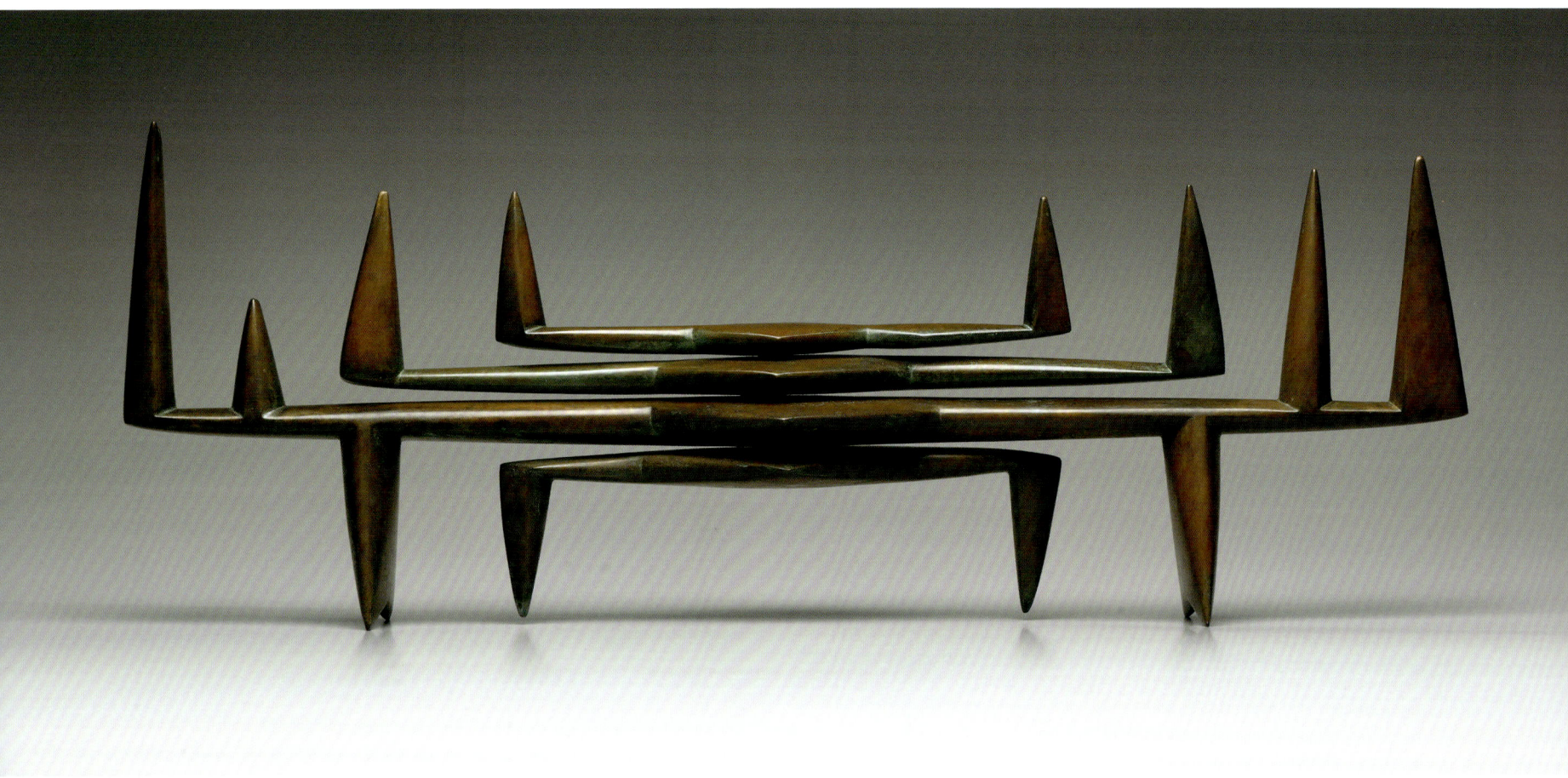

FIG. 3
Covid Summer, 2020
Bronze
9 3/16 x 25 5/16 x 4 5/16 in.
(23.4 x 64.3 x 11.4 cm)
Collection of the artist

Haines is a maker of exceptional skill; his finely honed surfaces in an array of materials are nothing short of masterful. Discipline, as the great American critic Gilbert Seldes once wrote, is what sets an artist free, and so Haines has been to pursue—and challenge—those towering legacies of art history entirely on his own terms.

His work is elegant and articulate, bending the strict rules of his Modernist forbears to his particular whims. There's a lightness, a joy, to Haines's art that I think mirrors his spirit. On my last visit, the soft daylight space above his workshop was clustered with an array of works on shelves that appeared as spiny alien creatures bursting with personality, or totemlike, rich and complex, as though from some unknown civilization.

Haines, wryly, gives nothing away: A spikey little bronze creature he titled *Covid Summer* (fig. 3) reveals only when it was made (2020); *Rooms with a View (2009)* (p. 84), also bronze, is a stack of soft-cornered squares burnished to a soft black, and belied my reading of it as a household spiritual idol.

Haines, surely, delves into notions of Primitivism, a high-Modernist building block that imagined a naive creative impulse that lived below conscious thought in ancient tribal cultures; a favorite book he showed me in the studio exploring the aesthetics of ancient stone tools was a clear touchstone in some of his own material explorations. But Haines is no literalist, and each of his works is built simultaneously with material fluency and an emotional richness that undermines—and indeed, rejects—hoary old notions of pure form and primal souls.

In this way, he pushes forward and past the strictures of that tradition. Many of his smaller works—hundreds, maybe more—are spontaneous iterations, the material leading the hand as much as the other way around, a principal joy of virtuosic ability following wood or metal or stone wherever it may lead; you can look at *100 Heads* (plate 69) to see what I mean.

But in the same breath, he refutes that practice as its own end and injects deft scrutiny to Modernism's essentialist doctrine. Haines dares to introduce to that time-honored tradition a sense of play, and joy; a congress of little bears (plate 64), for example, smatter the display of his work, positioned neither above nor below his more mysterious abstractions. They are elements of a practice that both reveres past pioneers and fast-held notions while refusing to be bound by them.

I'm drawn—because how could you not be?—to one piece in particular, *Flaneur*, a robustly handsome armless bunny, stood upright with a graceful swoop of line from its toes to the powerful arc of its ears (p. 18). It's Brâncuşian, intentionally so, I'll suggest, in the smooth sheen of its bronze hide; one might think for a moment of Brâncuşi's *Bird in Space*, an oblong arc of polished bronze, its title more intimation than descriptor.

Where Brâncuşi was opaque, Haines, instead is leading, inviting the imagination instead of confounding it. Haines's piece is an avatar of detached but generous observation, making space for a subjective view of the world by being within it (a flaneur, of course, is a solitary meanderer who quietly observes his or her surroundings from a distance). Its obvious charm aside, *Flaneur* is a piece that teases at inscrutable mystery, but lets its guard down and makes space for you.

In 2023, Haines held an exhibition at the Boston Sculptors Gallery, his longtime home for the public display of his work. The exhibition, *Archaic Echoes*, was either one piece, or hundreds, depending how you look at it; a broad tabletop featured *Archaeology of the Subconscious* (fig. 4), dozens of small objects in a breathtaking

NEXT SPREAD:
FIG. 4
Peter, his brother Chris, and his assistant Pedro installing *Archaeology of the Subconscious* at the Boston Sculptors Gallery, October 2024.

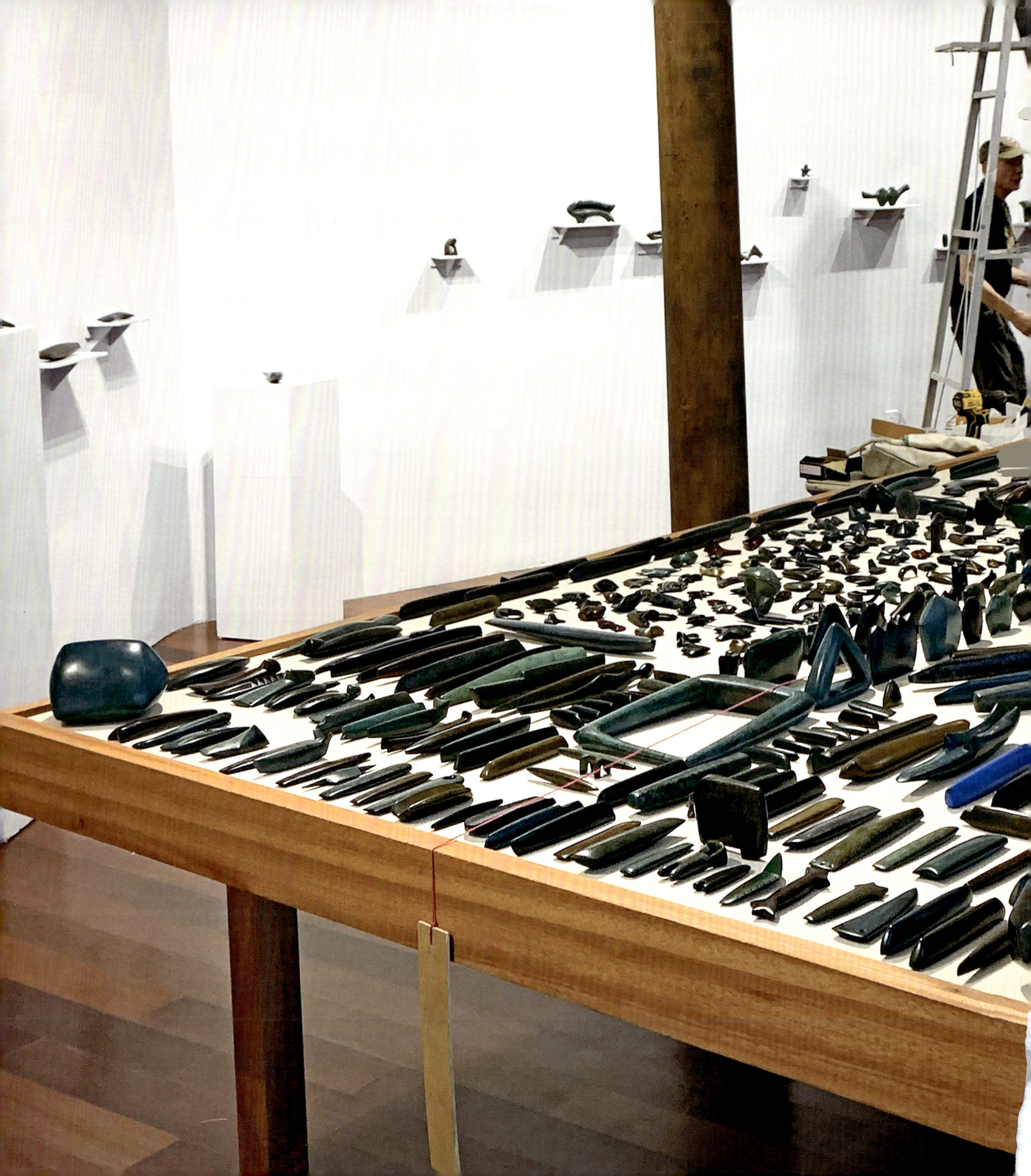

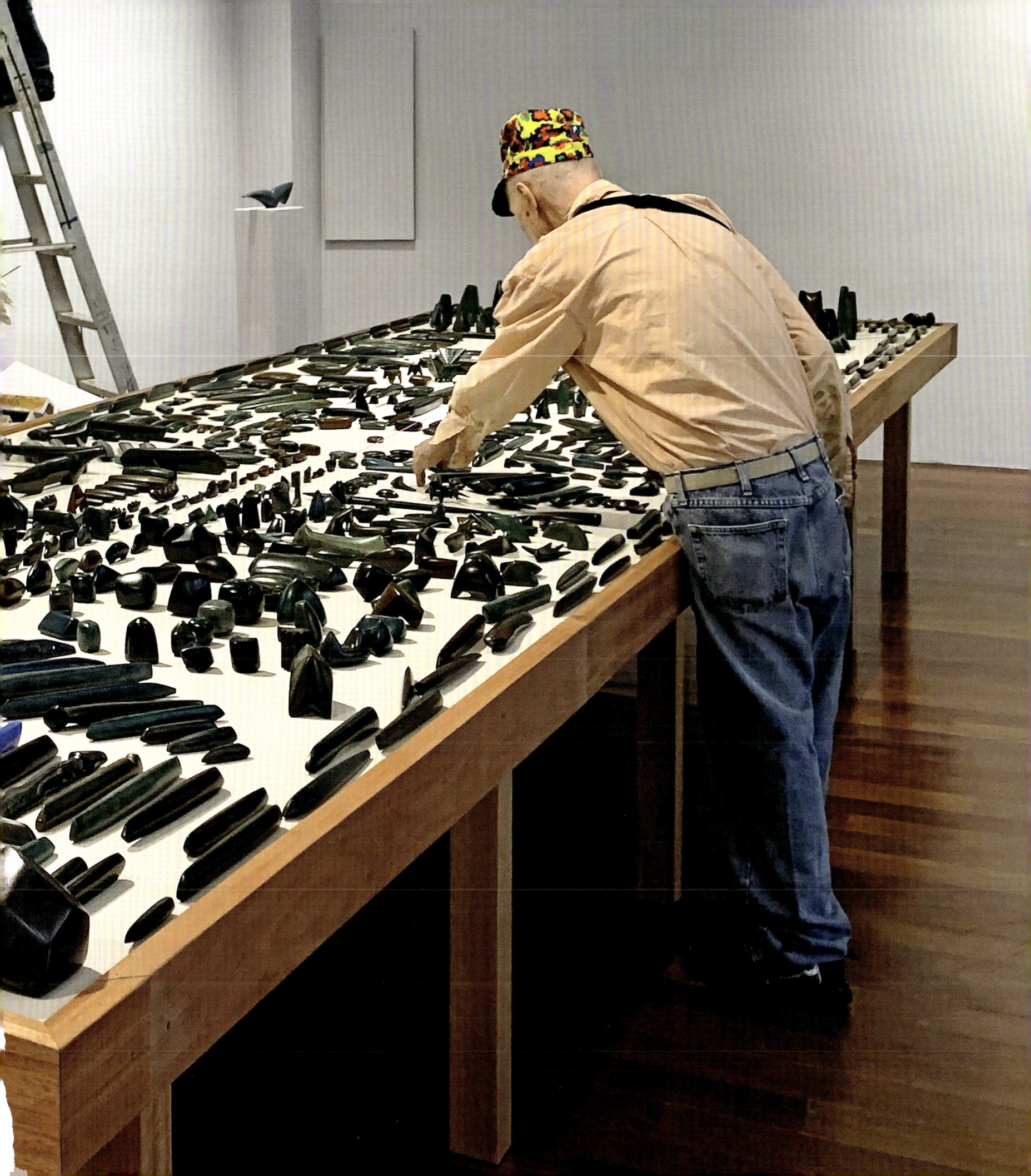

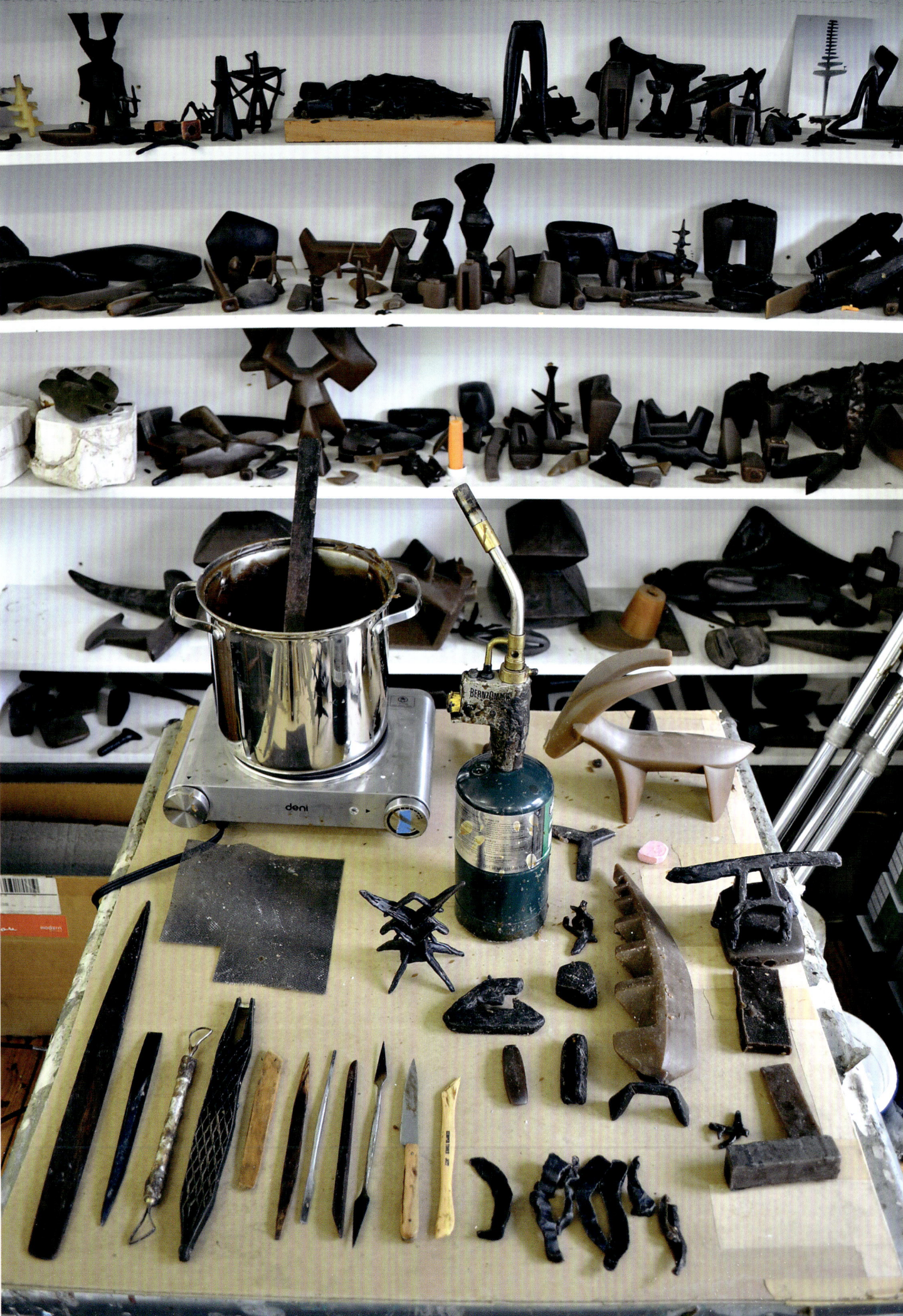

range of shapes and sizes carefully arranged in small groups radiating from a central core. One could almost think of it as a map, or an aerial view, of an ancient city; or, perhaps, a coded pattern of some unknown language.

The echoes, if I may borrow from the title, are of those formative high-Modern practices that inspired him from the start: smooth, mysterious forms arrayed like ancient runes, guarding secrets never to be surrendered. But in their vertiginous display, as though from 20,000 feet, their invitation counterbalances inscrutability; they are an entreaty to imagine, to play, and to dwell within.

I end here from where I started: in the studio (fig. 5), I was able to see how *Archaic Echoes* lay in the soft light of that upper display space, much as it did downtown—though of course, not exactly and that is the point. Here, in the space in which Haines's personal and artistic life has long grown and flourished intertwined, the piece has shifted. It can never be exactly as it was; it is something to live with, because it is something that lives—like Haines himself, both generative and generous: an intricate monument to a life well lived and art with the emotional clarity of home.

Ipswich, MA
2024

FIG. 5
Wax table in Peter's studio

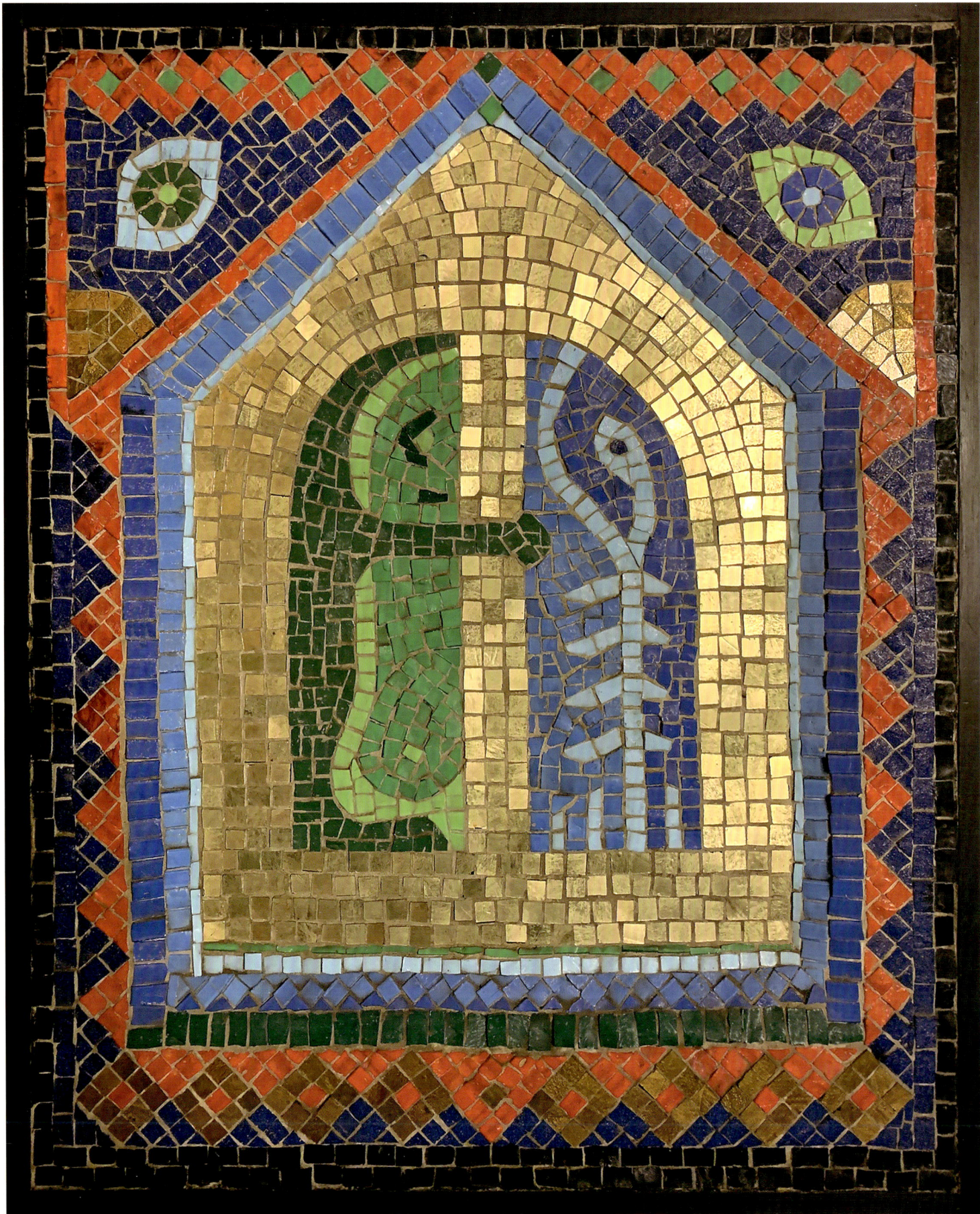

PETER DECAMP HAINES

Belinda Rathbone

It all begins with a lump of wax. The form is in there; it's a question of finding it. "My ideas come from the muck," Peter Haines has said of his work in sculpture.[1] As he kneads it with his fingers, the wax softens under his pressure and begins to respond. Prodding, pinching, he adds and subtracts. An oblong shape might become a fish, or it could be a spear that grows legs and becomes a bear. The "muck" Haines refers to is, on the one hand, the actual material that he shapes with his hands into sculptural forms, later to cast them in bronze. From another perspective, it is the archaeological site of his imagination, where ancient artifacts are unearthed and their messages given new life.

Peter DeCamp Haines was born on the Marine Corps base in Quantico, Virginia, in 1942, the first of three sons. His father, John Percy Haines, known as "Pete," was a Marine Corps fighter pilot who, during World War II, was the youngest squadron commander in the Pacific. John Glenn, later the first astronaut to circumnavigate the earth, flew on his wing. After the war, the family was transferred to Columbus, Ohio, where Peter's father was the head of the Naval Air Station (fig. 6).

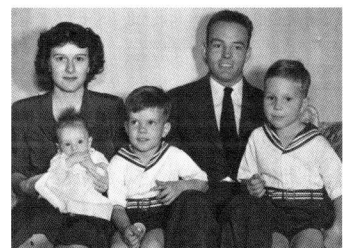

FIG. 6
Haines family portrait; back:
Pendery (mom), Pete (dad);
front: Chris, Perry, Peter

Peter's mother, Pendery Spear Haines, was a homemaker with a strong personal aesthetic and decorating skills to match. She was an accomplished sewer and a savvy frequenter of secondhand shops. In the Columbus suburb of Bexley, the Haineses gamely bought a rambling Arts and Crafts "fixer upper" with 13 fireplaces, elaborate woodwork, and stained-glass windows. Peter remembered how his mother's eclectic taste fueled the never-ending project of restoring and decorating the house, room by room. His maternal grandmother, who lived with the family after the war, was also artistic. Like her daughter, she worked in textiles, sewing and embroidering in bright colors inspired by traditional folk art. These homemade and second-hand materials, combined with assorted treasures Peter's

Icon, 1973
Glass tesserae mosaic
24 x 19 x ⅝ in. (61 x 48.2 x 1.6 cm)
Collection of the artist

Peter's student work from the Museum School

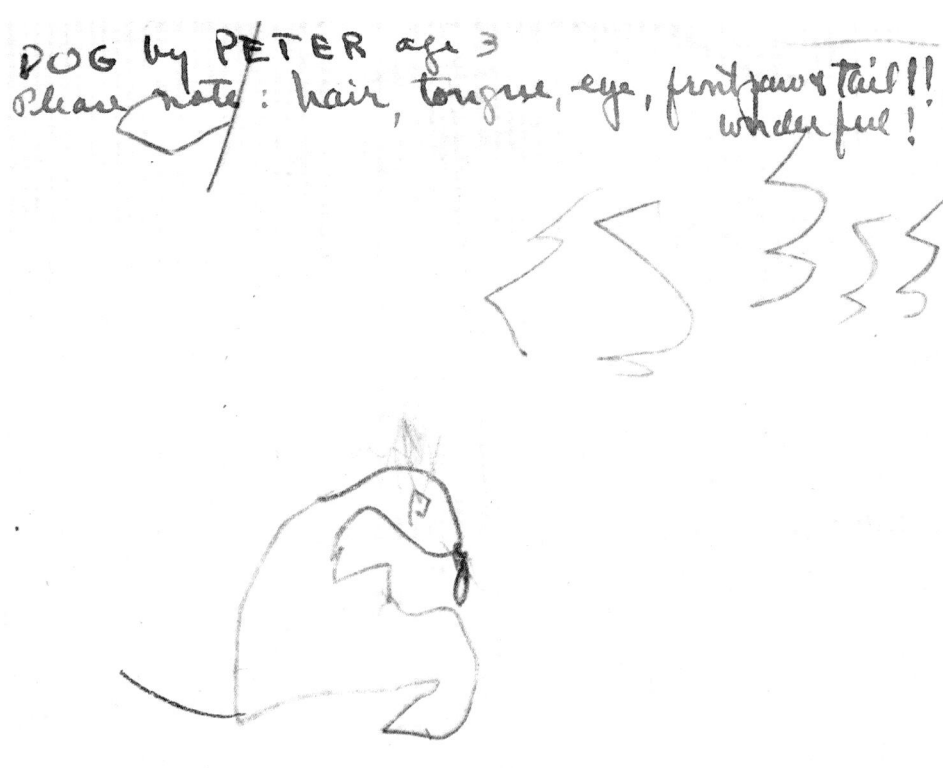

FIG. 7
Dog drawing by Peter at age 3, saved
by his mother

father brought home from China during the war, made for an unconventional environment. Peter grew to appreciate that, compared to other people they knew in Columbus, his parents were adventurous in their travels and in their taste for the art of other cultures.

Peter's natural talent for art was encouraged from an early age (fig. 7) and not just at home. At school he recalls being assigned to draw an object for each letter of the alphabet, an exercise at which he excelled. His fifth-grade teacher, Mrs. Dellenbaugh, urged Peter to participate in a citywide art contest. As the top prize winner, he was awarded a year of art classes on Saturday mornings at the Columbus College of Art and Design (fig. 8). Moving on to an all-boys day school— Columbus Academy—a year later, his artistic impulses were mostly restricted to compulsive doodling in the margins of his textbooks, following the loops and threads of his adolescent subconscious. In high school, he continued to paint in his spare time. Of the three Haines boys, Peter was the artist in his family, the one who was given art supplies for Christmas. But as much as his talent was nurtured at home, it never occurred to him that he could make a career as an artist.

In 1961, Peter was accepted at the University of Colorado in Boulder on a Navy ROTC scholarship. His father had promoted the choice as a way to get his first-born son educated for free. At college, Peter double majored in anthropology and psychology, reluctant to choose between them and intrigued by their interdisciplinary potential, which never quite gelled. Coasting through the academic year, he spent every summer in a ROTC program, the third of these returning him to his

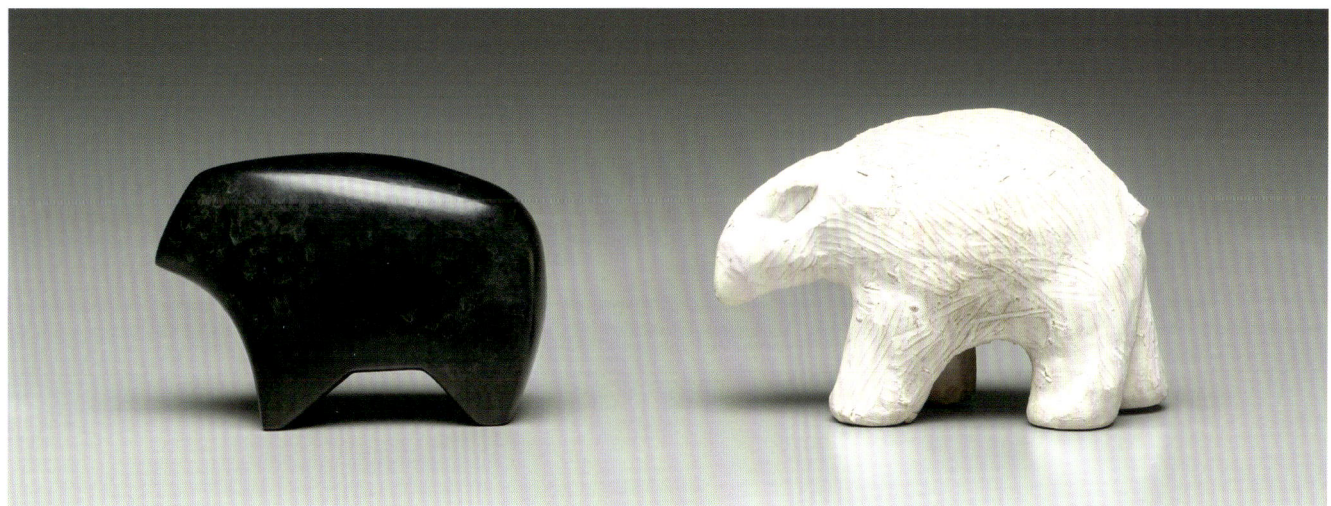

birthplace—the rigorous Marine Corps Officer Candidates School in Quantico, Virginia. As part of his ROTC requirement, he took two years of military history with Bernard Trainor, a retired three-star general who went on to be a military analyst and correspondent for *The New York Times*. For Haines, Trainor's course was fundamental, for it was not just a history of battles and wars won or lost; it also examined the humanistic side and the moral component of military engagement. "The Marines issued me a flak jacket," Haines recalled, "General Trainor issued me moral armor."[2] He reinforced the values Peter had absorbed by osmosis from his father's powerful example growing up.

Haines graduated from the University of Colorado as a second lieutenant in 1965; his next step was the Corps' Basic School. The war in Vietnam was accelerating, and it was almost certain that he would be deployed there in 1967. The anthropologist in him was curious about the culture he was about to engage with, so in addition to his basic training he elected to study Vietnamese at the Defense Language Institute in Monterey, California. This prepared him to command a 300-man Combined Action Company—two-thirds Vietnamese troops and one-third American. He was 25 years old.

The company's mission was to protect villages and hamlets with small patrols to guard against the Viet Cong. For most of Haines's tour of duty, company life on the front was relatively calm, and he even occasionally had the time and tranquility to engage in his favorite pastime—painting. With the Tet Offensive in late January 1968, that all changed. He saw heavy action for the first time, and it came, just as it was supposed to, as a surprise. "It was the first time in two weeks I slept without my boots on," he recalled, "and we were attacked."[3]

After 13 months in Vietnam, Haines left in May 1968. For his courage and composure in the battlefield, he earned a Bronze Star. To this day he attributes the mental health he was able to maintain on the front and following his tour in Vietnam to Bernard Trainor's course for the ROTC midshipmen at the University of Colorado. For the remaining six months of his four years of military duty Haines was stationed in Iceland—from summer solstice to winter solstice—and then he was a free man.

It wasn't immediately clear to Haines what to do next. His brother Perry was at Harvard Business School and, sensing Peter's need for direction, urged him to consider it, too. Peter had an aptitude for math and some curiosity about the business world. He applied and was accepted. One of his professors, Anthony "Tony" Athos, taught a course in interpersonal behavior with just the kind of pitch that appealed to Haines—a psychological approach to business. Athos was inclined to be receptive to a student's creative interpretations of course assignments and had enough clout in the school to pave the way for their realization in unconventional ways. So when Haines suggested that he substitute his final thesis with a nonverbal interpretation of a case study in the form of a painting, Athos said OK. "Tony's affirmation went a long way," remembered Haines.[4] The result was an acid-colored diagrammatic treatment of the case of a young woman at a crossroads, a satirical marriage of modern business school practices with tribal mythology (fig. 9). More a question mark than a statement, *Gracia* might have been a subconscious self-portrait of his own position at a turnstile of personal change. Whatever it was, Haines's painting as a thesis won the highest grade from Athos.

In 1971 when Haines was almost 29 years old, his father died after a long illness. That same year, Peter graduated from Harvard Business School. Both events were a shock to his system, and absorbing the shock, he later said, brought about a conversion experience. Watching his father succumb to the debilitating effects of Hodgkin's disease and as a recent survivor of the Vietnam War, he asked himself what he was living for and, with a new urgency, what mattered to him most. It was

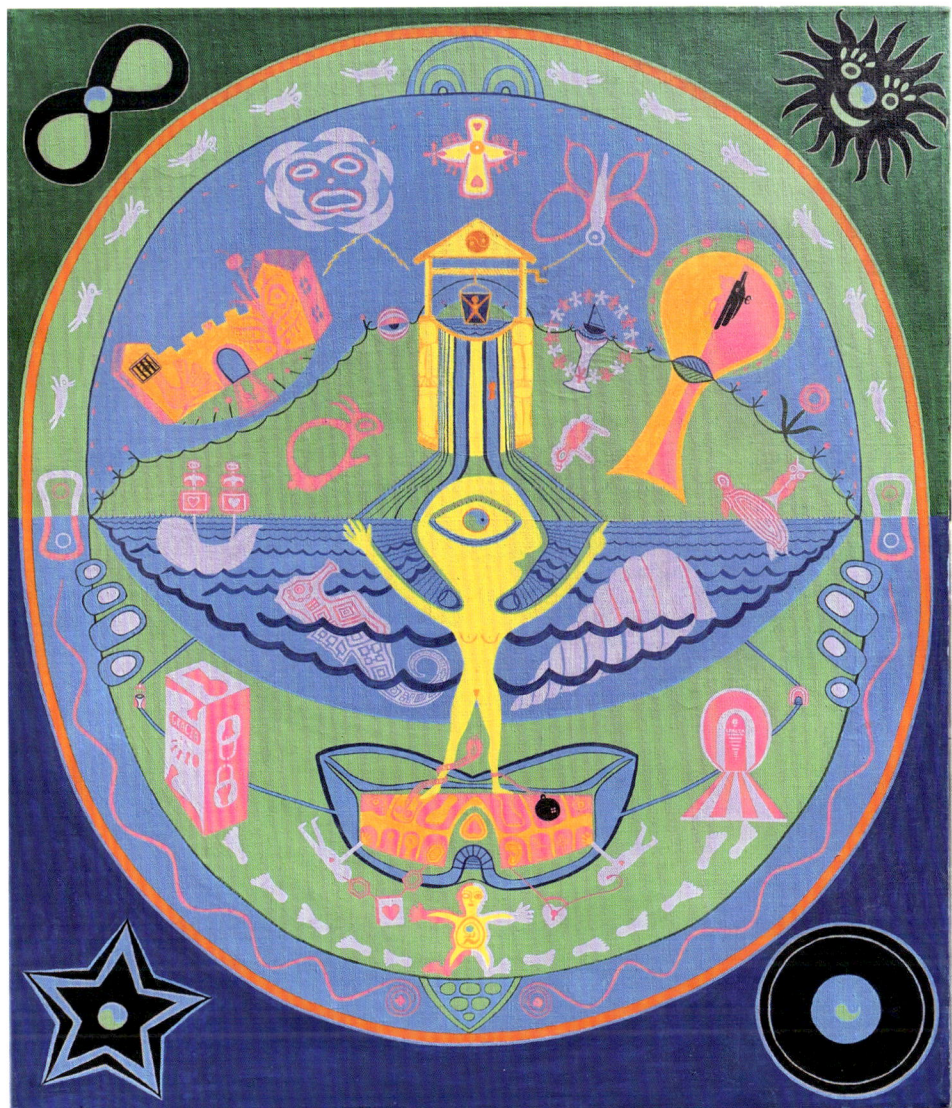

FIG. 9
Gracia, 1971
Acrylic on canvas
36 x 30 in. (91.4 x 76.2 cm)
Collection of the artist

Peter submitted *Gracia* as his final
thesis at Harvard Business School.

now radiantly clear that what really mattered to him was making art. So instead of
pursuing consulting work with McKinsey & Company, where he had already held a
summer job, with some credit left over from the GI bill he applied to the School of
the Museum of Fine Arts in Boston.

Although he was about 10 years older than most of the students at the school,
Haines discovered that he was way behind in his painting skills and out of touch
with the art discourse of the day. He had painted all his life, but he was an autodi-
dact. At the time, Color Field painting was the dominant style at the school and
the critic Clement Greenberg retained his powerful influence in asserting the
preeminence of abstract art in the midst of emerging counter movements such

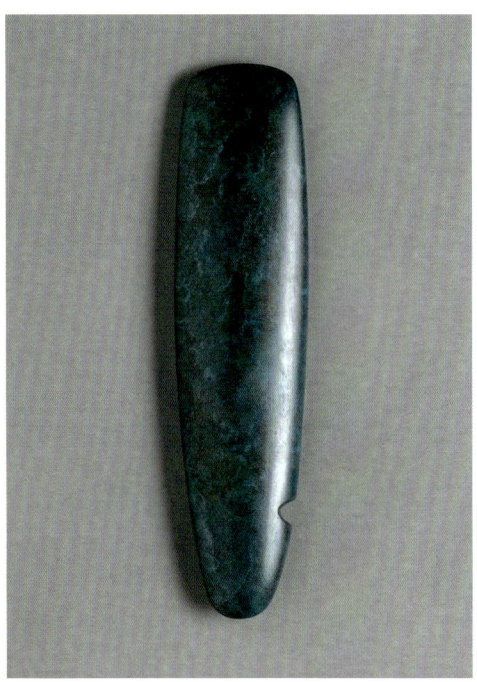

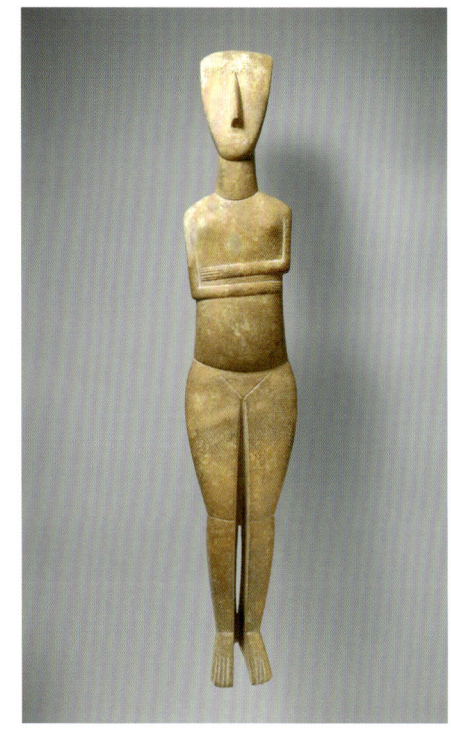

FIG. 10
Dream Axe, 1981
Bronze
8¾ x 2¼ x ¾ in. (22.3 x 5.6 x 2 cm)
Collection of the artist

This piece was inspired by Peter's
"Big Dream"; it is the first of many
axes he sculpted.

FIG. 11
Marble female figure attributed
to the Bastis Master, early
Cycladic II period, 2600–2400 BCE
Marble
24¾ in. (62.8 cm)
The Metropolitan Museum of Art,
New York, NY
Gift of Christos G. Bastis, 1968;
acc. no. 68.148

as Pop art, performance art, and Minimalism. In search of his own way forward,
Haines put theories aside in favor of craft, and treated his art education like an
à la carte menu, sampling a variety of skills and media. He tried woodcut printing,
silkscreening, bronze casting, welding, ceramics, and jewelry making (p. 28).

After graduating, Haines rented studio space in the Bromley Heath building
in Jamaica Plain with three fellow Museum School artists—2,000 square feet
divided by four cost $50 a month—while he lived in a shared apartment in Boston's
Back Bay. In 1975 he moved across the river to Cambridge. In what is now part of
Boston's booming tech sector, he found a former manufacturing building for sale
on Sidney Street in Cambridgeport for $30,000 (p.44). A concrete block on a slab
with high ceilings, Sidney Street, Haines later said, was his "blank canvas."[5] The
foundation was solid, the walls were straight, there was plenty of room for living
and working, as well as an adjacent yard as big as the building. In his first five years
on Sidney Street he created a home for himself at the center of the structure,
erected interior walls from sheet rock, fashioned a basic kitchen in one corner and
a loft for sleeping in another, while reserving ample space on either side for his
studio. He heated the space with a homemade woodburning stove forged from two
oil barrels, which ate about five cords of wood a year.

Soon after moving to Cambridge, Haines joined a book group that was led by
independent publisher Bill Webb. The group had formed, at the instigation of local

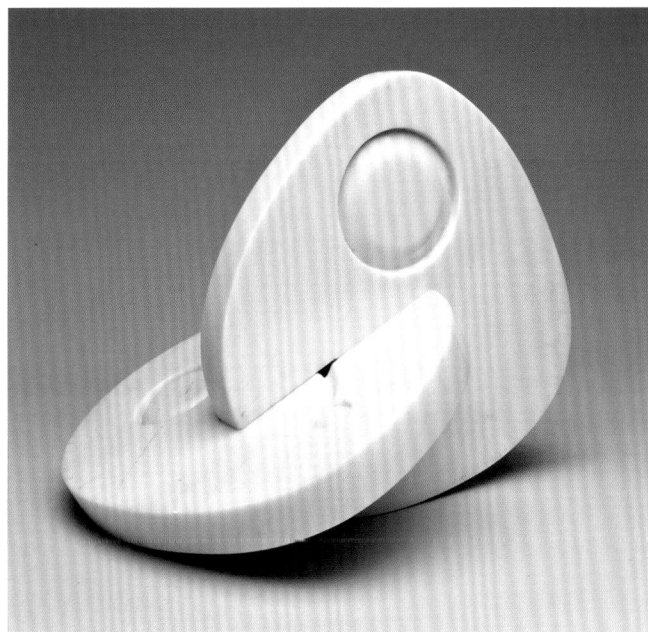

gallerist Victoria Munroe, around an interest in Carl Jung, but it soon meandered into other topics. As the discussion of one reading suggested the next, Webb would choose the book, "and it was always perfect," remembered Haines, " . . . he was the most well-read person I have ever known."[6] These readings and conversations nourished his artistic imagination in unexpected ways. It was around this time that he had what he called a "Big Dream." In the dream, he was on an archaeological expedition and he found a stone axe. He woke up full of excitement. Following Jungian practice, he wrote of the experience in his "dream journal," and drew a picture of the axe. It would still be a few years before he translated that image into a bronze casting, *Dream Axe* (fig. 10), which combined his enduring interest in anthropology and psychology with his discovery of sculpture's potential to express Jungian ideas.

Haines's *Big Dream* would guide his development as a sculptor over the next four decades. The axe form contained all the basic lessons of shaping an edge and of how light lines and silhouette can flow together to resolve a compound curve. The axe also demonstrated by example the universality of forms, or, in Jungian terms, the collective unconscious. The shapes of ancient tools, of wild animals, and ritual objects made by the Olmecs of Mexico and the Cycladic peoples of ancient Greece (fig. 11), by China's Shang Dynasty and North America's Indigenous tribes converged and merged in his imagination and in his hands.

As much as their imagery resonates with antiquity, Haines's bronze sculptures show his appreciation of modern masters such as Henry Moore, Constantin Brâncuşi, and Isamu Noguchi (fig. 12)—sculptors who also owe a debt to non-Western art and

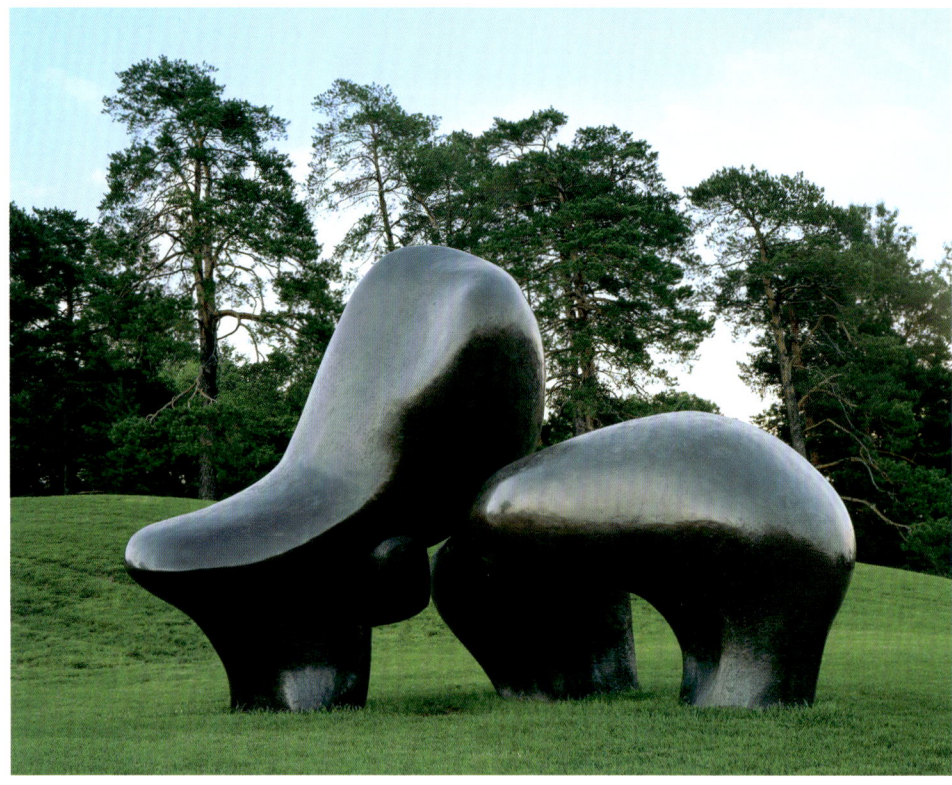

ethnographic models. Haines's work follows the same Modernist current of the so-called "primitive" in its inspiration and its break from the classical canon, or as Moore espoused, "a universal continuous activity, with no separation between past and present."[7] Many of Haines's sculptures therefore "sit comfortably in a modernist tradition," to quote Sebastian Smee, while his work also serves "to remind us that this familiar language is tremendously elastic and vital."[8] In his use of negative space, ambiguous allusions, and love of pure form, Haines speaks a multilingual Modernism in his own dialect.

With a generous travel grant Peter had won at his graduation from the Museum School and put aside, he took off for several weeks in 1981 to absorb the wonders of Egypt, Rome, Florence, Paris, and London. A visit to Henry Moore's studio in Much Hadham, Hertfordshire, where the master trusted him alone in his studio for 45 minutes to contemplate his maquettes and collections of natural forms, left a deep impression (fig. 13). Naturally enough, Haines followed this historic visit with a pilgrimage to Stonehenge.

In 1980, as a guest at a Seder in Cambridge, Peter met Sekyo Nam, a Korean new-comer to the city. Sekyo had left Korea for Germany to work as a registered nurse and later migrated to the United States. After working as a nurse in Tennessee, she moved to Cambridge to study and practice acupuncture. As much as she was an adventurous world traveler with an independent mind, Sekyo was loyal to the traditions and way of life she had learned growing up in rural South Korea, which she carried over her many changes of habitat. These were soon to add a new aesthetic to Peter's domestic life, along with the stability of a strong and capable partner.

Peter and Sekyo were married in 1982. With funds left over from his Museum School travel grant, the couple took a honeymoon trip to Ireland, driving around the rural countryside exploring stone circles and other archaeological sites that reinforced the connections between Modernism and antiquity, sculpture and nature.

In the years that followed, the building on Sidney Street evolved from an artist's studio into a family home with the birth of two daughters, Pendry in 1983 and Julia in 1985. Sekyo gave up acupuncture to focus on homemaking and, in her spare time, translating Korean poetry. They turned the vacant lot adjacent to the building into a hidden garden oasis, full of flowers and fruit trees. They laid a patio out of old bricks scavenged from demolished industrial buildings in the neighbor-hood. An apricot tree, a wedding present from a friend, grew into a large shade-tree centerpiece. Sekyo's traditional Confucianist parents were heartbroken that she hadn't married a Korean but eventually came to accept her choice, and Peter and Sekyo visited her family in Korea a number of times over the years, while icons of Sekyo's family heritage ultimately found their way into Peter's work by osmosis. Vacations with their girls—to Eaton Ranch in Wyoming, to Yellowstone Park, and rafting in the Alaskan wilderness—stirred Peter's creative imagination in innumer-able and unaccountable ways. The caribou migration at the Arctic National Park left a deep impression that resulted a few years later in his exhibition, *Migration* (fig. 14), consisting of over 300 small bronzes moving across a platform. The family traveled abroad to Greece, Turkey, India, Mexico, and Namibia. On a rafting trip on the Zanskar River in the Himalayas, Peter hiked to ancient Buddhist temples and witnessed the creation of sand mandalas, a visual concept that fascinated him in its infinitude and invitation to mystery. Wherever they went, Peter would absorb the emblems of the culture organically and intuitively, building on his polysemous vocabulary of forms in an ever-widening universal language.

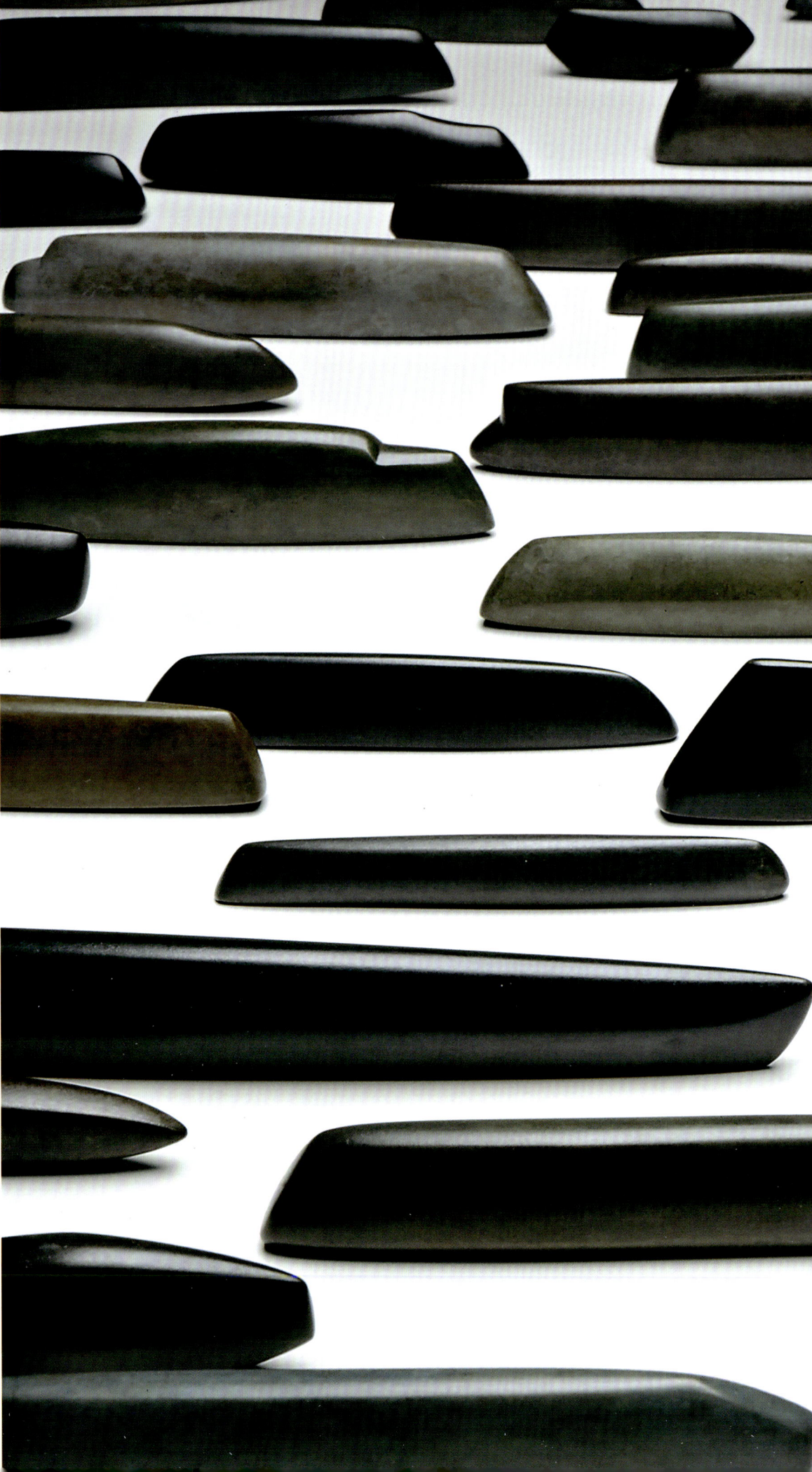

FIG. 14
Migration, 2001 (detail)
Bronze
Longest: 14 in. (35.6 cm)
Collection of the artist

Over 300 of these small bronzes
were shown at Chapel Gallery
(originally the Boston Sculptors Gallery),
Newton, MA.

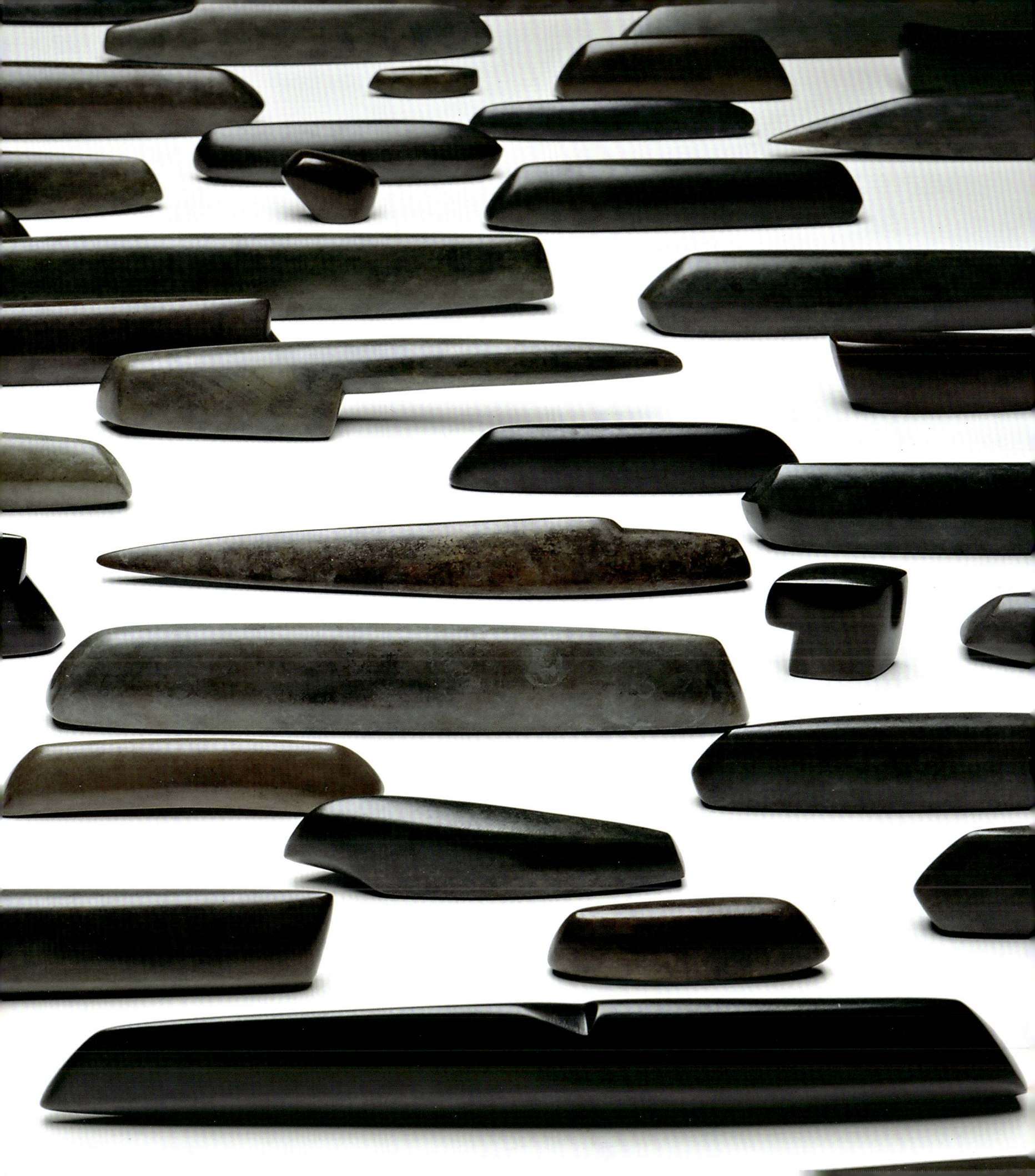

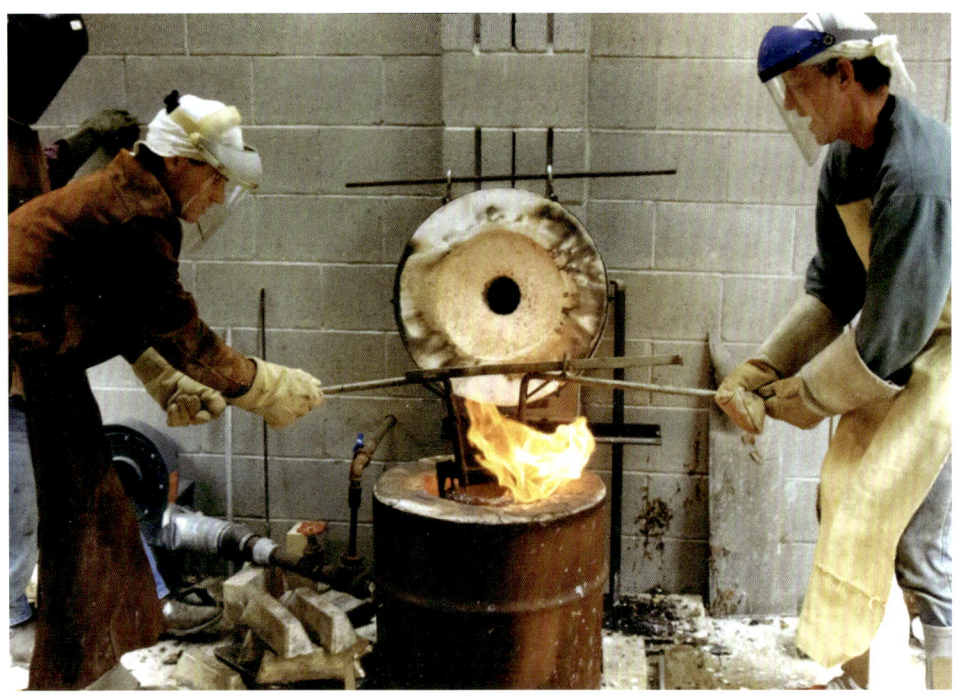

FIG. 15
Robert Schelling and
Joe Wheelwright pouring bronze at
Vermont Gentlemen's Foundry.

A sculptor working in bronze needs a foundry. To begin with, Haines traveled to Beacon, New York, to work with Dick Polich at Tallix, a foundry that specialized in the unusual requirements of contemporary sculptors. Unlike many of the artists Polich worked with, such as Frank Stella and Richard Serra, Haines was relatively easy to please, and never complained when things didn't come out perfectly, since he was capable of perfecting the work himself. It was a thrill to work with Tallix, but it was expensive. In the early 1980s, fellow sculptor and Cambridge book-group member Joe Wheelwright and his wife Susan bought 30 acres of land in East Corinth, Vermont. Joe invited Haines and two other Boston sculptors, Robert Schelling and Larry Pollans (fig. 15), to chip in for a ceramics kiln that Boston College was unloading at the time. They had to take the car-sized kiln apart just to remove it from the building before reconstructing it in Vermont.

Compared to Tallix, this would be low-tech bronze casting. For the artists, it was a vast savings in foundry costs. The kiln required a gradual raising of its temperature to 1,000 degrees, which meant that in the first step of the lost-wax bronze-casting method, it would take altogether three days for the molds to dry out without breaking. The next step was preparing the mold for the bronze pour. In the summer months, when the temperature was favorable for casting and the weather was fine for camping, Peter would arrive with his tent and his dog, Amos, for a three-day bronze pour. After the pour and while they waited for the bronze to solidify, Peter

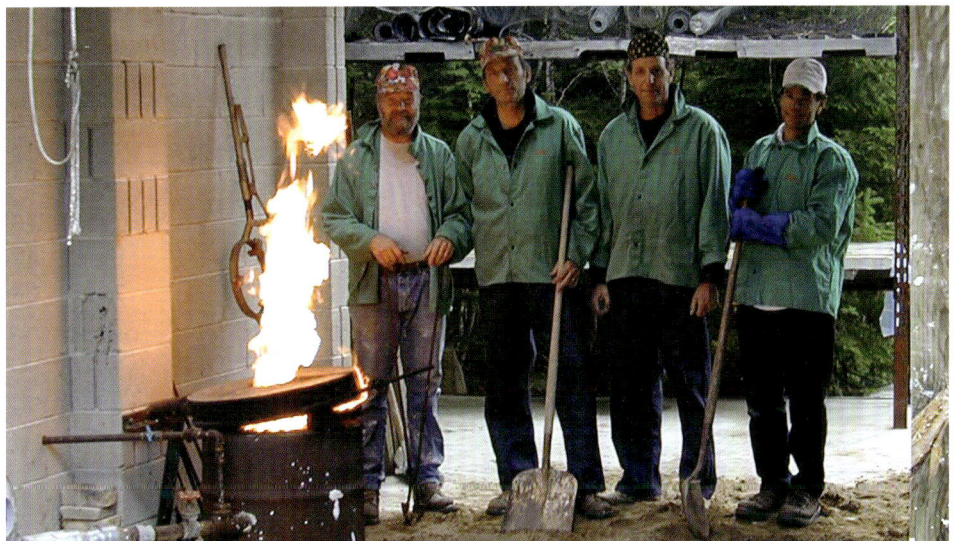

FIG. 16
The Vermont Gentlemen's
Foundry

and Joe played endless games of chess with pieces they'd sculpted themselves. With tongue in cheek, they called it "the Vermont Gentlemen's Foundry" (fig. 16).

As their families grew, the Haineses with their two young daughters convened in East Corinth in summer with the Wheelwrights, who also had two daughters around the same age. For Joe and Peter, work continued according to its particular rhythms, while for their wives and children there were the pleasures of pond swimming, campfires, stargazing, and walks in the woods. In Boston at around this time, a popular annual art event was initiated by artists Clara and Bill Wainwright— the First Night Festival on New Year's Eve. They called on local artists to make sets and costumes and Haines and Joe Wheelwright were regularly drafted into carving giant ice sculptures for the First Night spectacle.

In the early 1980s, another young Boston sculptor, Murray "Mac" Dewart, began hosting sculptors' dinners in his studio in Brookline. A recent transplant from Vermont, Dewart had longed for the kind of community a city could offer. These studio gatherings evolved into the idea of a cooperative sculpture gallery of which Haines and the Vermont Gentlemen's Foundry artists were among the 18 originating members. For a gallery, they rented an unused Sunday school space with vaulted ceilings in West Newton that they named the Chapel Gallery, and over time developed a base of collectors there.

Meanwhile, Boston's South End district was beginning to gentrify. Big commercial developers welcomed the art community to add interest to the street life and help tame the neighborhood. In 1992, the Boston sculptors group moved from West

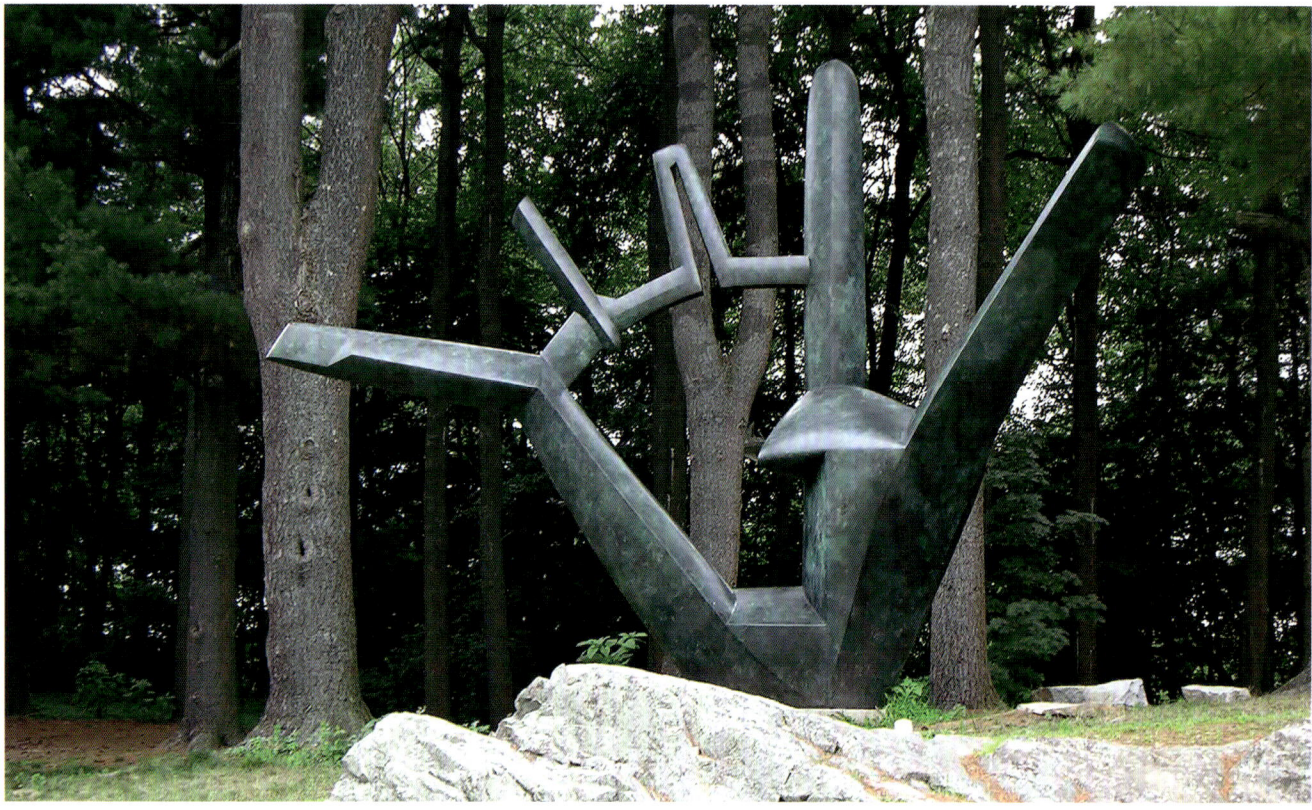

FIG. 17
Hand, 1988
Bronze
11 x 17 x 5 ft. (3.3 x 5.2 x 1.5 m)
Collection of the artist

Installation at deCordova
Sculpture Park Museum

Newton to the heart of the fledgling gallery district; they opened a large space on Harrison Avenue and renamed themselves the Boston Sculptors Gallery. The neighborhood's innovative "First Fridays" of every month, when the galleries stayed open into the evening hours, became an important connection point for artists from around the city. Another sculpture-friendly place in the Boston area was the deCordova Museum in Lincoln, with its 30-acre sculpture park. Haines's monumental *Hand* sculpture (fig. 17) enjoyed extended exposure there from 2006 to 2010. At the time, the deCordova actively collected and exhibited Boston artists and as a result enjoyed a loyal following of local artists and collectors.

Thanks in large part to financial support from Peter's brother Perry, in 1995 Peter and Sekyo expanded their Sidney Street building to make a second floor, creating more living space and greater privacy for themselves and their adolescent daughters. At around the same time, Peter added two floors to his studio, as the demand for his work grew and the need for studio assistants and more storage space arose. The domestic side of the building retained its bunker-like atmosphere with much of the natural light coming from above, enclosed from the outside world. Packed with works of art by mostly local artist friends and many acquired by exchange, it brims

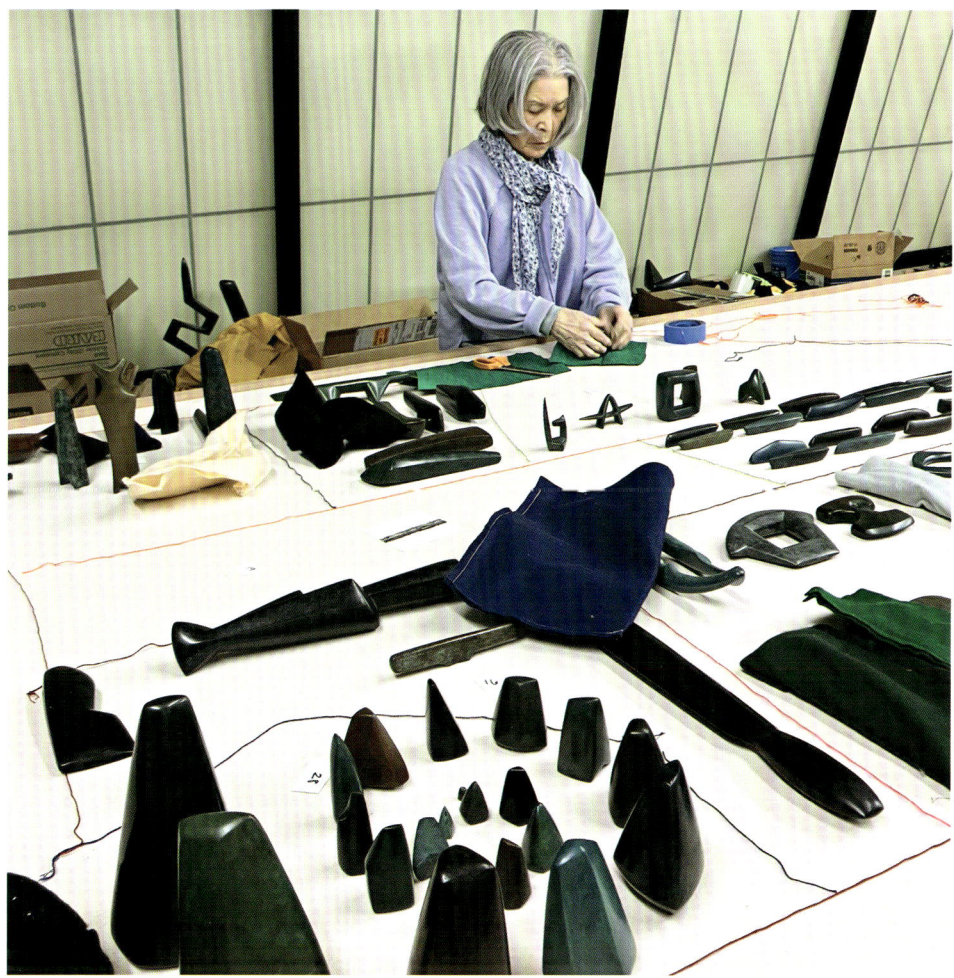

FIG. 18
Sekyo in the studio wrapping
bronzes for *Archaic Echoes* in
preparation for transport to the
Boston Sculptors Gallery.

with color, life, and personal histories. The garden outside is also enclosed, adding to the unusual sense of quiet and privacy in the middle of a city.

Over the years, Haines's body of work has grown to thousands of pieces, while his themes have remained remarkably constant. He liked to admit, with equanimity, that he was a hedgehog, not a fox.[9] "Art like this," wrote Joseph Masheck of Haines's work, "may hold up the possibility of expressions of wholeness, composure, serenity . . . not just their gritty opposites."[10] Taken individually, each sculpture is serenely self-contained, but also invariably enigmatic. Seen together, the mysteries multiply.

Haines received a Stage 4 cancer diagnosis in April of 2023. Undeterred, he was determined to have one last show and display his life-long theme—archaeology. He constructed a 22-foot long, 6-foot-wide table for the display of 1,000 small sculptures, drawing on a large inventory of objects made over the course of 45 years. He called the show *Archaic Echoes* (fig. 18) and it drew upon earlier themes

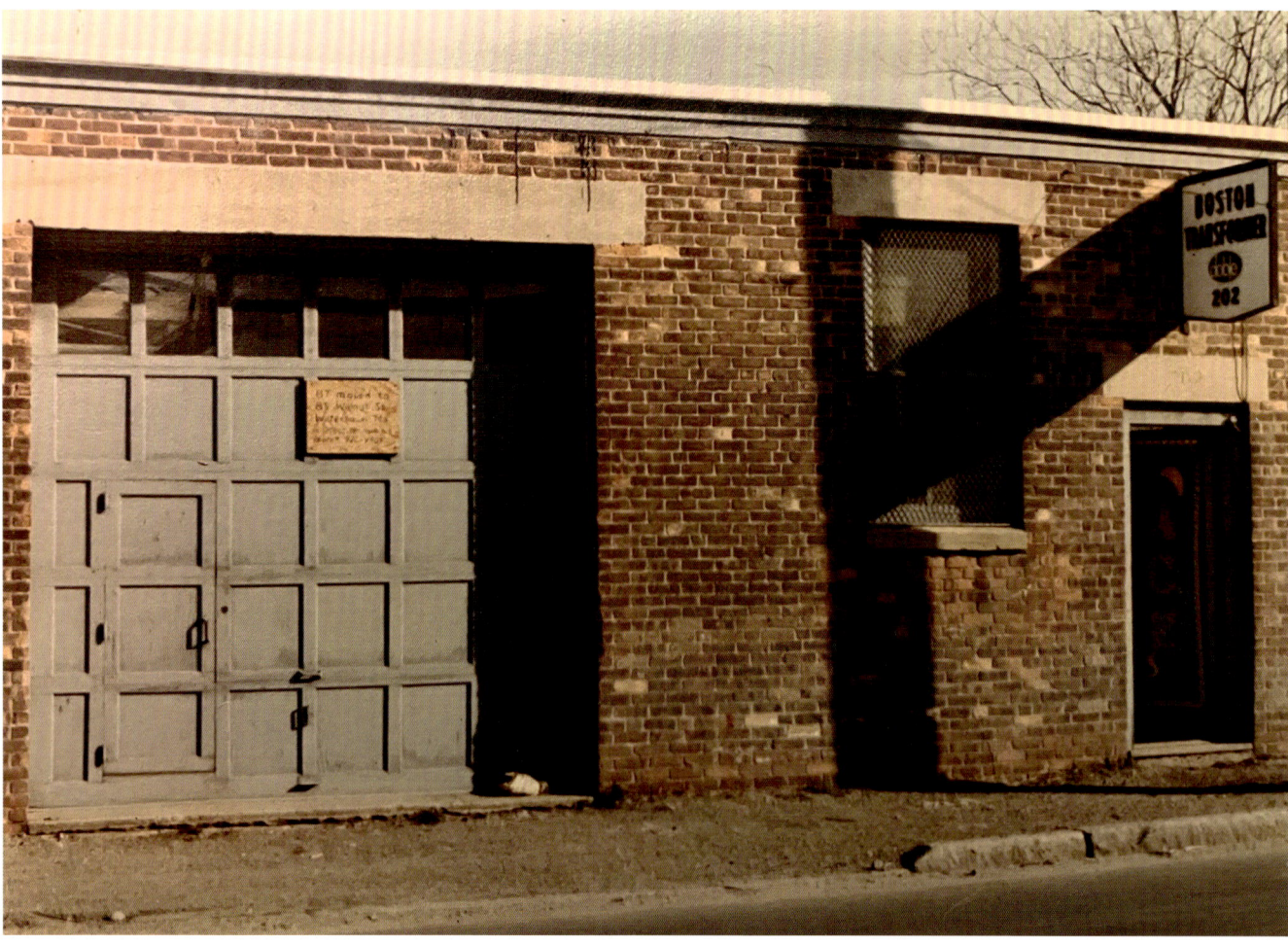

Peter's original building on Sidney Street, ca. 1977

with a mandala shape at the center, but with openings—gateways—leading in all directions. Haines then organized the sections like an anthropologist of his own ancient culture. There was a bird section, another for blades and hand tools. There were "things with holes," and "lozenge shapes," and objects that looked like heads.[11] The borders were a continuous migration of animal-like forms. The overall effect was suggestive of a natural-history-museum display, the difference being there were no labels, the display case was open, and the viewer was invited to touch, to handle, and to imagine. Haines called it an *Archaeology of the Subconscious*[12] putting the viewer in the role of archaeologist, making connections between what we see and a primal sense of what we know (fig. 19). As much as looking, he invites the viewer to engage by touch and for his sculptures to transmit their timeless messages from hand to hand.

PAGE 46
FIG. 19
Selection of pieces from table
installation of *Archaeology of the Subconscious*, 2024, a collection of 1000 small abstract bronzes the sculptor worked on for 45 years
Longest: 14 in. (35.6 cm)
Collection of the artist and
private collection

Archaic Echoes would be Haines's last exhibition at the Boston Sculptors Gallery. A year after closing the show and several months of filling orders in his studio and undergoing palliative chemotherapy treatment. He died peacefully at home in Cambridge on October 25, 2024, surrounded by family and friends. He was 82.

Cambridge, MA

2024

ENDNOTES

1   Author's conversation with the artist, Cambridge, MA, January 15, 2024.

2   Ibid.

3   Ibid.

4   Author's conversation with the artist, Cambridge, MA, January 28, 2024.

5   Conversation with the artist, Cambridge, MA, January 15, 2024.

6   Ibid.

7   Henry Moore, "Primitive Art," in *Listener*, April 24, 1941, 598.

8   Sebastian Smee, "A Convergence of Boston Sculpture," *Boston Globe*, June 27, 2013.

9   Author's conversation with the artist, Cambridge, MA, November 18, 2023.

10 Joseph Masheck, *Point 1: Art Visuals/Visual Arts* (New York: Willis Locker & Owens Publishing, 1984), 48.

11 From a transcript of a recorded conversation on Zoom between Haines, Tom Singer, and Barry Svigals, October 30, 2023.

12 Conversation with the artist, Cambridge, MA, November 18, 2023.

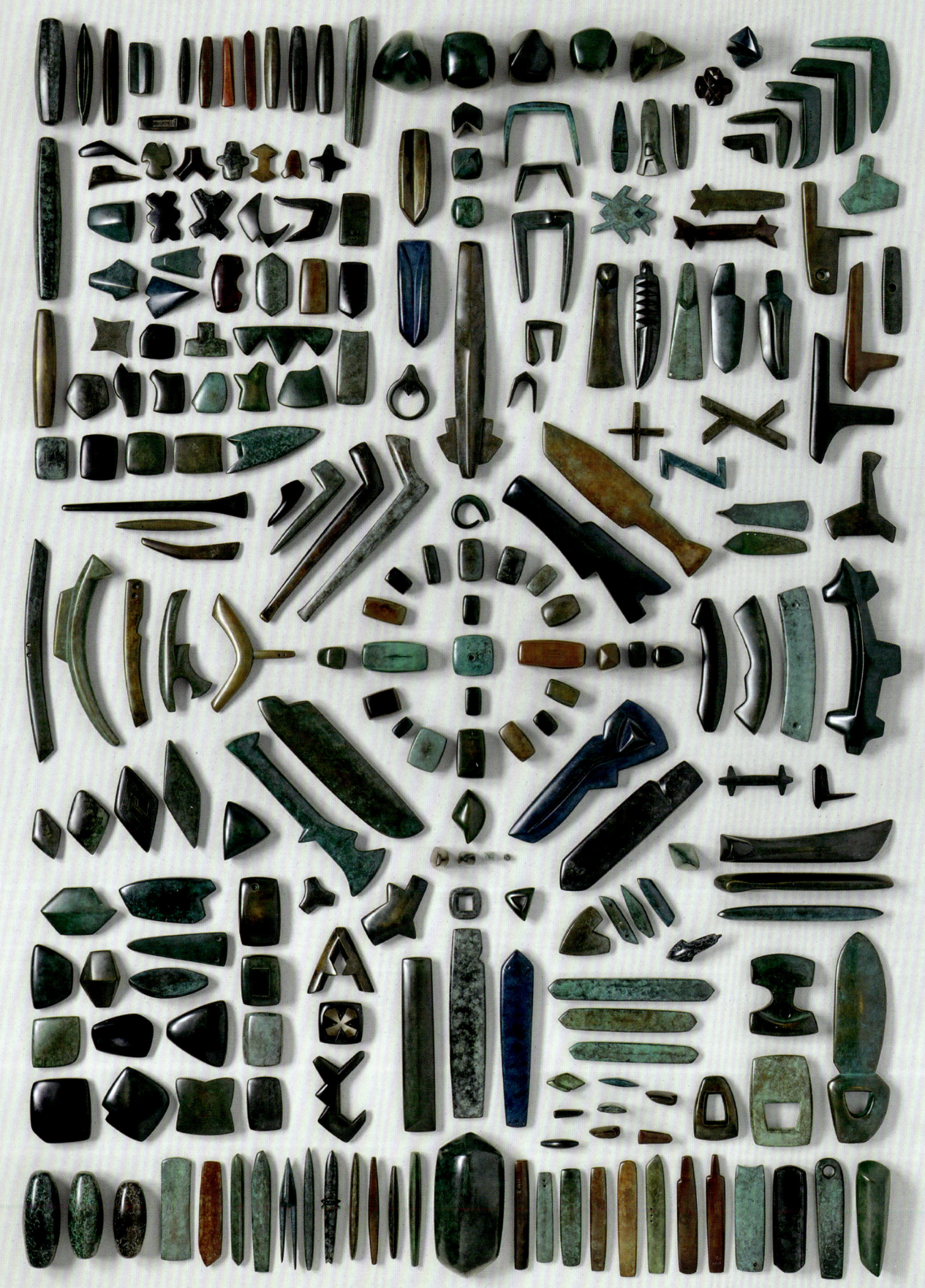

I think of the artifacts

as universal archetypes

that recall

the archaic materiality

of our ancestors.

Peter DeCamp Haines

Plates

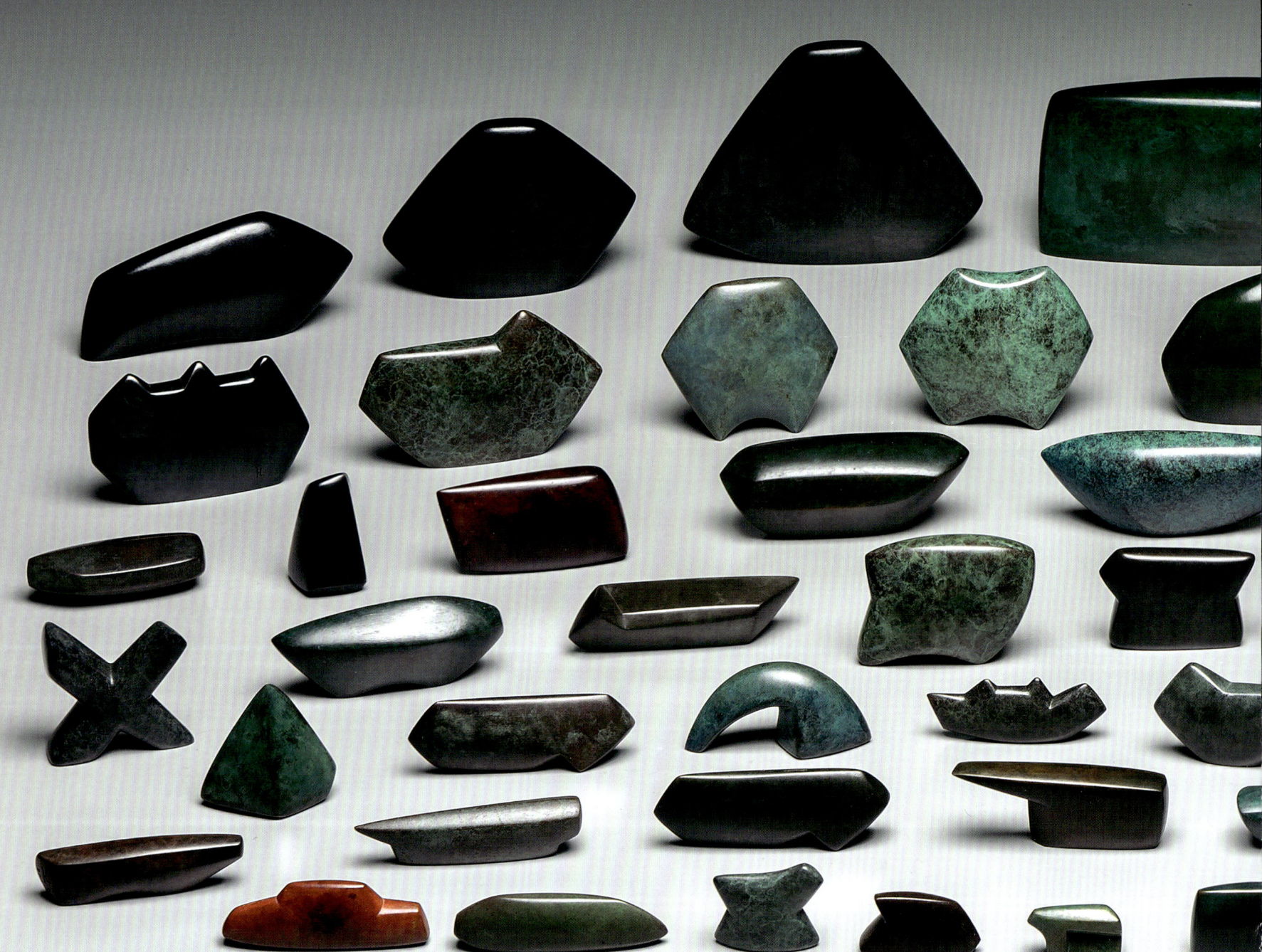

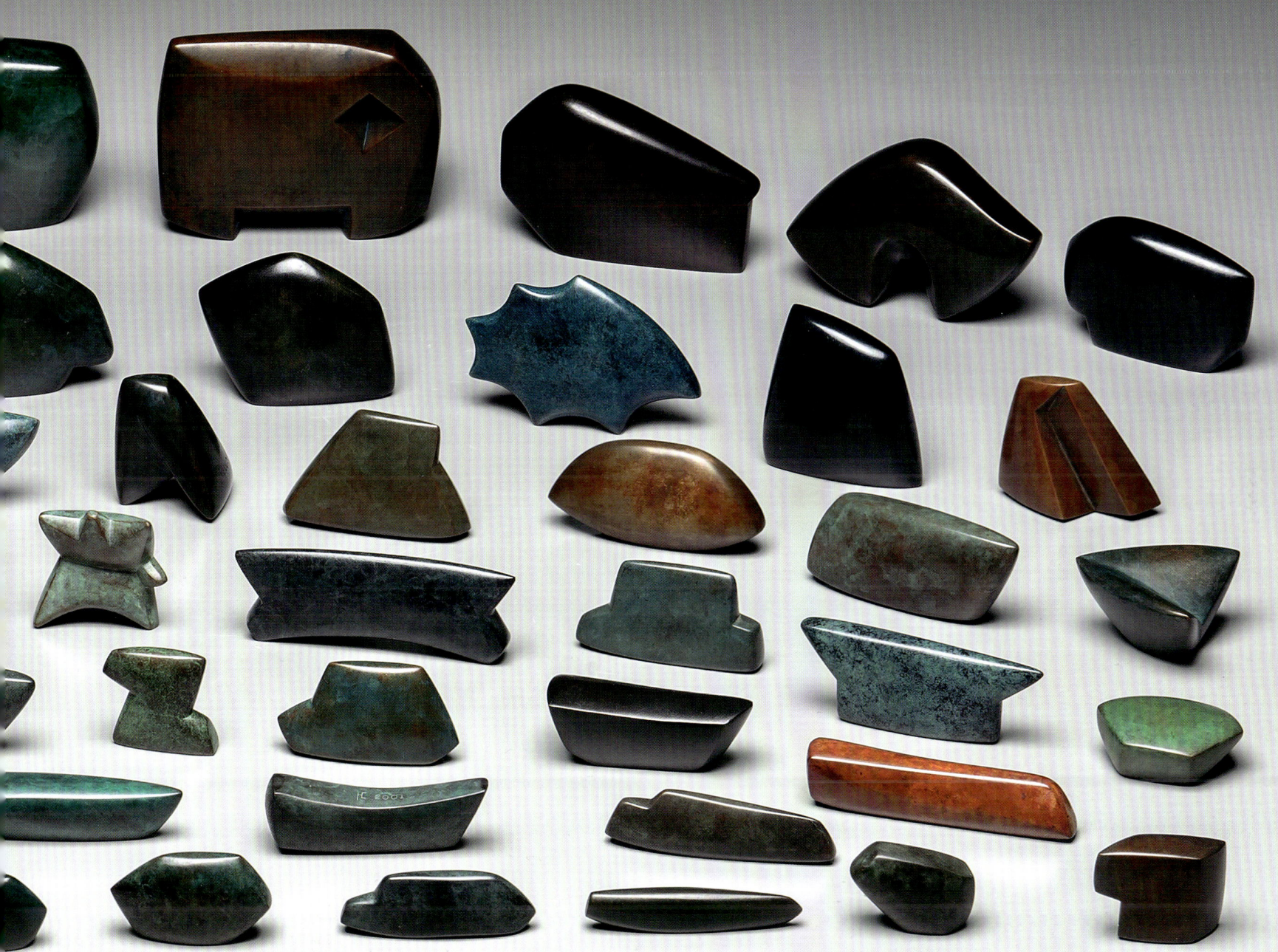

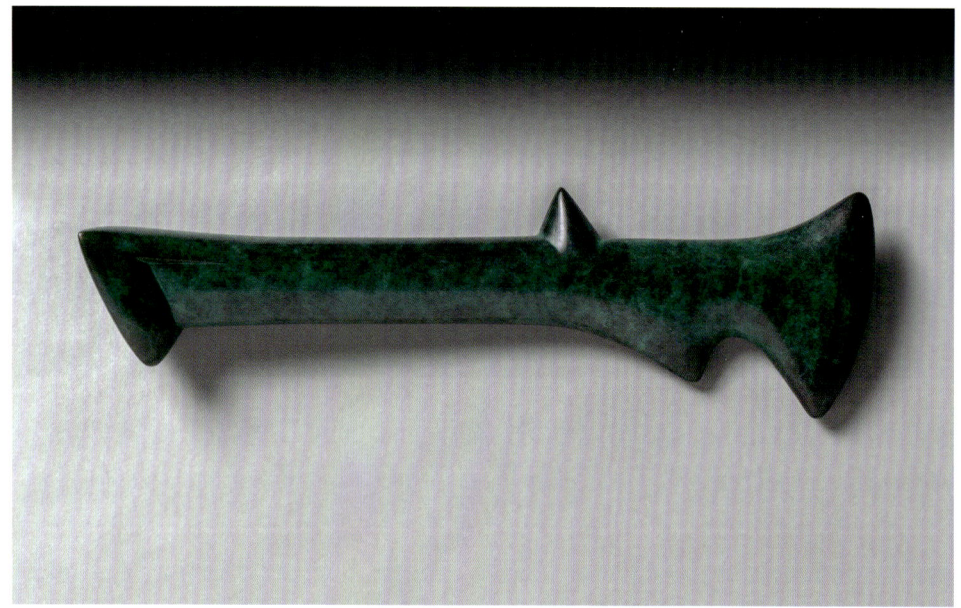

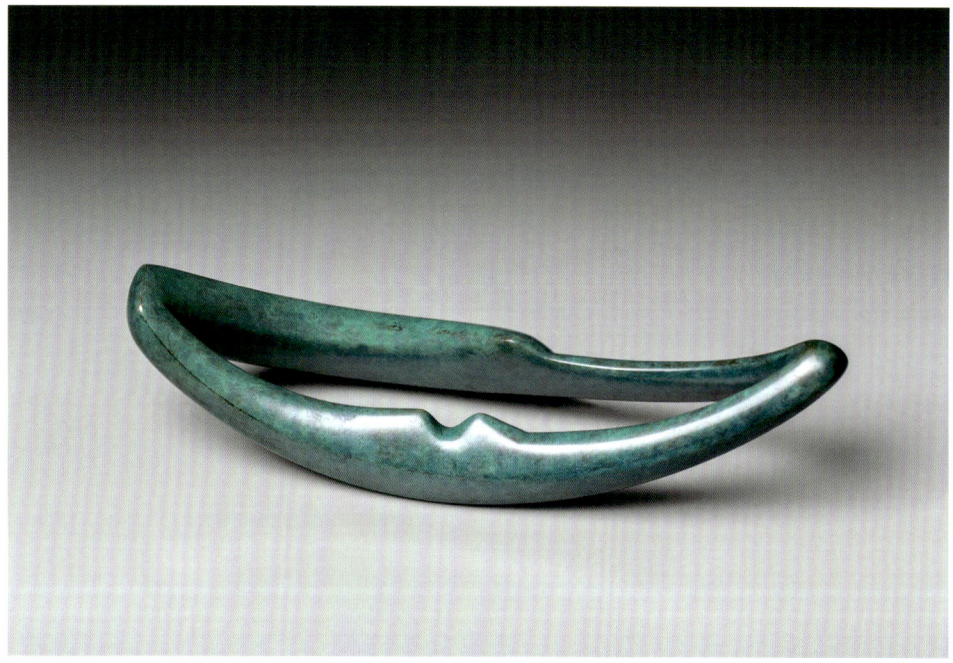

PREVIOUS SPREAD

PLATE 1

Animal Elements, 1978–2023
Bronze
Tallest: 3¹³⁄₁₆ x 4¹³⁄₁₆ x ¹⁵⁄₁₆ (9.6 x 12.2 x 3.3 cm)
Smallest: ¹¹⁄₁₆ x ¹⁵⁄₁₆ x ³⁄₈ (1.8 x 3.3 x 1.0 cm)
Collection of the artist and private collection

PLATE 2

Hand Wand, 1985
Bronze
2¹⁵⁄₁₆ x 10 x 1⅝ in. (7.4 x 25.4 x 4.1 cm)
Collection of the artist

PLATE 3

Reclining Moon, 1987
Bronze
3 x 9 x 2⅝ in. (2.5 x 7.6 x 6.67 cm)
Collection of the artist

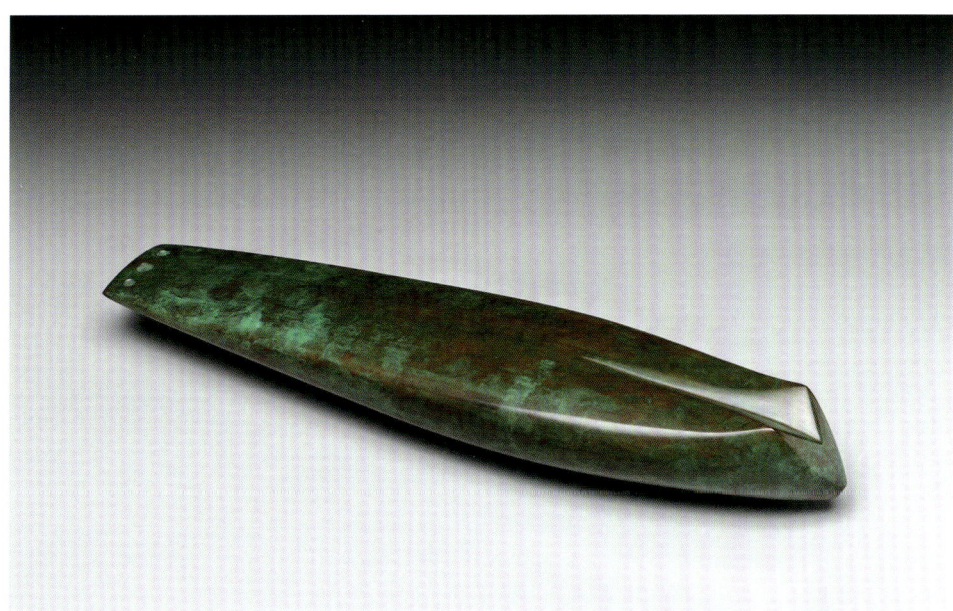

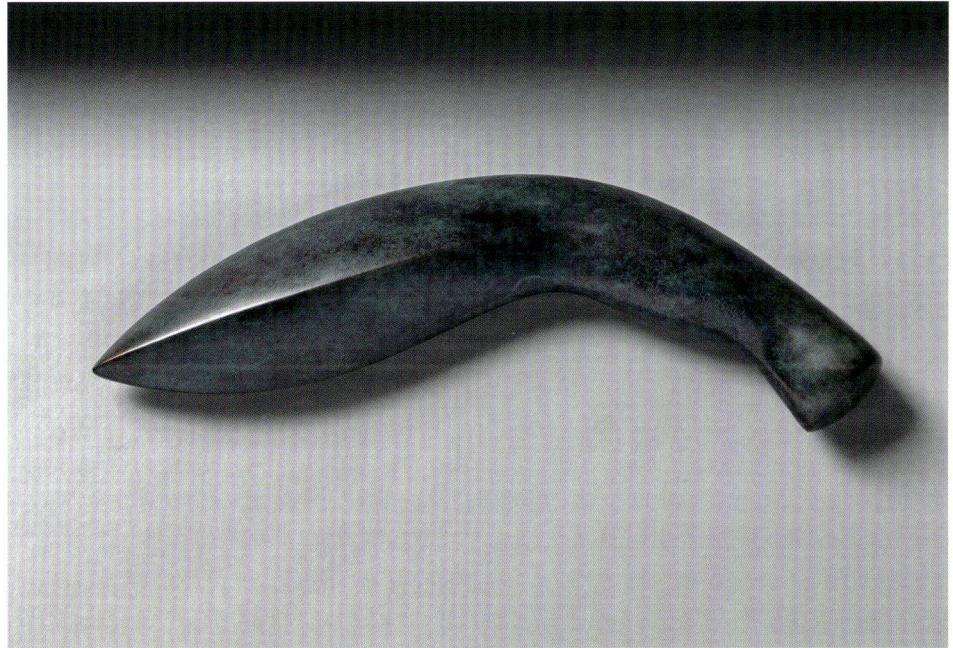

PLATE 4

Artifact, 2022
Bronze
1¼ x 10⁷⁄₁₆ x 2½ in. (3.2 x 26.4 x 6.3 cm)
Collection of the artist

PLATE 5

Bear Poker, 2024
Bronze
3 x 9½ x 11¹¹⁄₁₆ in. (7.6 x 24.1 x 29.8 cm)
Collection of the artist

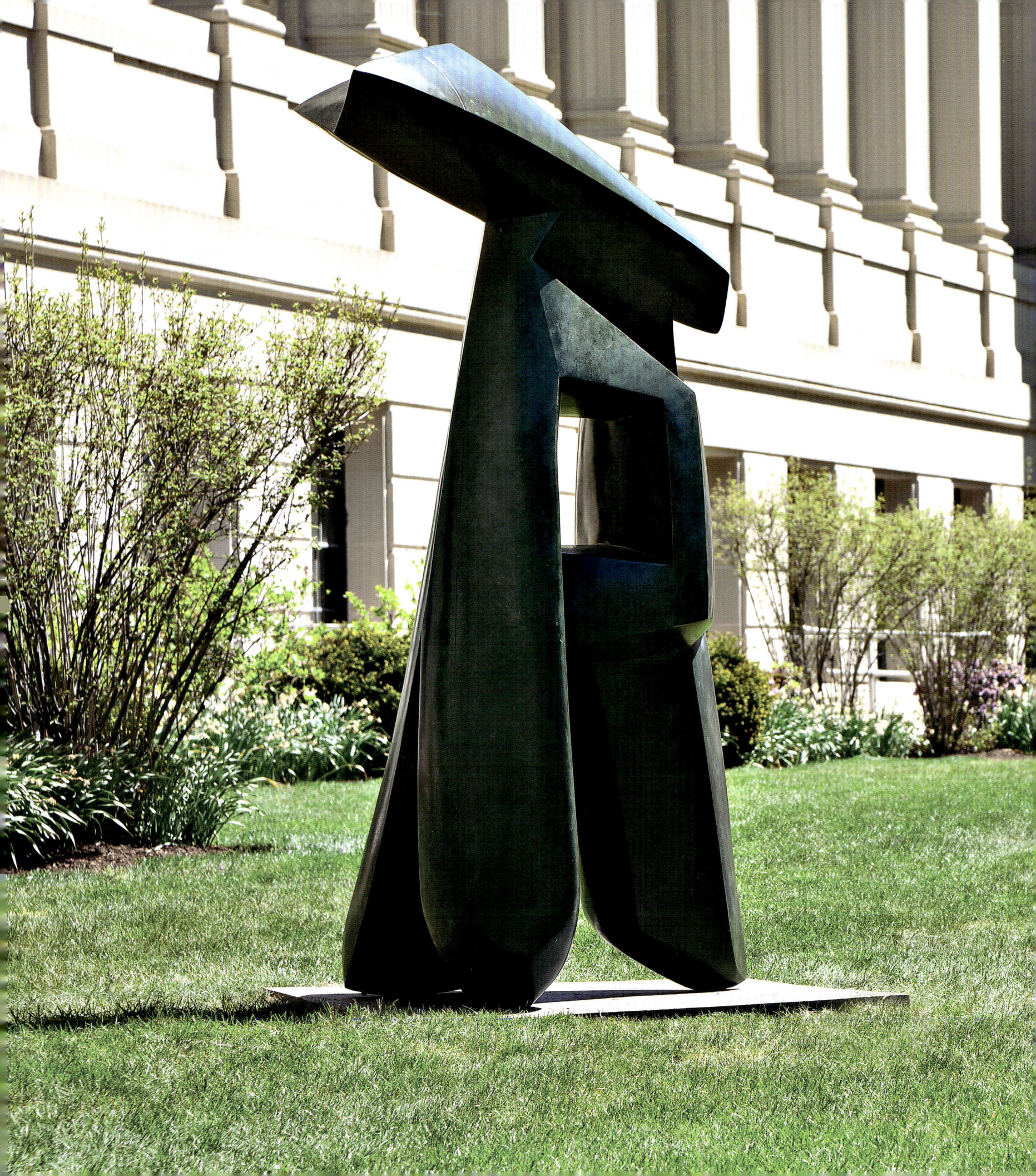

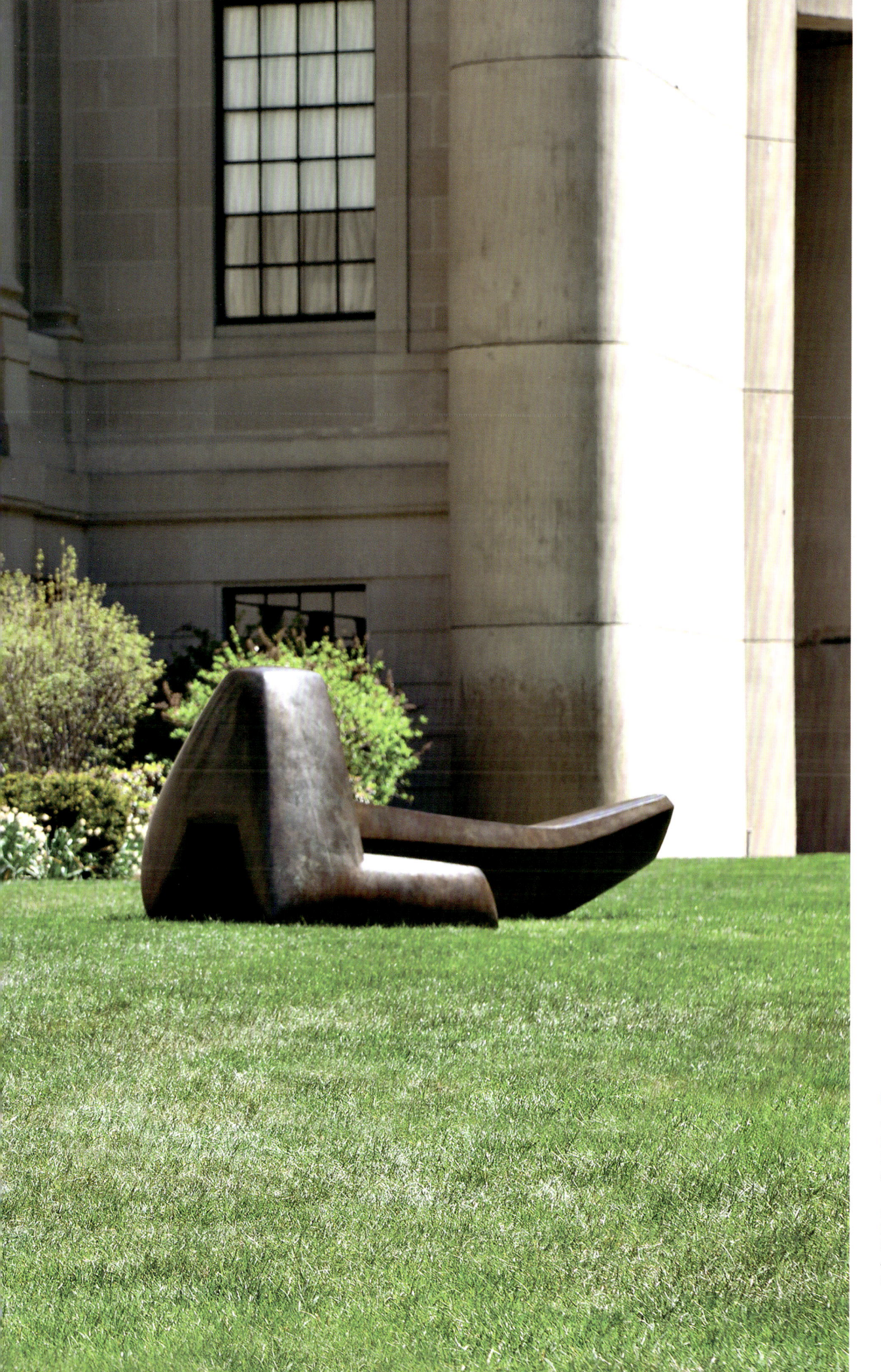

PLATE 6

LEFT
Inner Eagle, 1988
Bronze
86 x 49 x 34 in. (218.4 x 124.4 x 86.4 cm)

RIGHT
Reclining Blade, 1988
Bronze
43 3/16 x 139 x 42 in. (109.7 x 353.1 x 106.7 cm)
Christian Science Center, Boston, MA

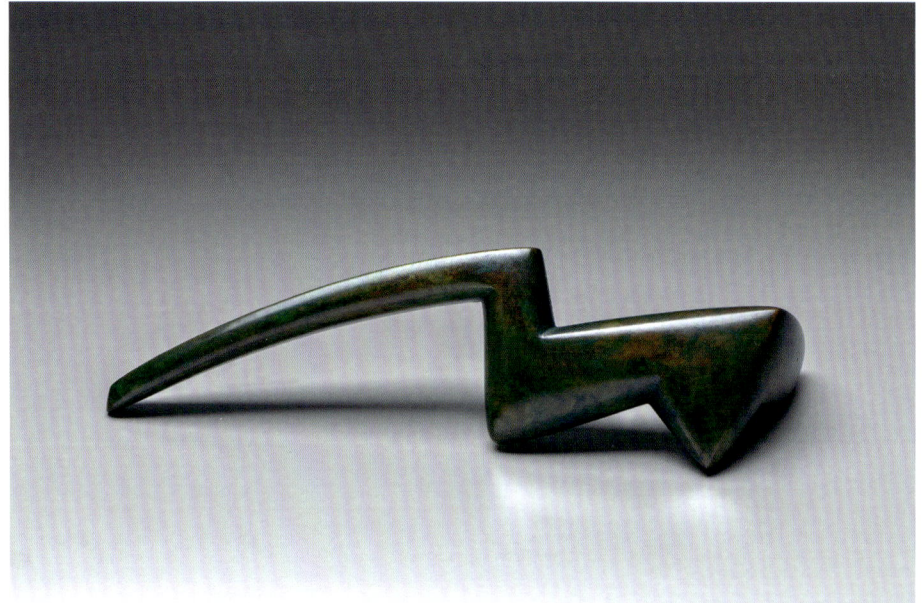

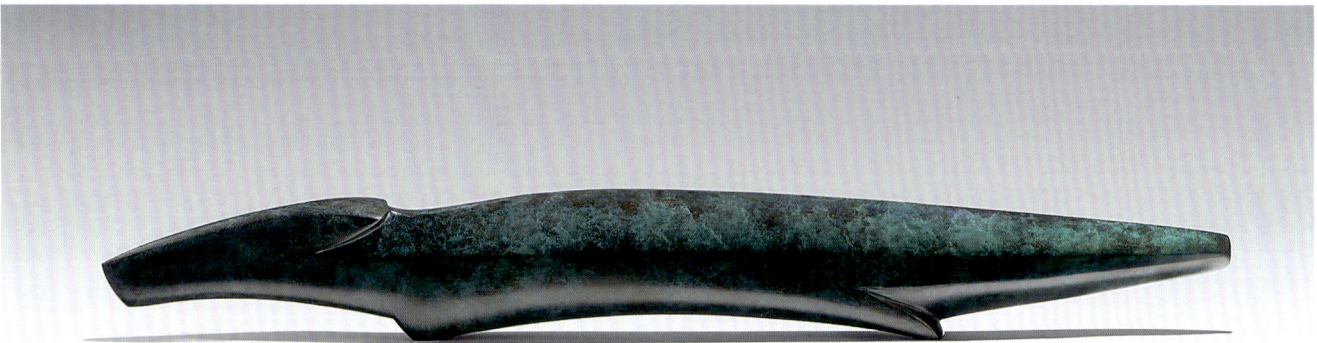

PLATE 7

Zigzag Snake, 1986
Bronze
1⅝ x 7¹¹⁄₁₆ x 2⅛ in. (4.1 x 19.6 x 5.3 cm)
Collection of the artist

PLATE 8

Fox Streak, 2011
Bronze
1½ x 12½ x ¹³⁄₁₆ in. (3.8 x 31.7 x 2 cm)
Private collection

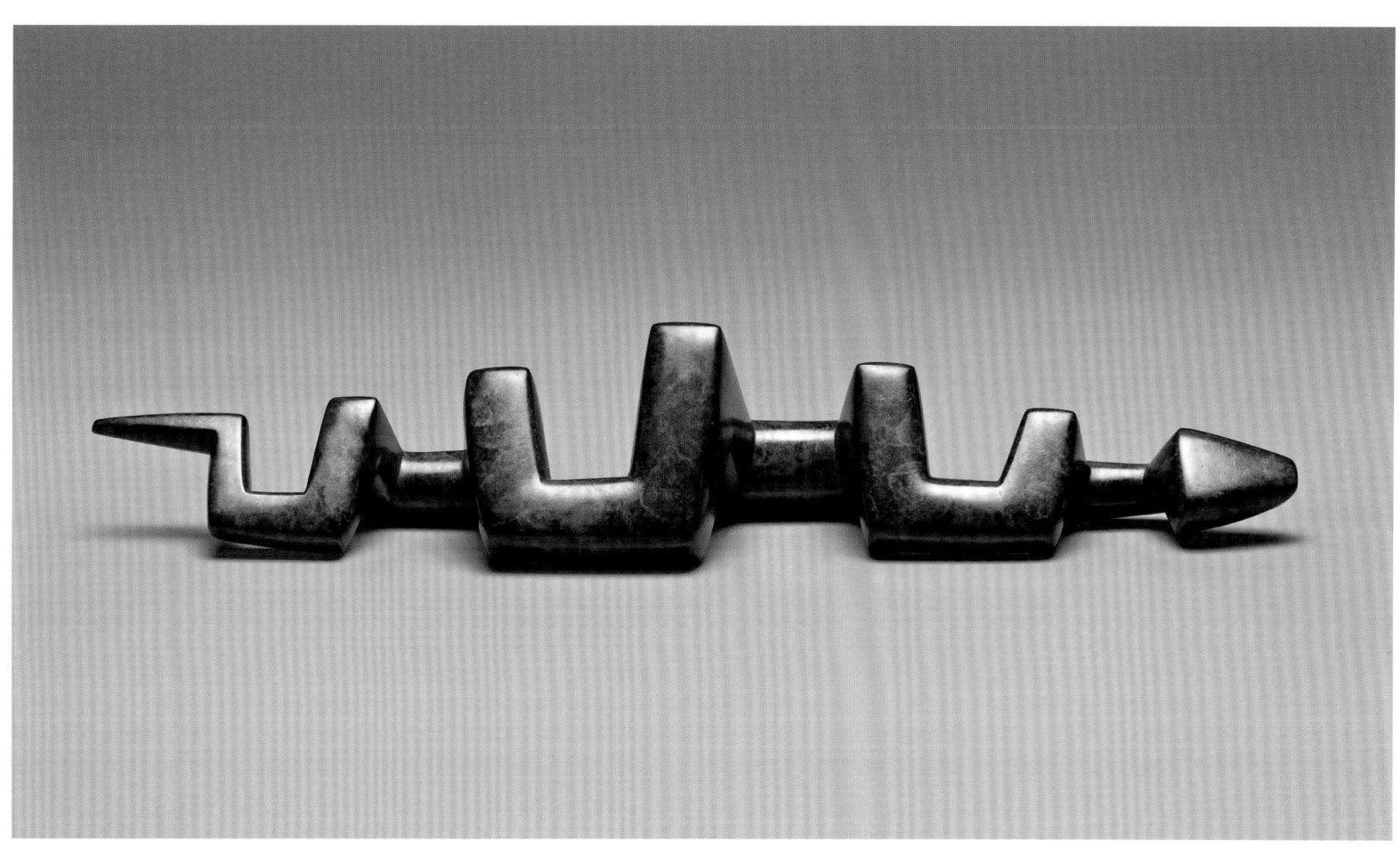

PLATE 9

Crank Snake, 2020
Bronze
2½ x 14 3/16 x 3½ in. (6.3 x 36.1 x 8.9 cm)
Collection of the artist

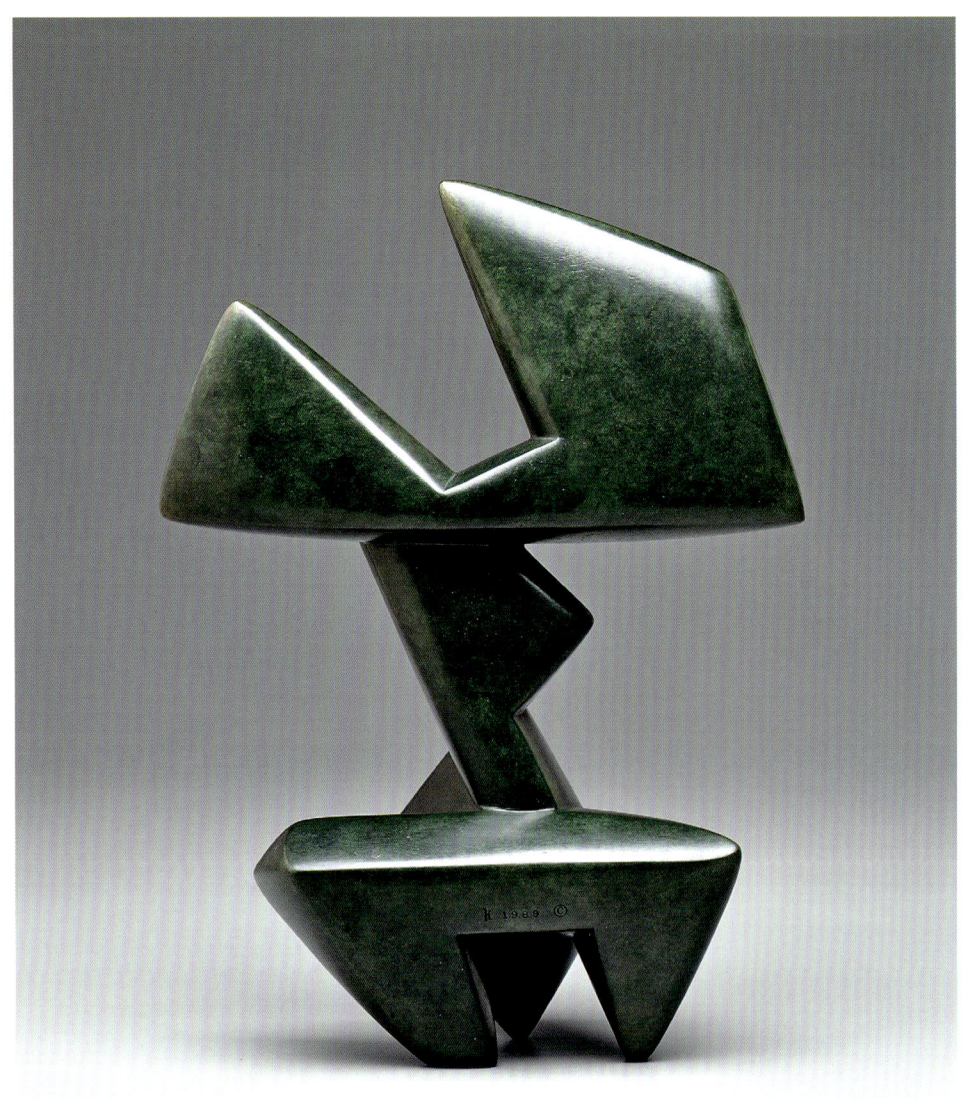

PLATE 10

Semaphore, 1989
Bronze
11 x 9¹¹⁄₁₆ x 4⅛ in. (27.9 x 24.6 x 10.4 cm)
Private collection

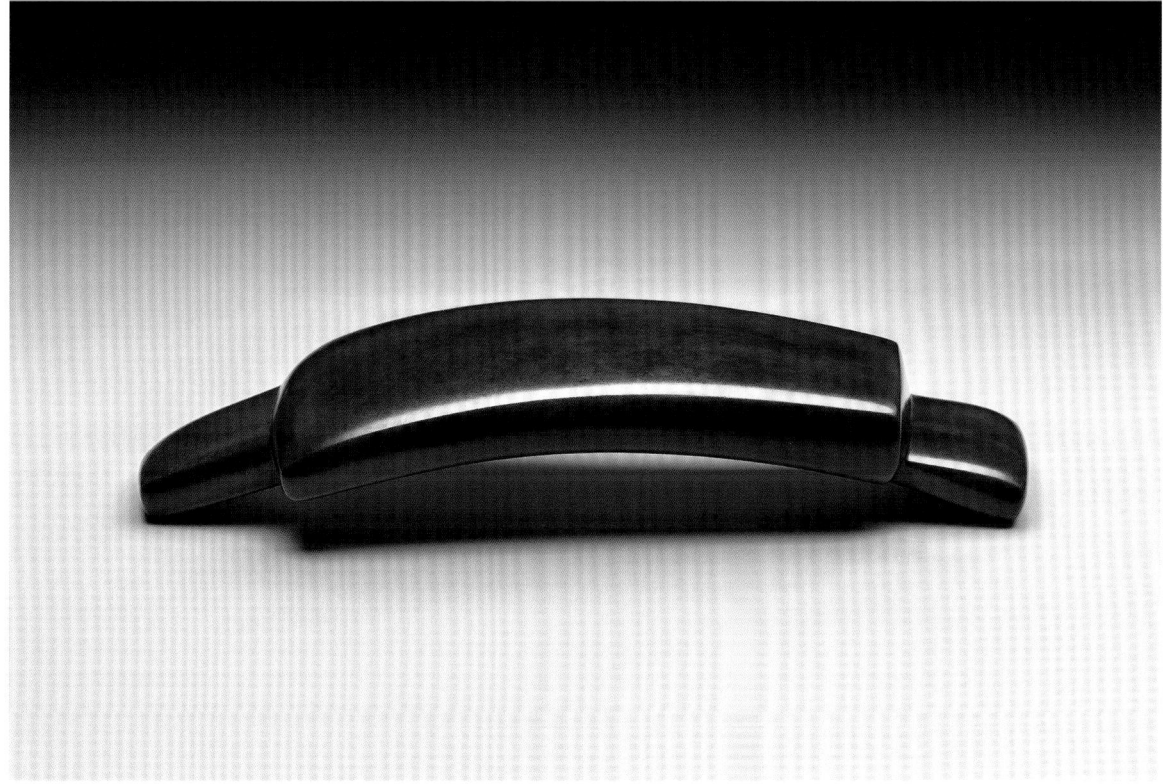

PLATE 11

Human Span, 1992
Bronze
2⅜ x 11¾ x 4 in. (6.1 x 29.8 x 10.2 cm)
Collection of the artist

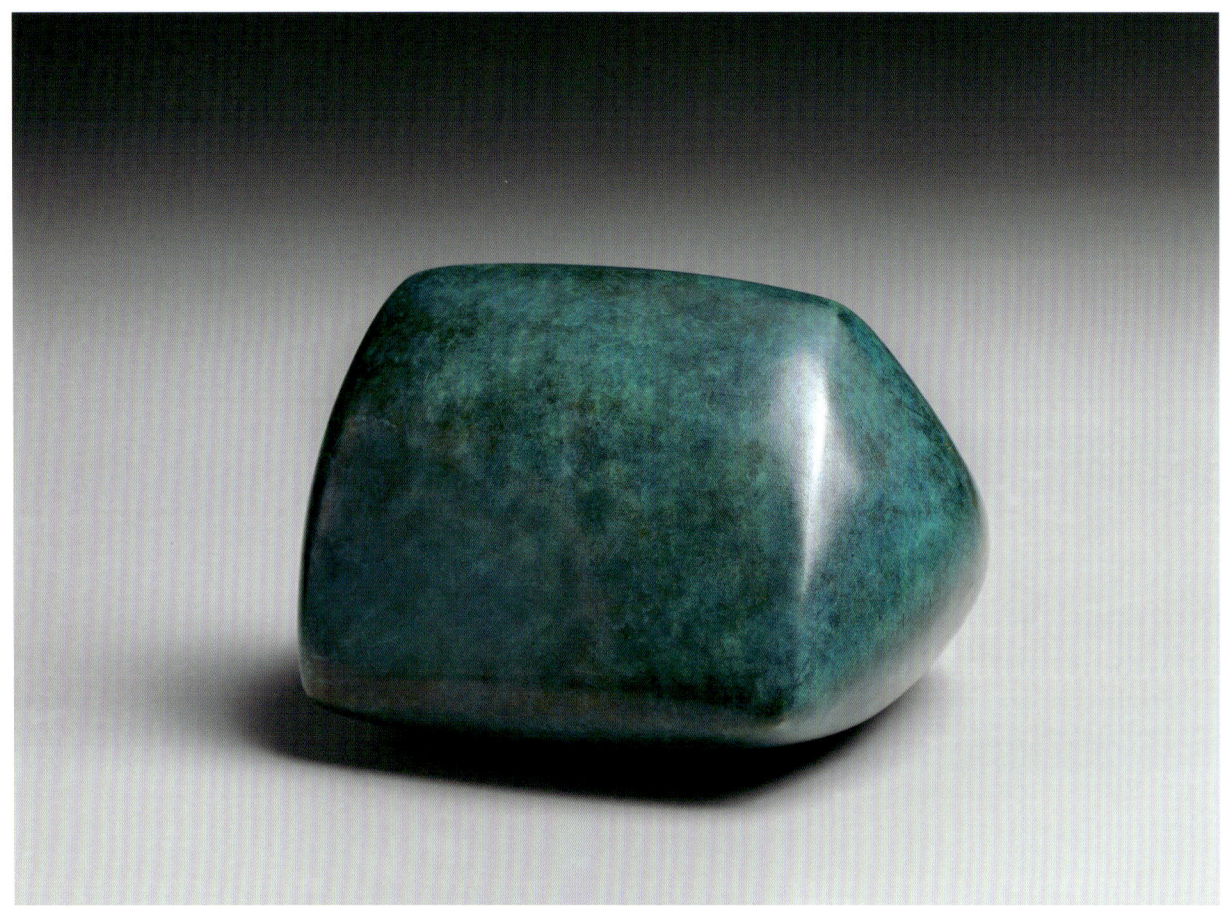

PLATE 12

Dragon's Egg, 1992
Bronze
4¼ x 6½ x 5¼ in. (10.8 x 16.5 x 13.3 cm)
Collection of the artist

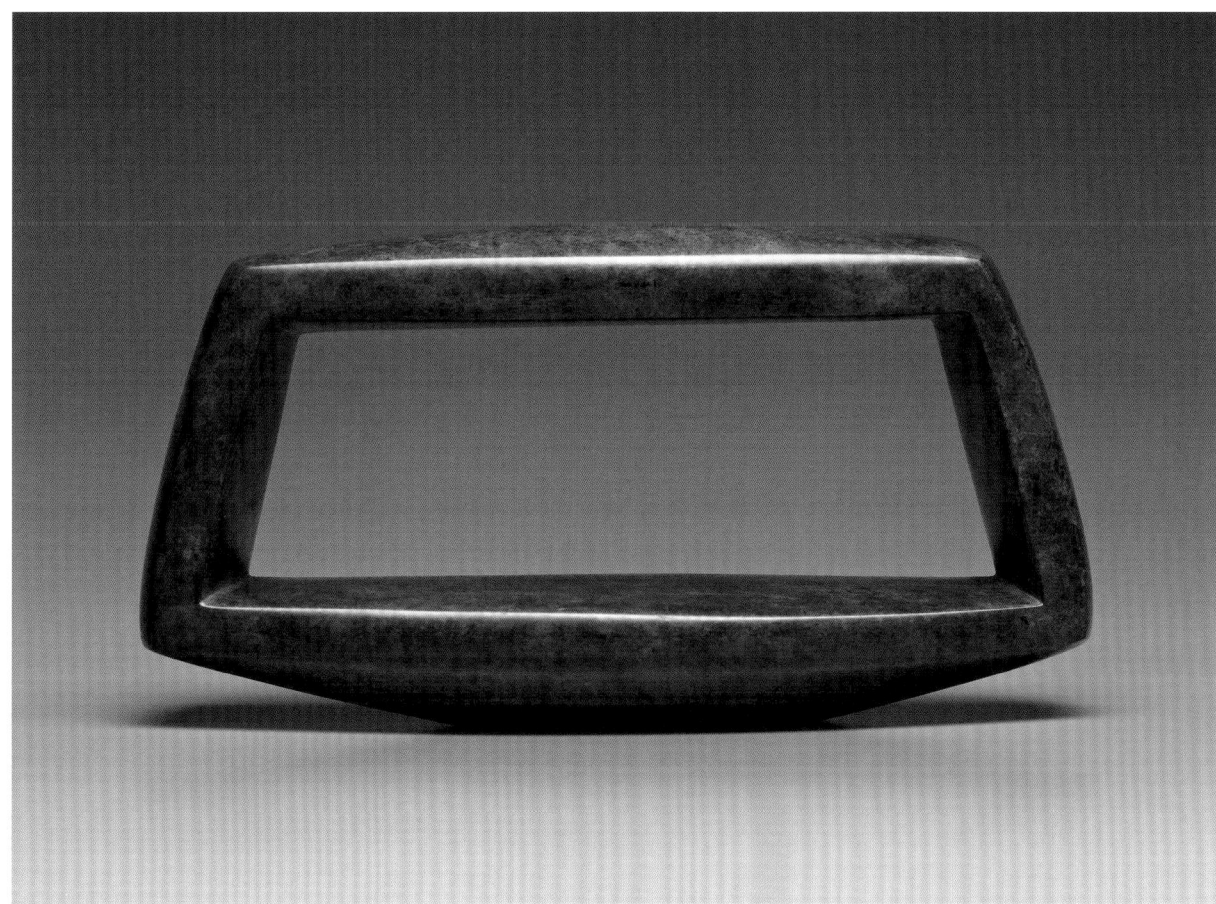

PLATE 13

Mouth of Truth, 2016
Bronze
4⁵⁄₁₆ x 8⁵⁄₈ x 3⅛ in. (10.9 x 21.8 x 7.9 cm)
Collection of the artist

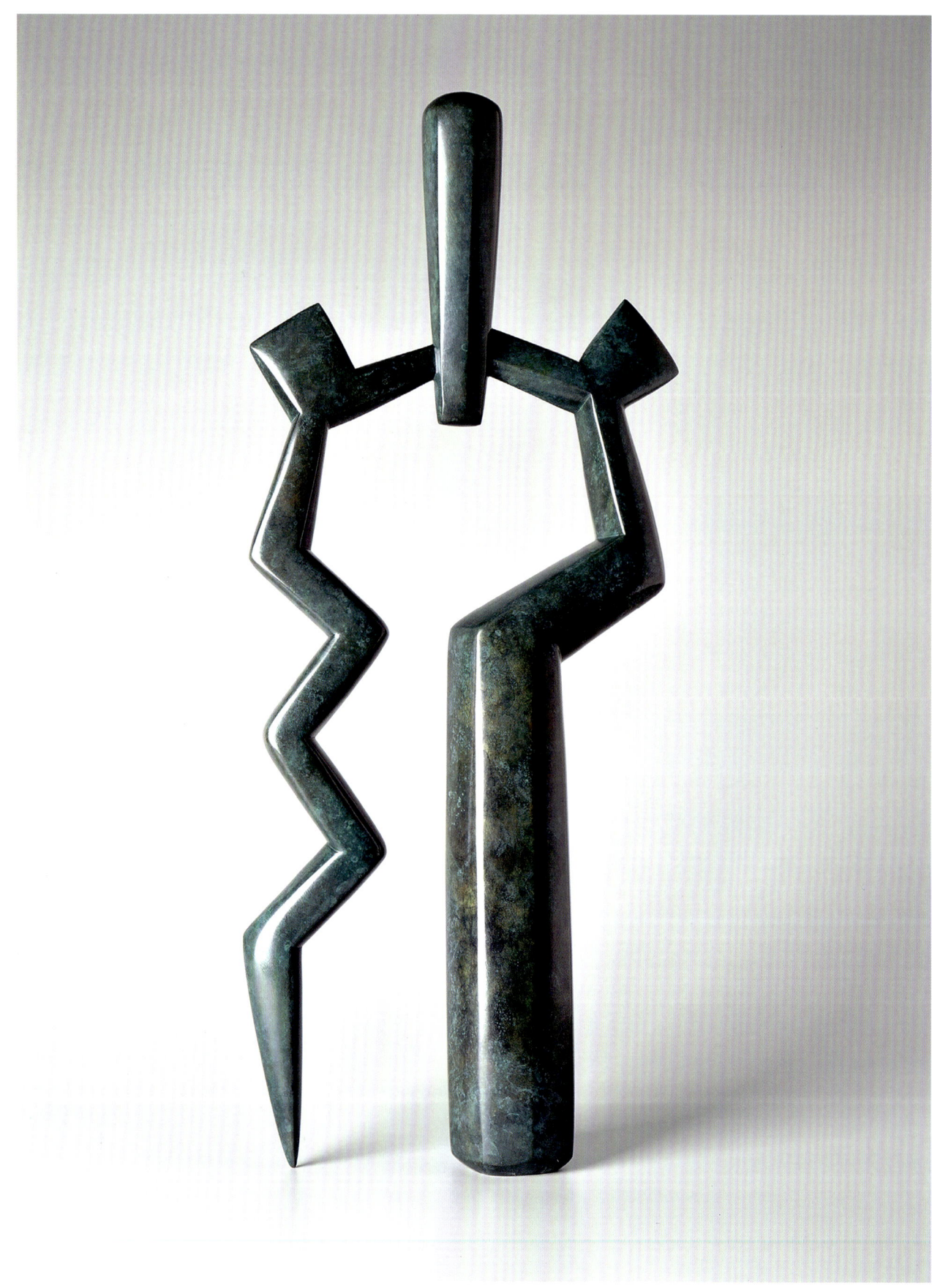

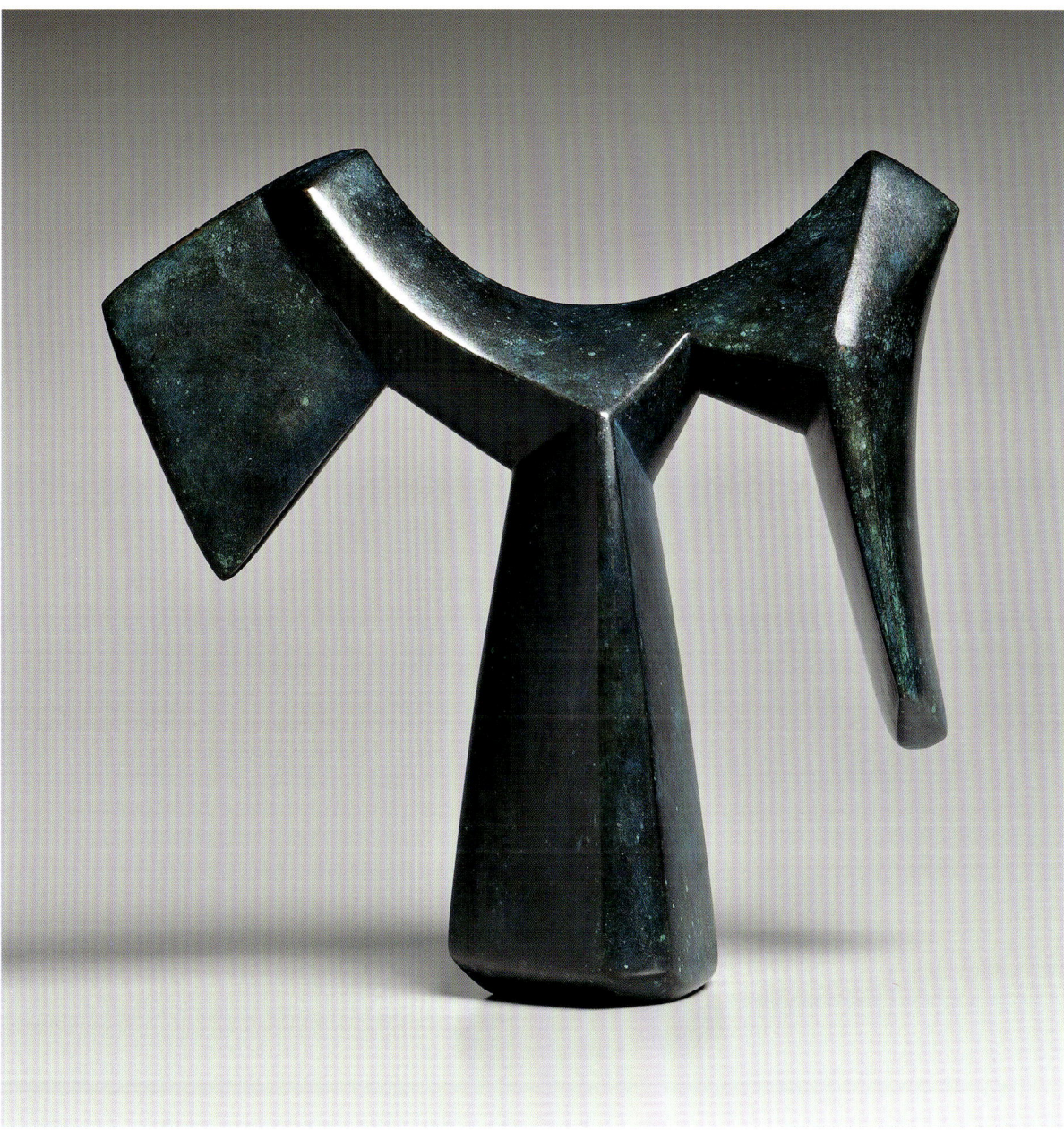

PLATE 14

Thunder and Lightning, 1994
Bronze
28³⁄₁₆ x 11¹¹⁄₁₆ x 3¹¹⁄₁₆ in. (71.6 x 29.7 x 9.4 cm)
Collection of the artist

PLATE 15

Monk Dancing, 1996
Bronze
11¹⁄₂ x 11¹³⁄₁₆ x 4¹³⁄₁₆ in. (29.2 x 30 x 12.2 cm)
Private collection

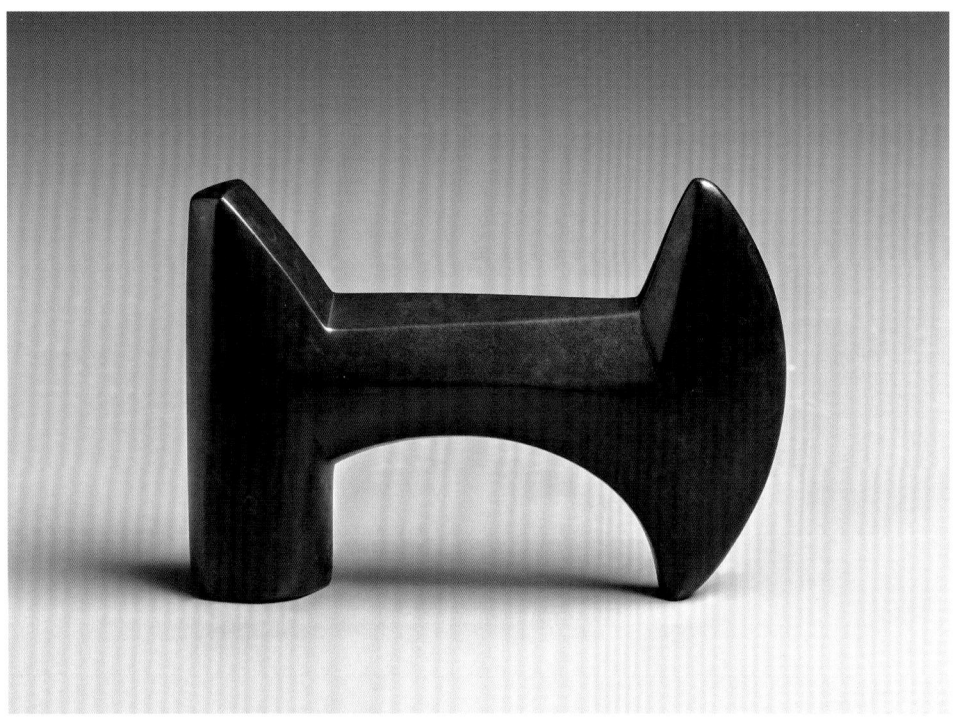

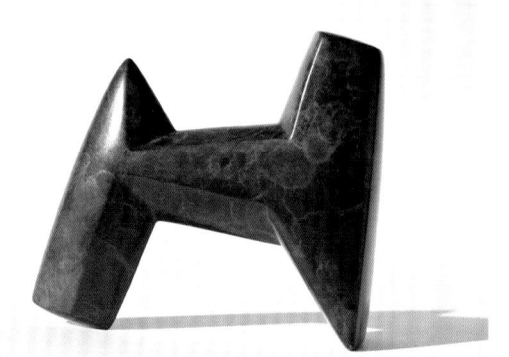

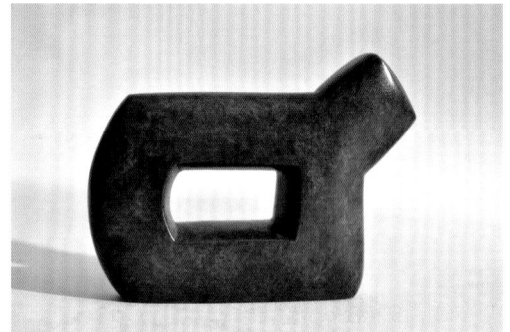

PLATE 16

Watch Dog, 1997
Bronze
4¼ x 6⅛ x 1⅜ in. (10.8 x 15.5 x 3.5 cm)
Collection of the artist

PLATE 17

Star Hound, 1997
Bronze
3½ x 3¹³⁄₁₆ x ¹⁵⁄₁₆ in. (8.9 x 9.6 x 3.3 cm)
Collection of the artist

PLATE 18

Empty Dog, 2013
Bronze
2 x 2¹³⁄₁₆ w x ⅝ in. (5.1 x 7.1 x 4.5 cm)
Collection of the artist

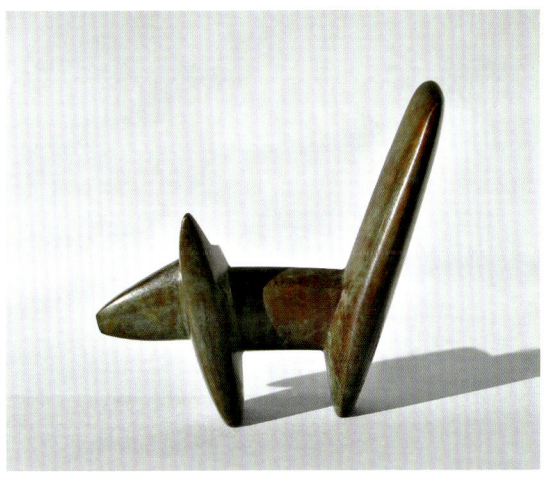

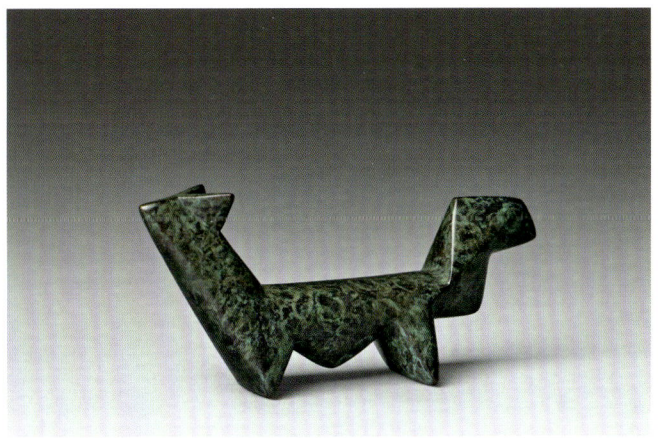

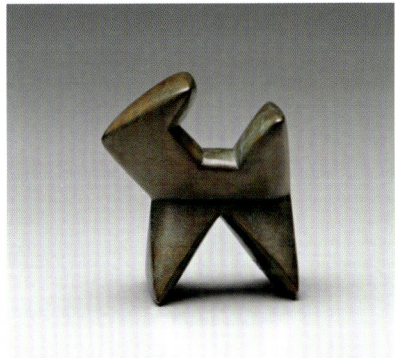

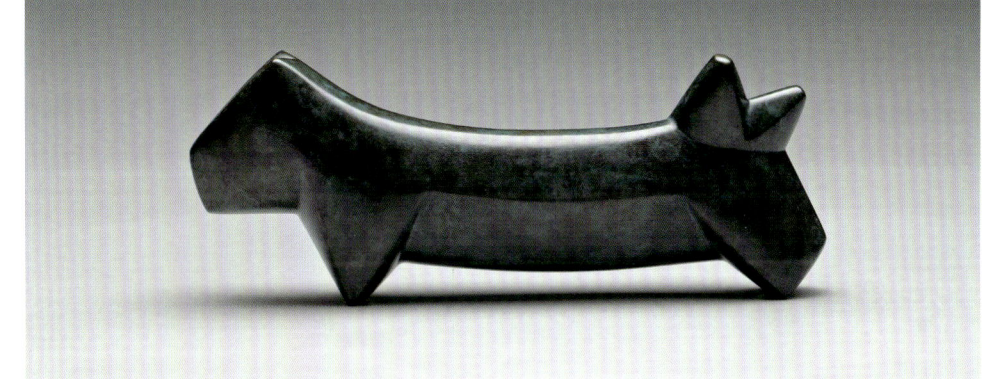

PLATE 19

Dog, 2009
Bronze
2⅝ x 3 x ¹³⁄₁₆ in. (6.6 x 7.6 x 2 cm)
Private collection

PLATE 20

Bronzadoodle, 2020
Bronze
1¹¹⁄₁₆ x 1½ x 1⅛ in. (4.3 x 3.8 x 2.8 cm)
Collection of the artist

PLATE 21

Best in Show, 2020
Bronze
2 x 4 x 1 in. (5 x 10.2 x 2.5 cm)
Private collection

PLATE 22

Rare Breed, 2021
Bronze
2¹¹⁄₁₆ x 7½ x ¹³⁄₁₆ in. (6.8 x 19 x 3 cm)
Private collection

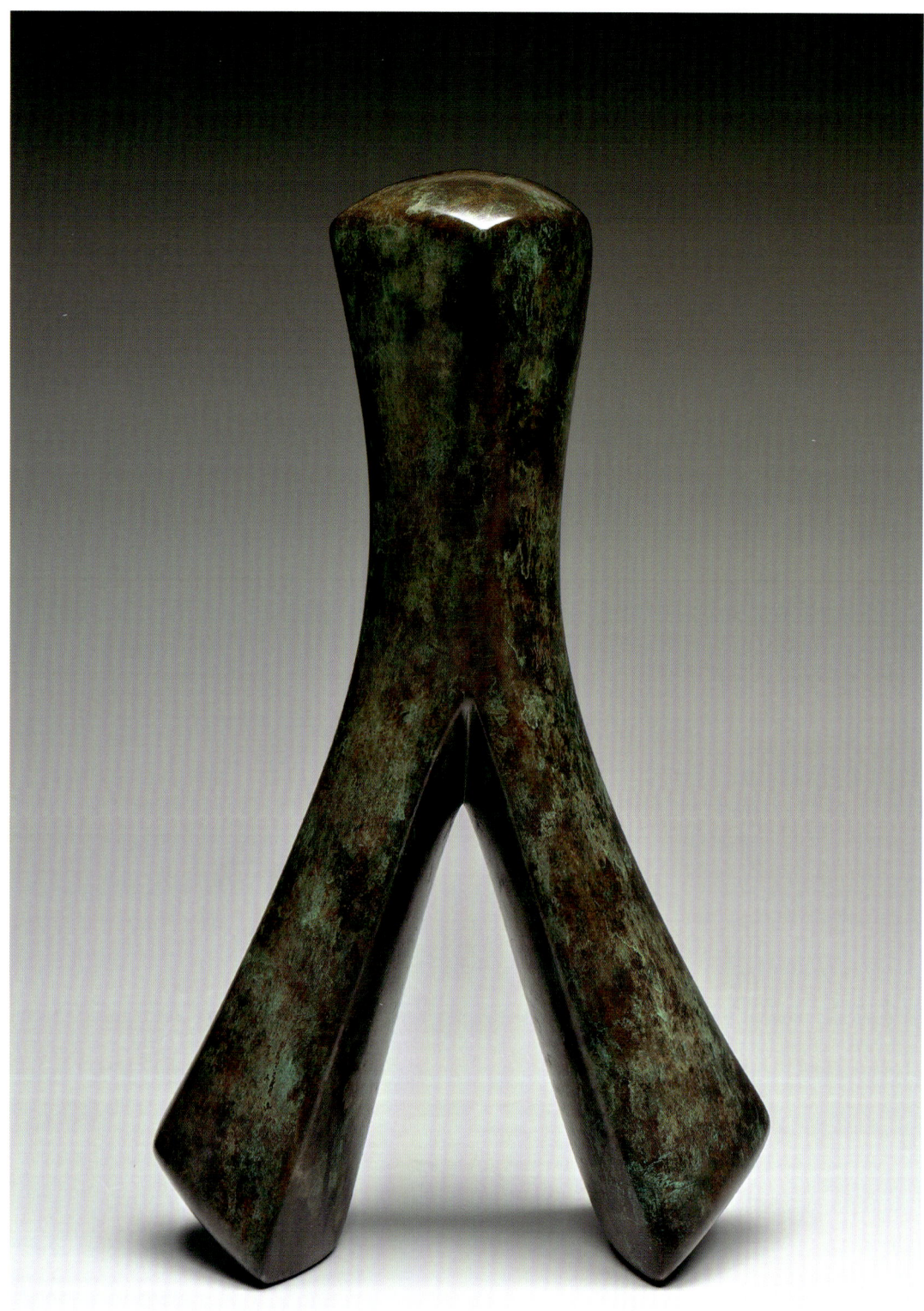

PLATE 23

They, 1998
Bronze
15 x 9 x 4¾ in. (38.1 x 22.9 x 12.1 cm)
Collection of the artist

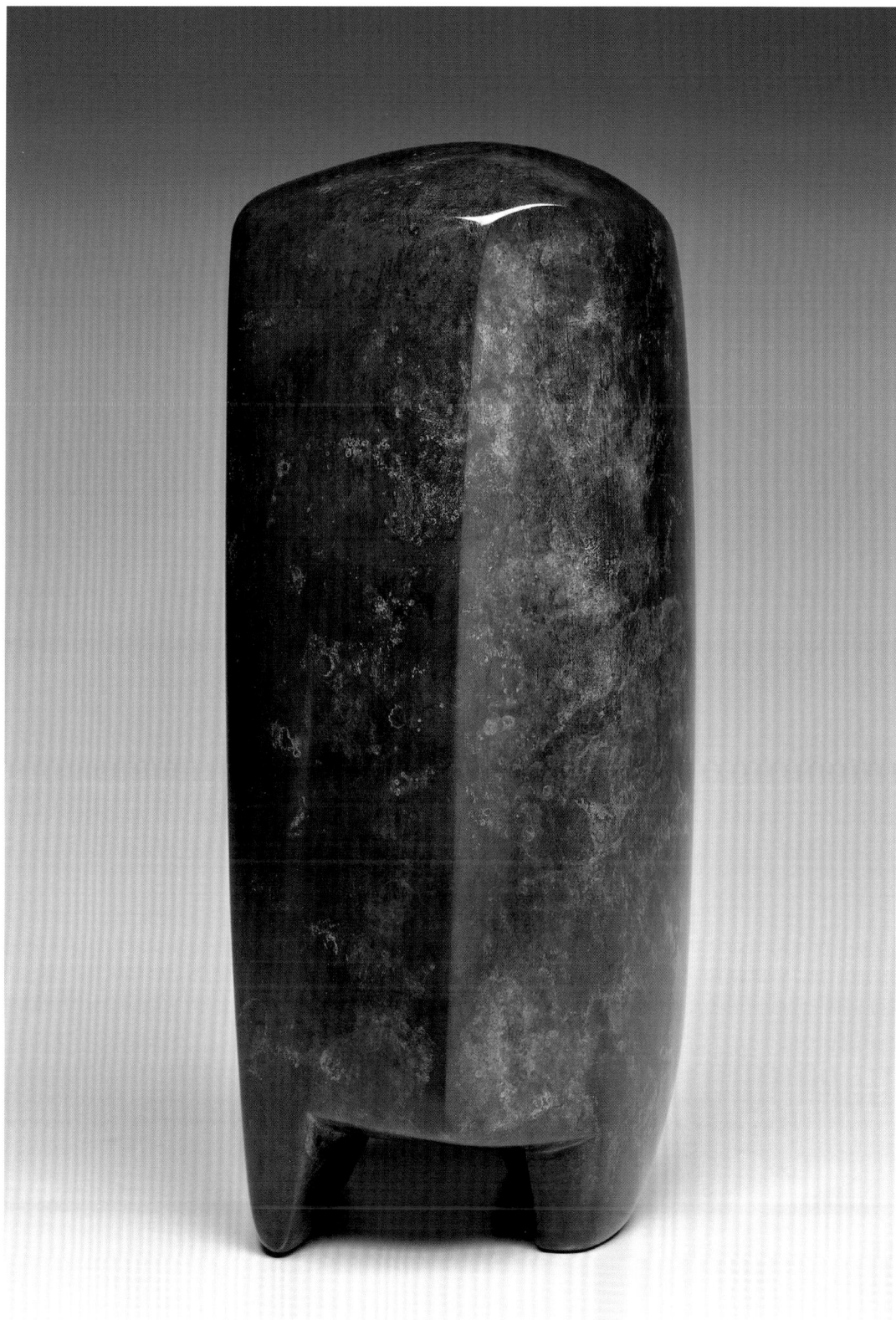

PLATE 24

Tower, 1998
Bronze
15½ x 6 x 5¾ in. (39.4 x 15.2 x 14.6 cm)
Collection of the artist

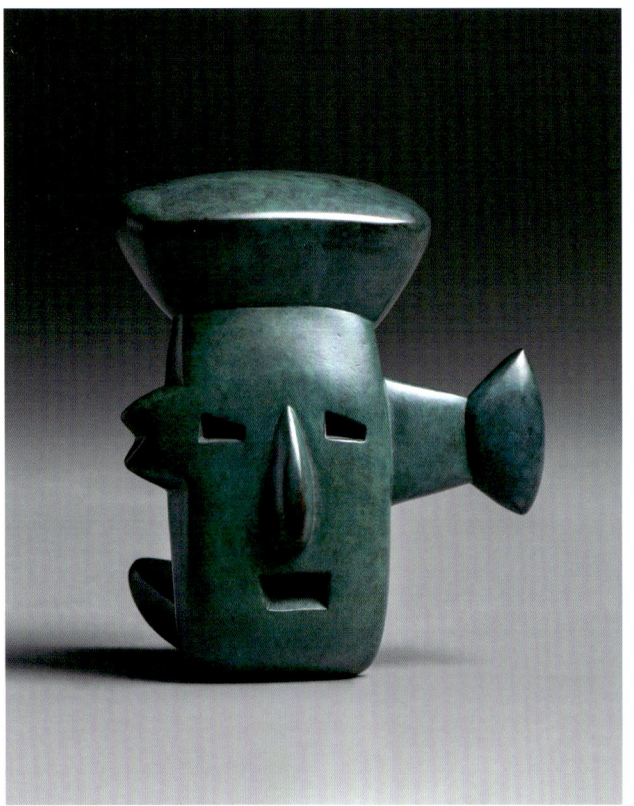

PLATE 25

Fishead, 2000
Bronze
4½ x 4 x 2¹¹⁄₁₆ in. (11.4 x 10.2 x 6.6 cm)
Collection of the artist

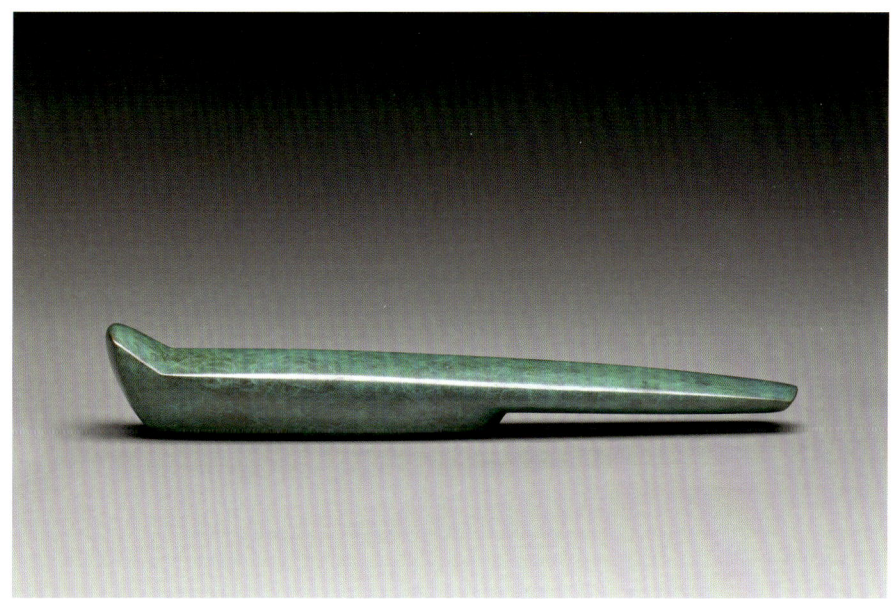

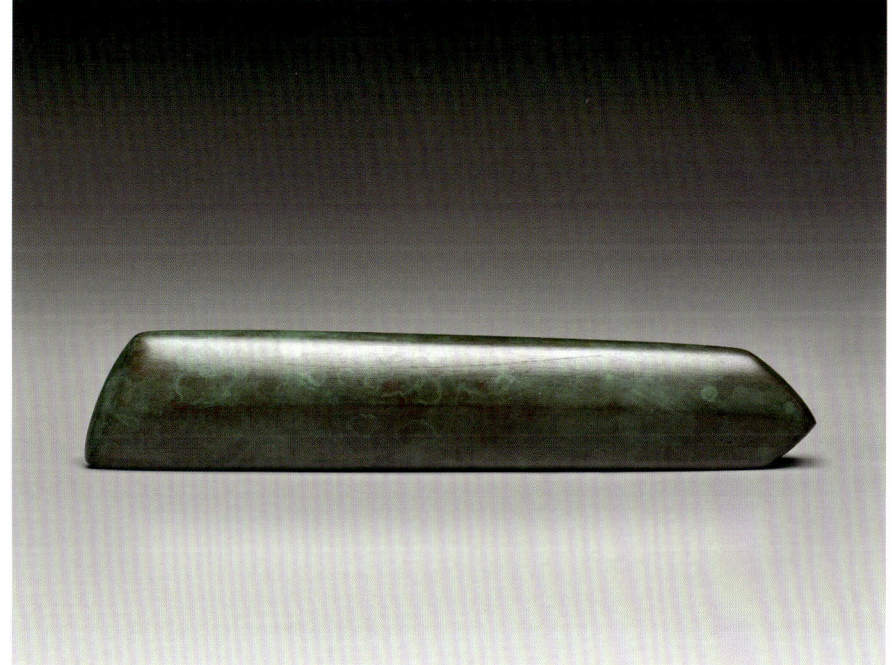

PLATE 26

Migrator 1, 2001
Bronze
8¹¹⁄₁₆ x 1⁷⁄₁₆ x 1⁷⁄₁₆ in. (22.1 x 3.5 x 3.5 cm)
Collection of the artist

PLATE 27

Migrator 2, 2002
Bronze
1⁵⁄₁₆ x 9⁵⁄₁₆ x ⁹⁄₁₆ in. (3.3 x 23.6 x 1.8 cm)
Collection of the artist

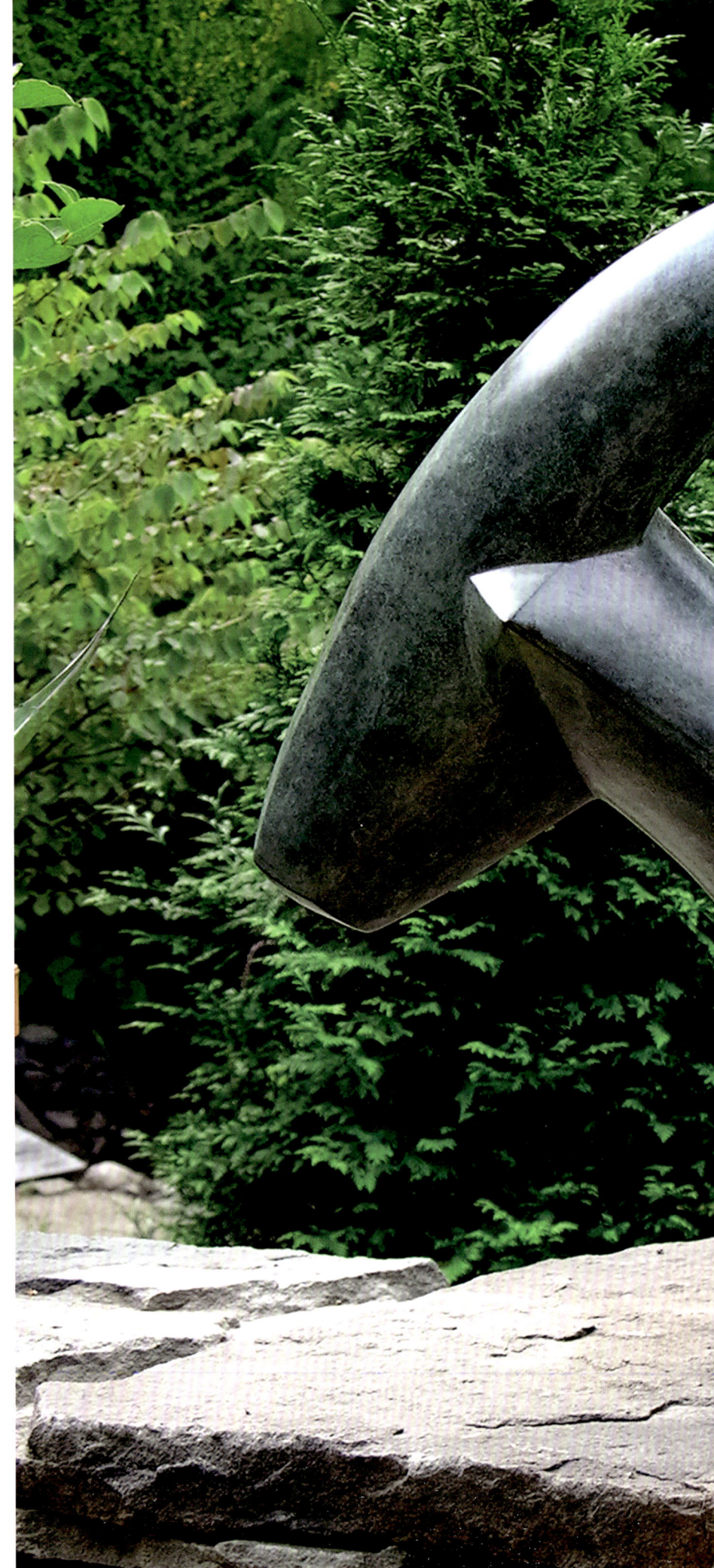

PLATE 28

Updated Goat, 2005
Bronze
23 x 29 x 9 in. (58.4 x 73.7 x 22.9 cm)
Private collection

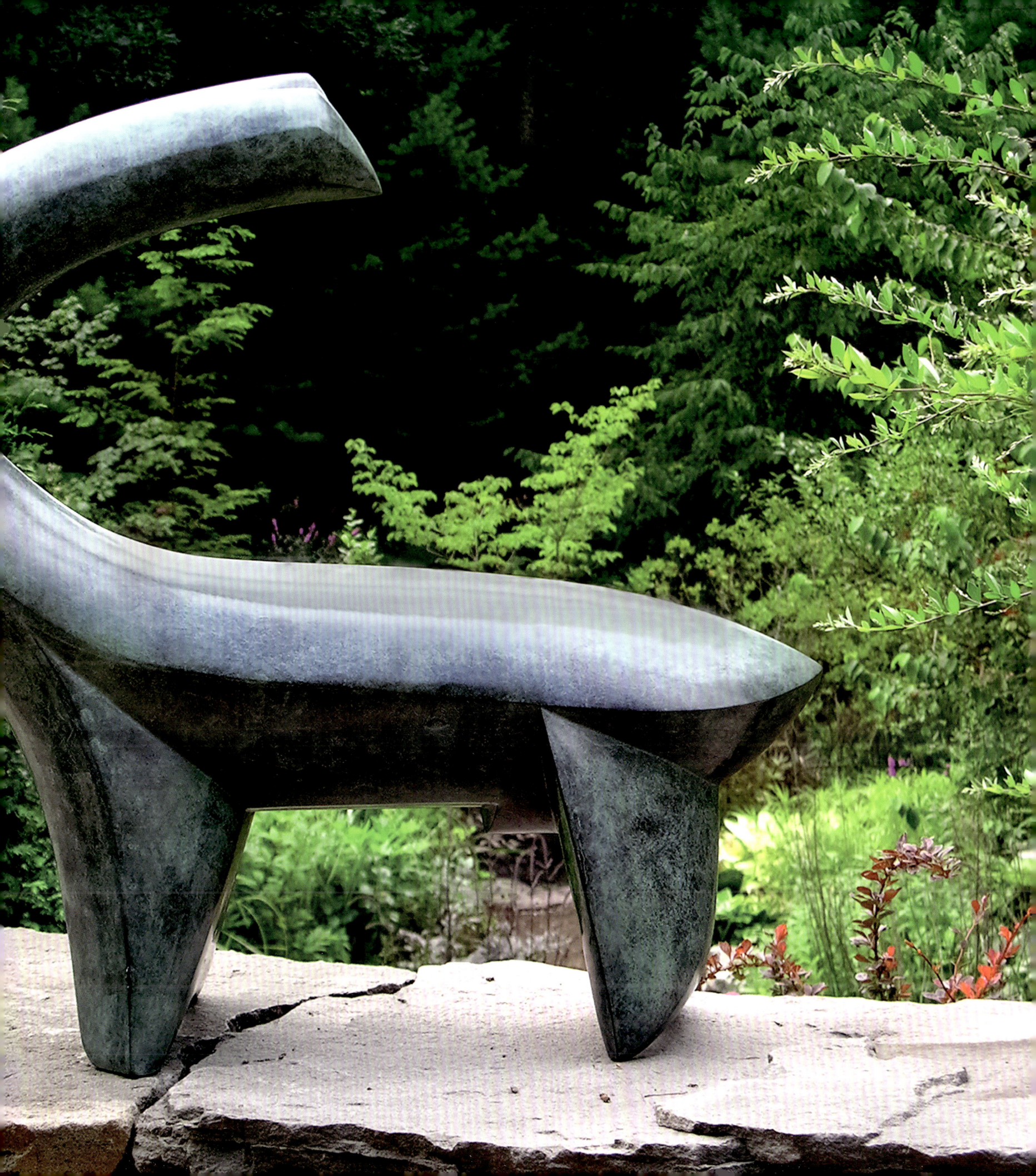

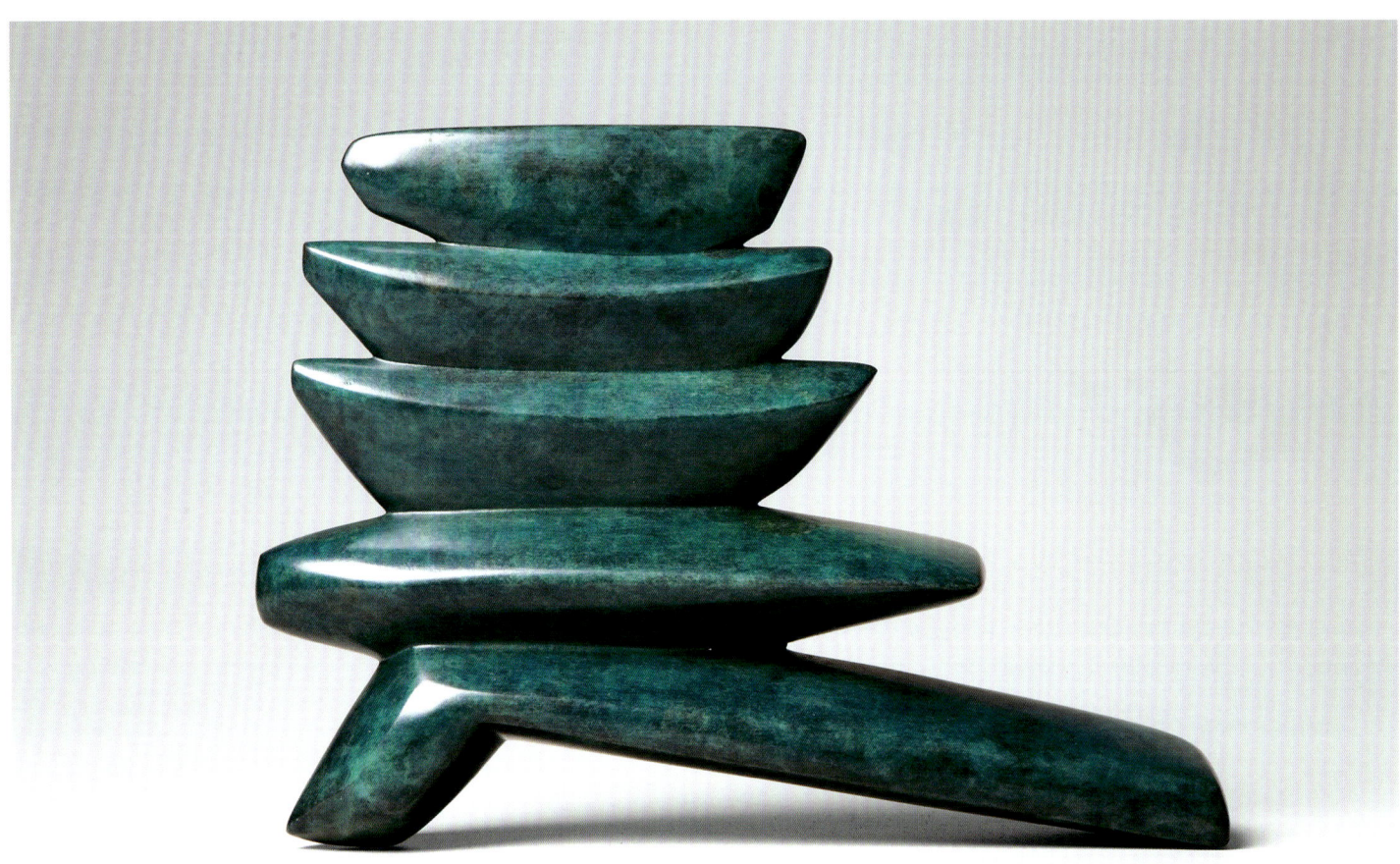

PLATE 29

Family of Five, 2006
Bronze
9 x 12 x 4 in. (22.9 x 30.5 x 10.2 cm)
Collection of the artist

PLATE 30

Space Rabbit, 2006
Bronze
20 x 11 x 8 in. (50.8 x 28 x 20.3 cm)
Collection of the artist

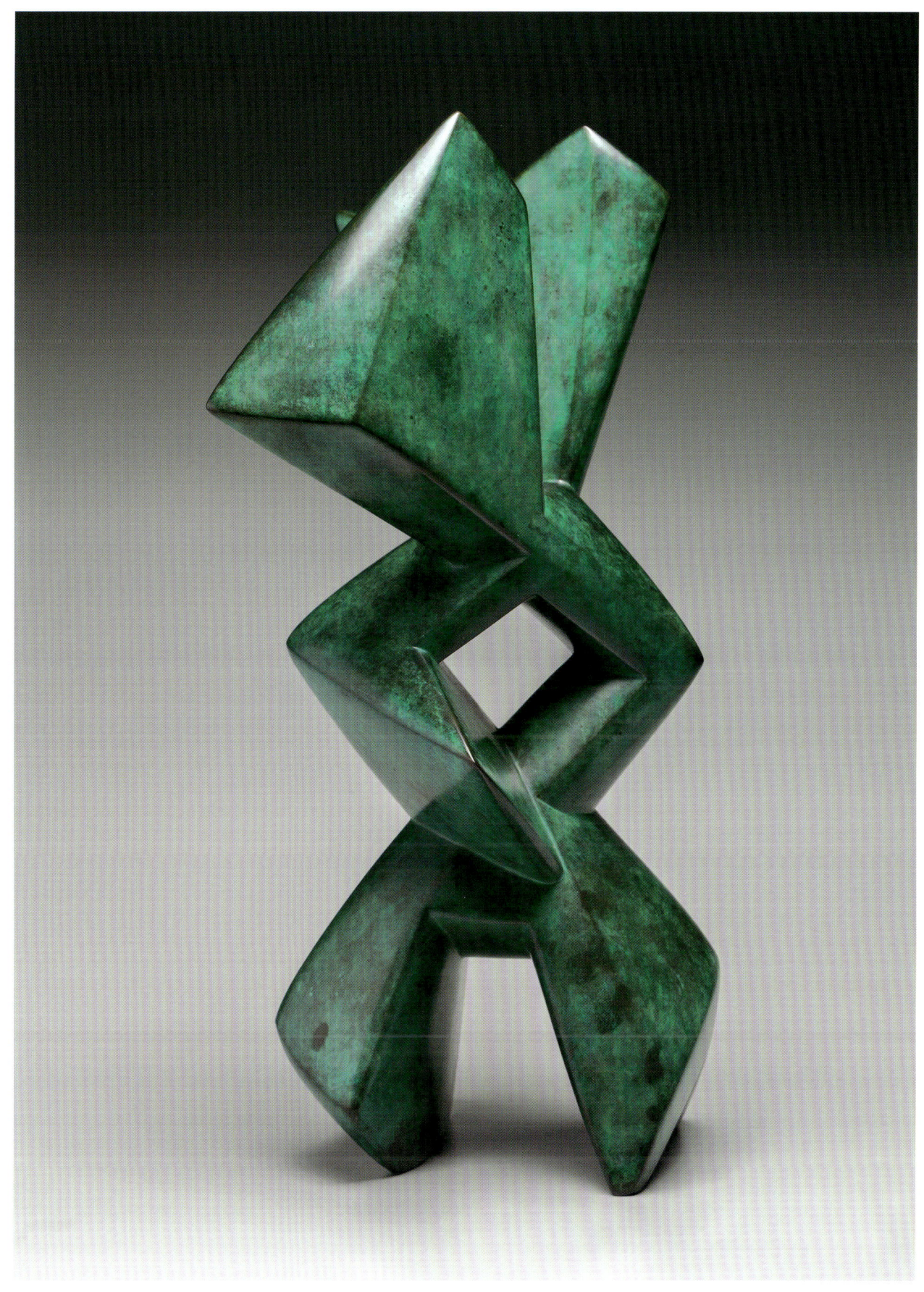

PLATE 31

Bird of Knowledge, 2007
Bronze
76⁷⁄₁₆ x 15³⁄₁₆ x 14¹⁄₂ in. (194.1 x 38.6 x 36.8 cm)
Collection of the artist

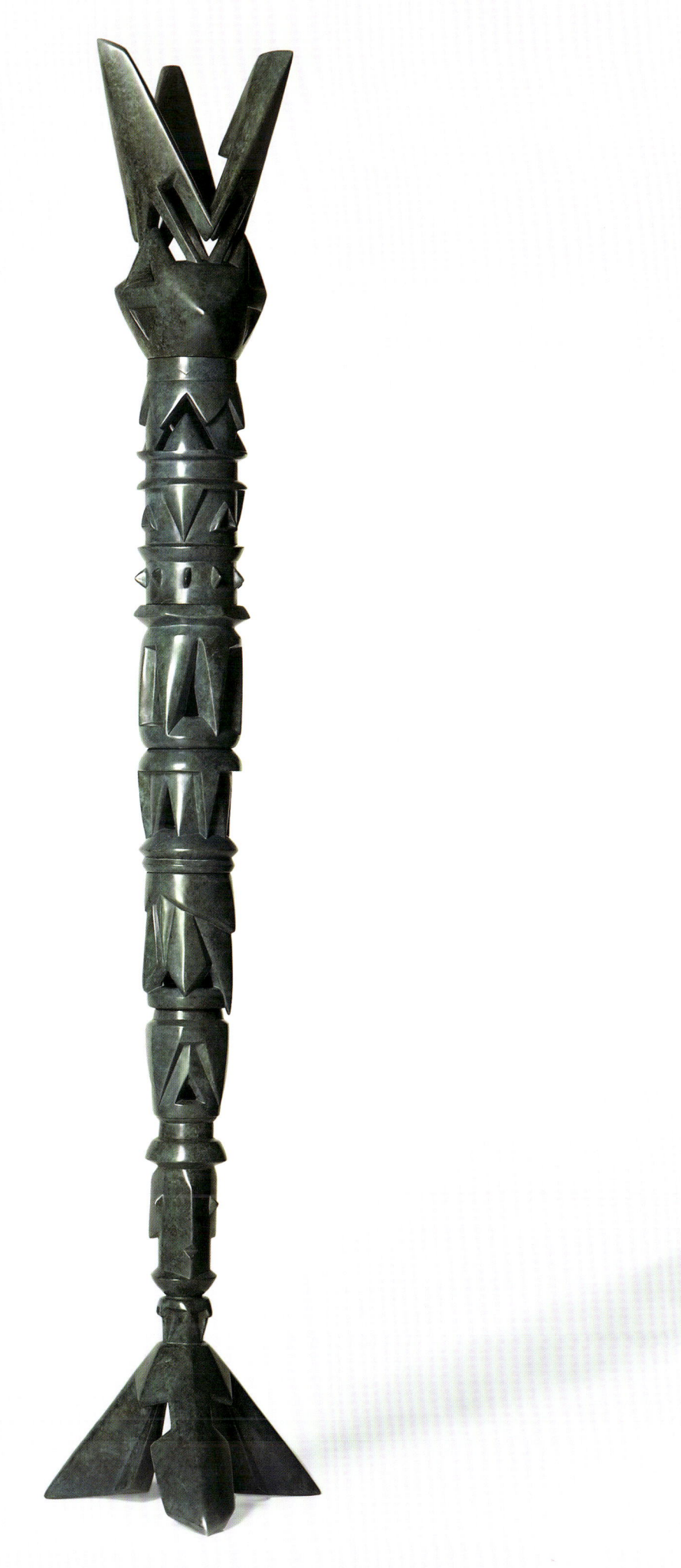

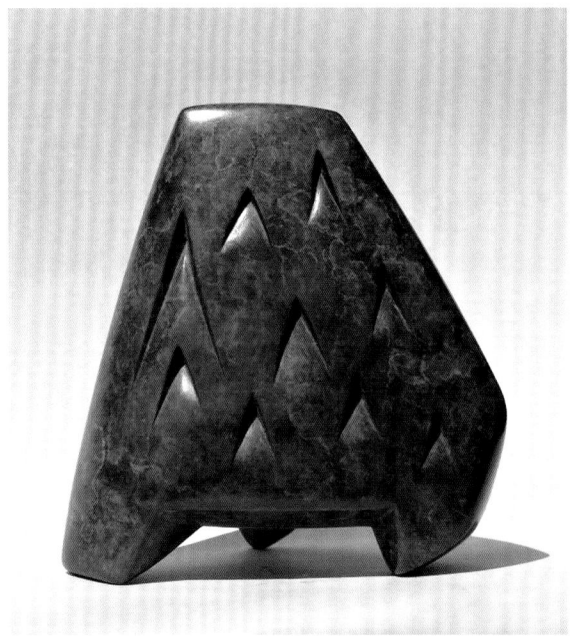

PLATE 32

Animal in the Forest, 2007
Bronze
7 x 6¹¹⁄₁₆ x 4³⁄₁₆ in. (17.8 x 17 x 10.4 cm)
Collection of the artist

PLATE 33

Crest, 2008
Bronze
29 x 13¹¹⁄₁₆ x 5⁷⁄₁₆ in. (73.7 x 34.8 x 13.7 cm)
Private collection

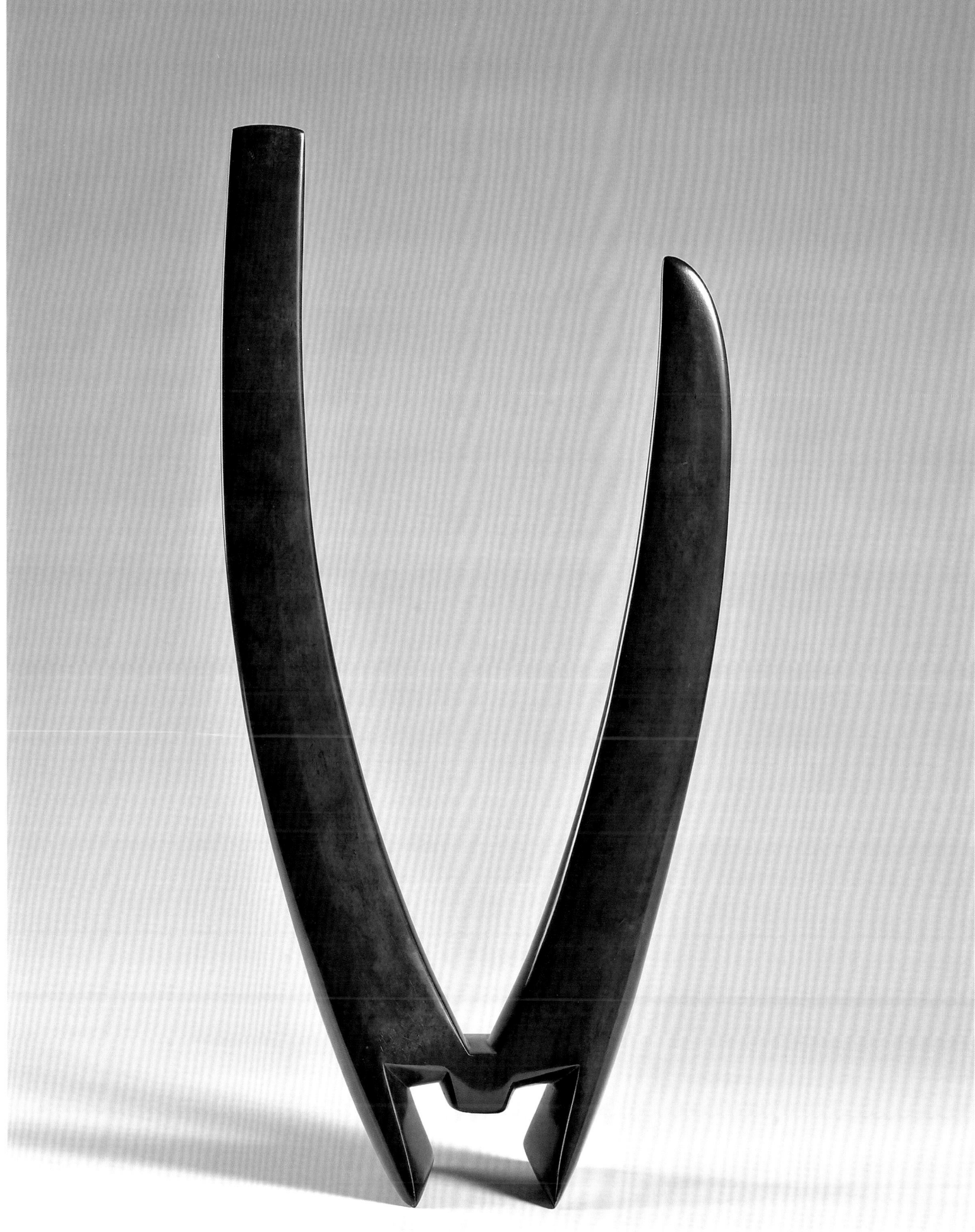

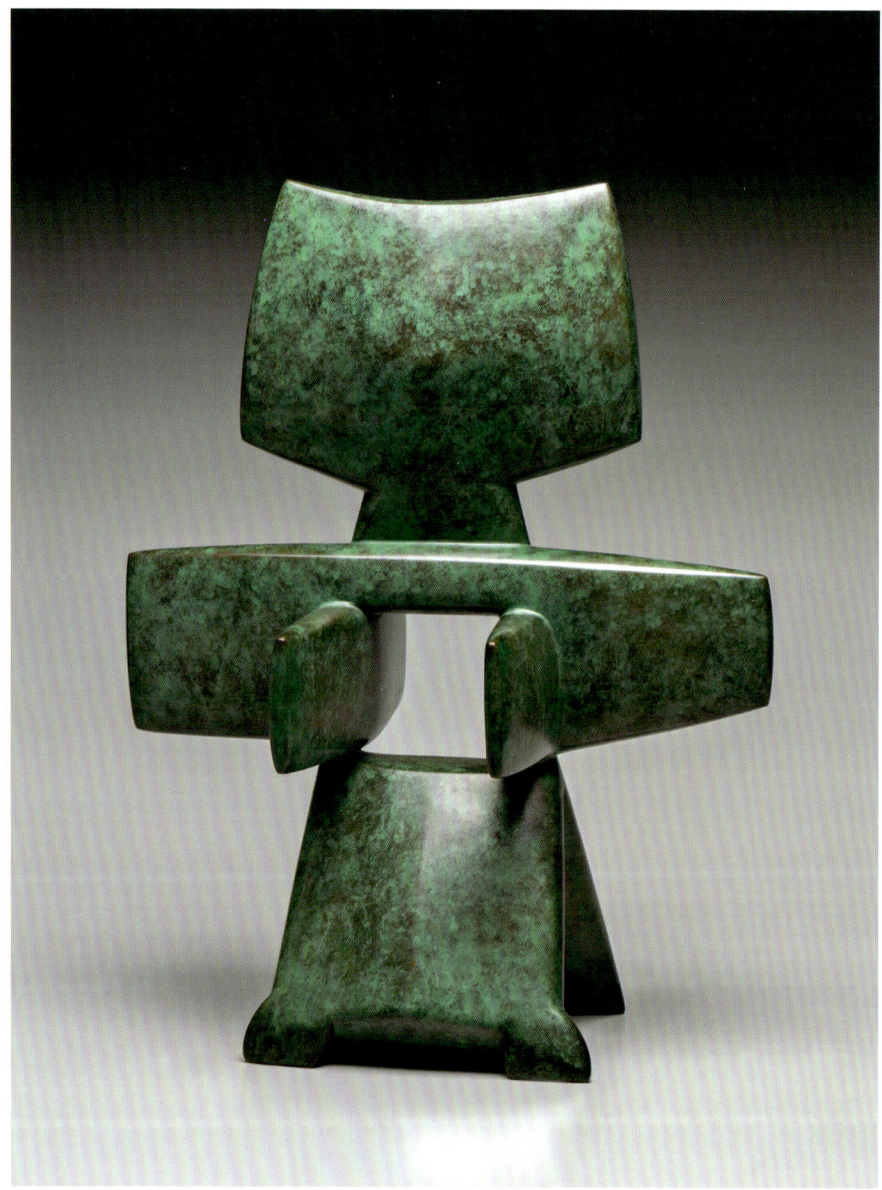

PLATE 34

Household Deity, 2008
Bronze
17 3/16 x 13 7/8 x 10 3/16 in. (43.7 x 35.3 x 25.9 cm)
Collection of the artist

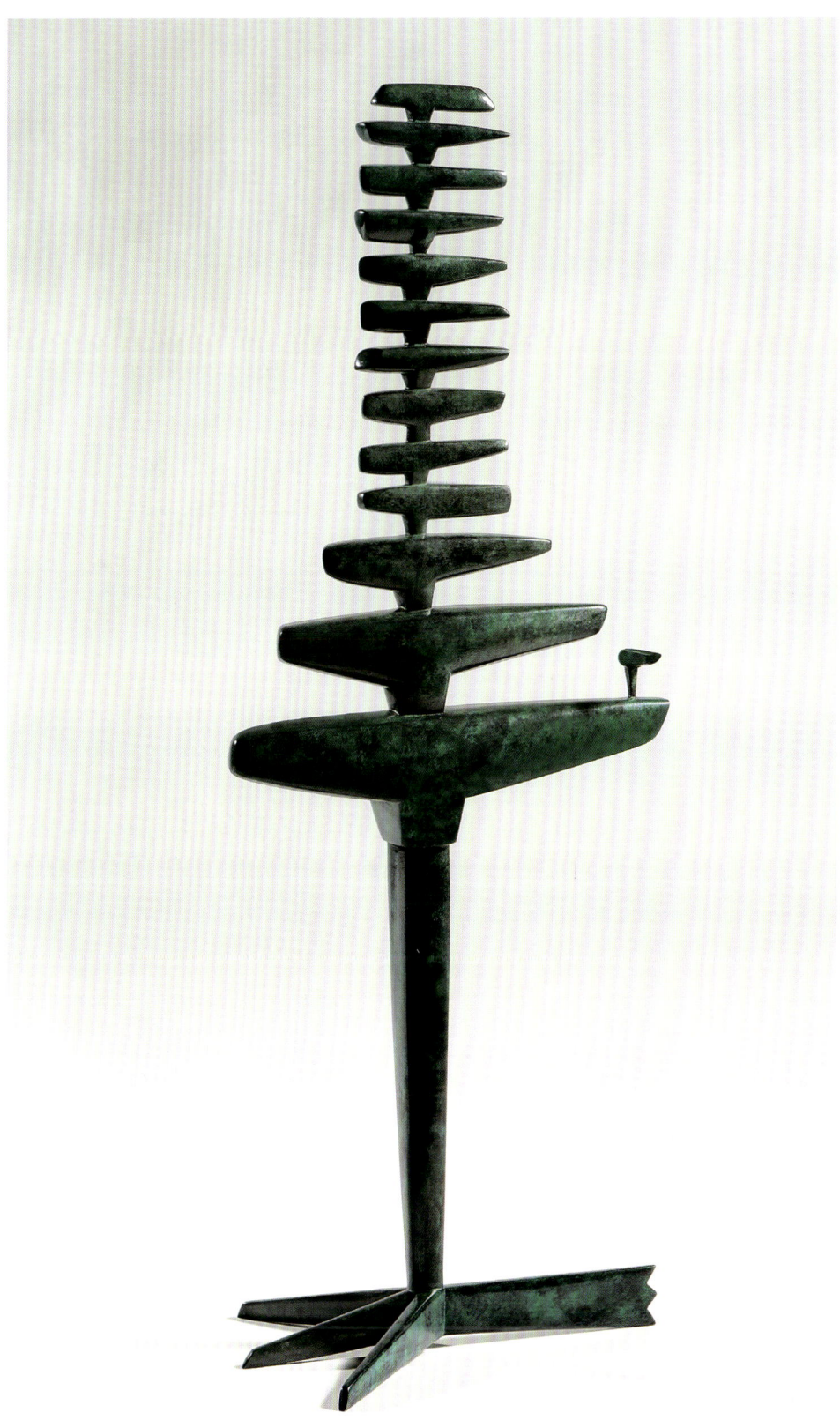

PLATE 35

Standing Murmuration 752, 2009
Bronze
24⁵⁄₁₆ x 9³⁄₈ x 6³⁄₈ in. (61.7 x 23.9 x 16.2 cm)
Collection of the artist

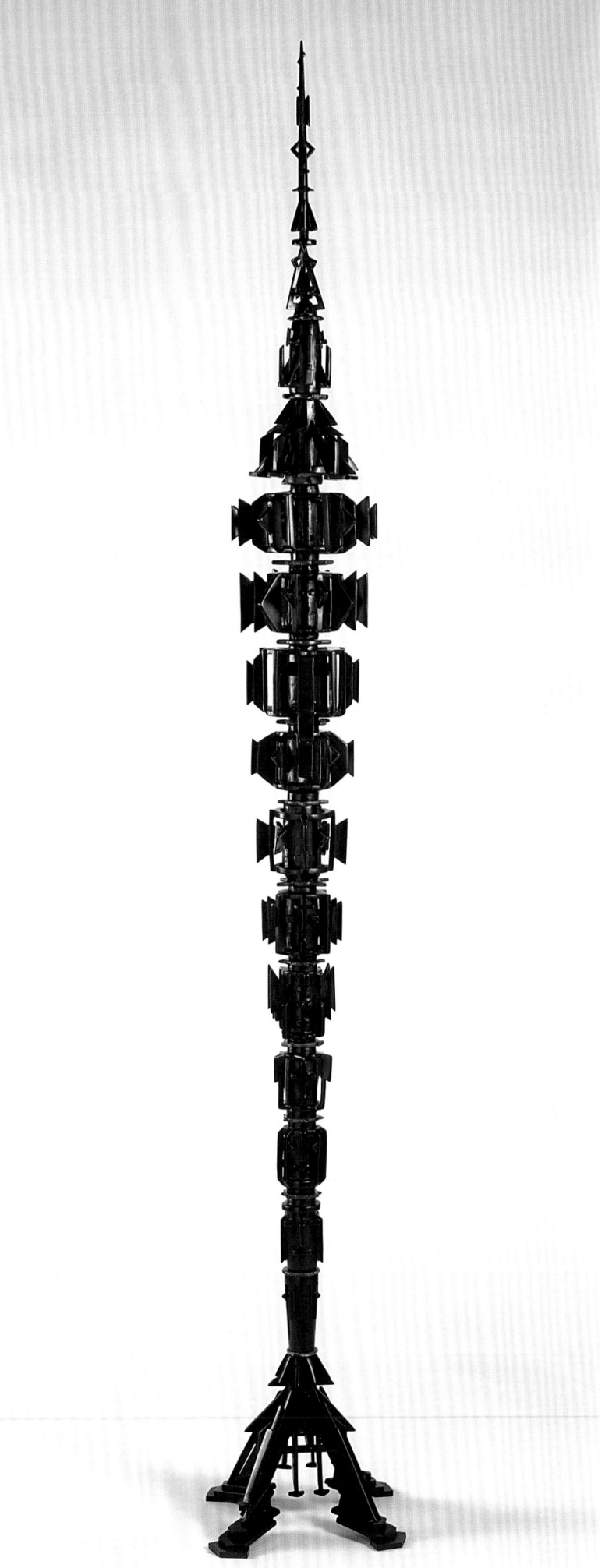

PLATE 36

Space Totem, 2009
Bronze
96 x 16½ x 16½ in. (243.8 x 41.9 x 41.9 cm)
Collection of the artist

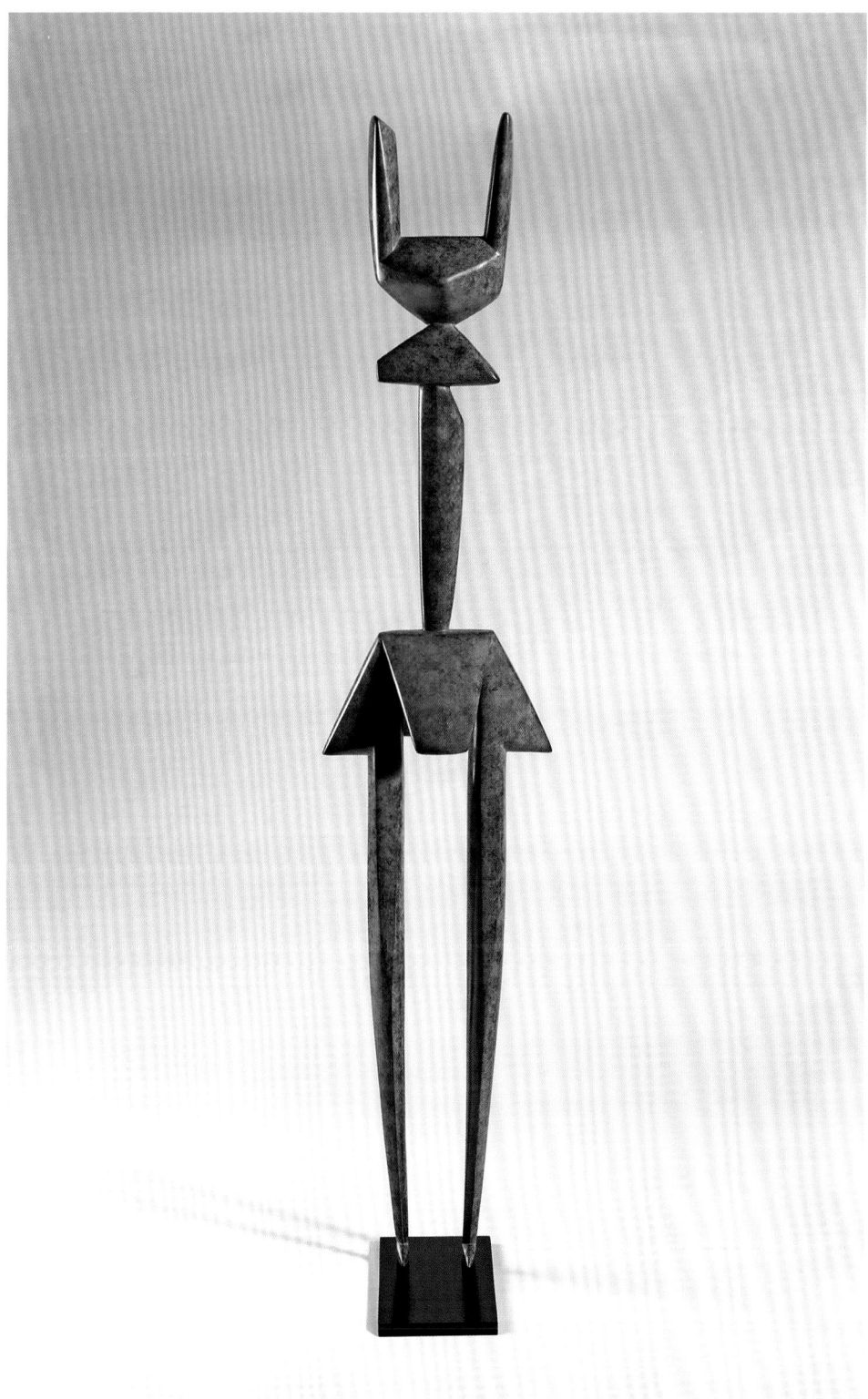

PLATE 37

Runway Rabbit, 2009
Bronze
46⅞ x 9½ x 6⅝ in. (119.1 x 24.1 x 16.8 cm)
Private collection

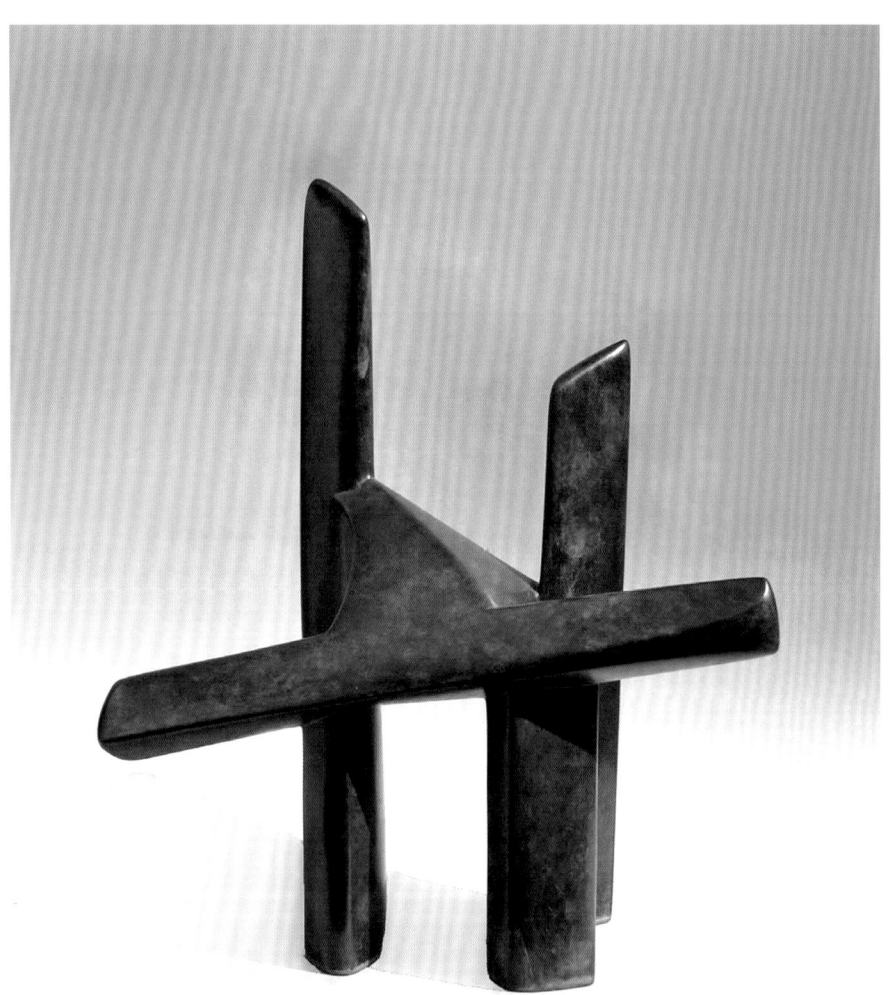

PLATE 38

Dream House, 2009
Bronze
11³⁄₁₆ x 9¹³⁄₁₆ x 3⅞ in. (28.4 x 24.9 x 9.9 cm)
Private collection

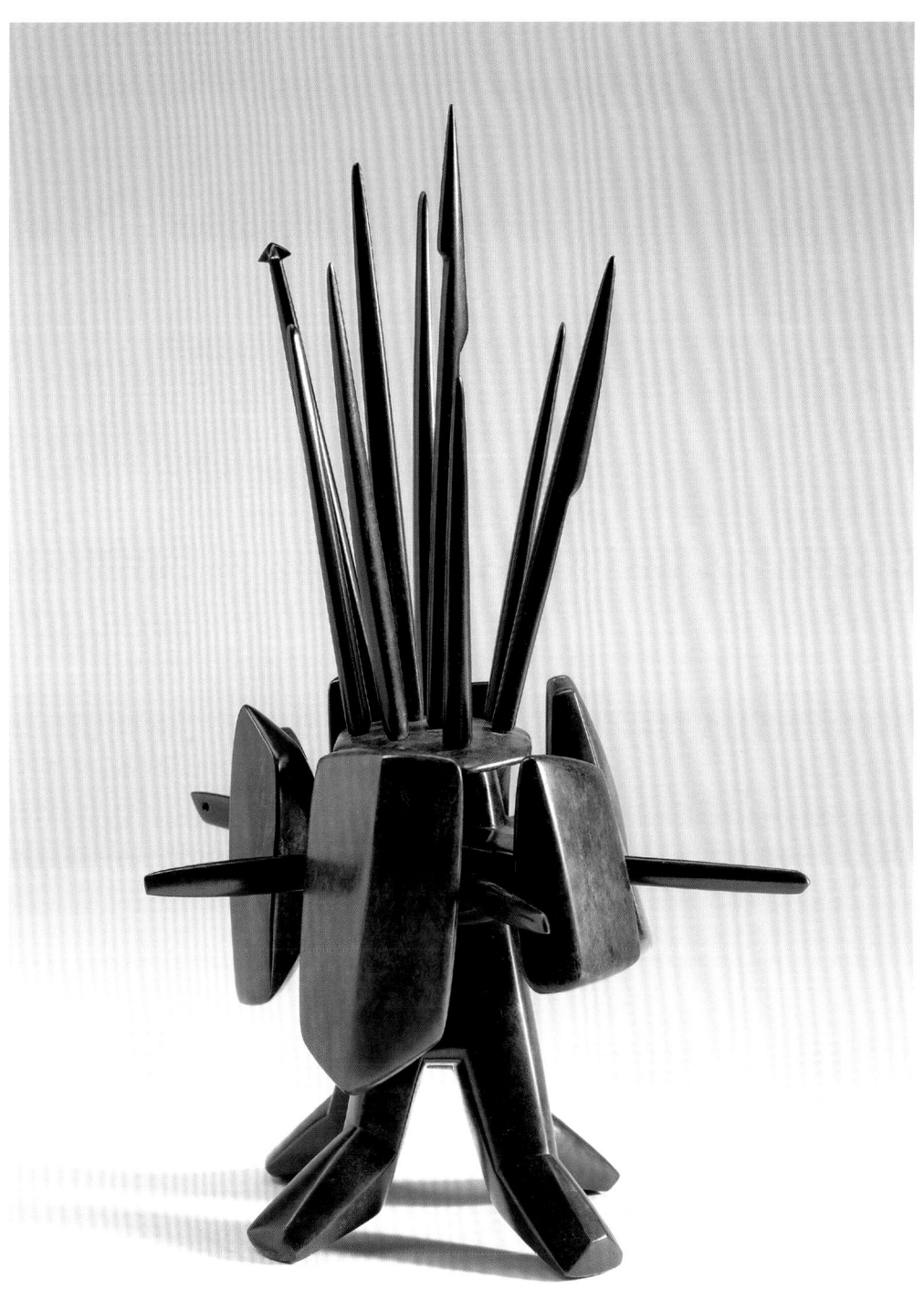

PLATE 39

Defense, 2009
Bronze
18¹³⁄₁₆ x 11⅛ x 11⅝ in. (47.7 x 28.2 x 29.5 cm)
Private collection

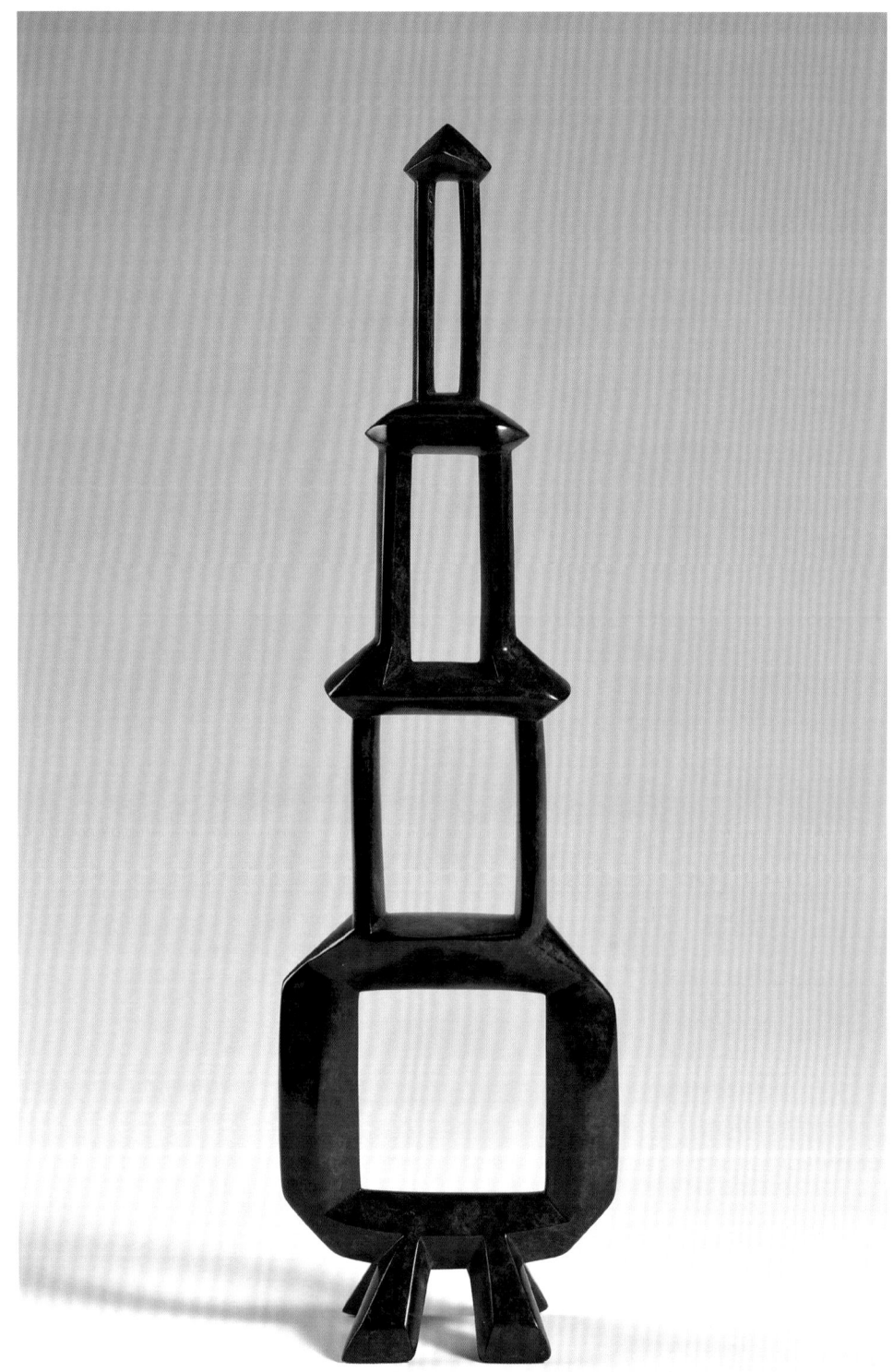

PLATE 40

Rooms with a View, 2009
Bronze
22 x 6⁵⁄₁₆ x 3¹⁄₈ in. (55.9 x 16 x 7.9 cm)
Collection of the artist

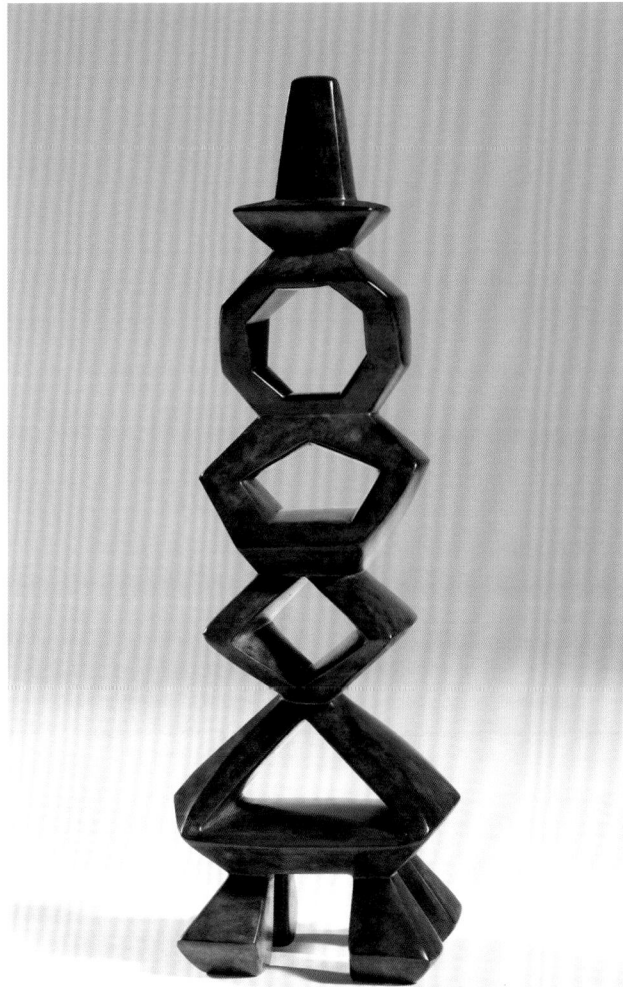

PLATE 41

Scholar, 2009
Bronze
12⅝ x 4³⁄₁₆ x 3¹⁵⁄₁₆ in. (32 x 10.7 x 9.9 cm)
Collection of the artist

The top of this piece references the traditional Korean horsehair hat
worn by gentlemen scholars.

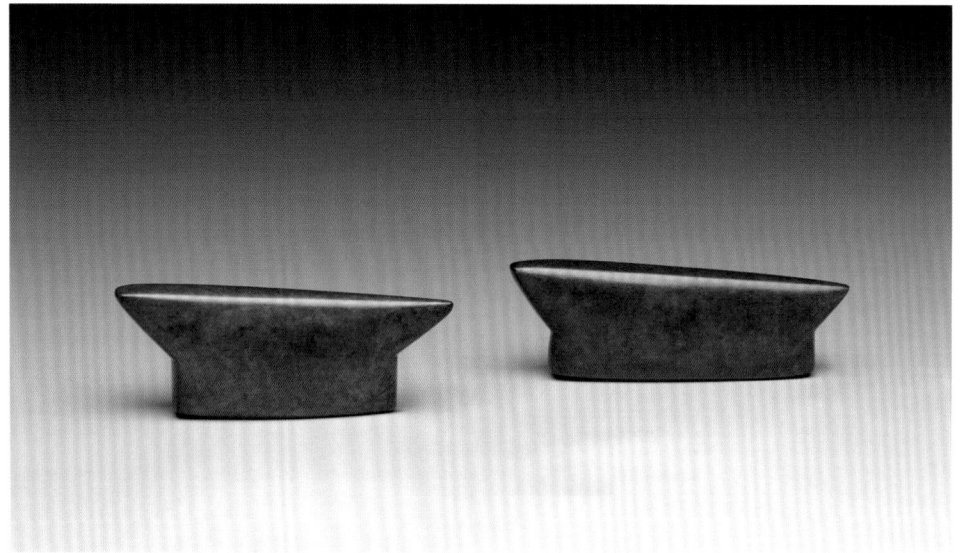

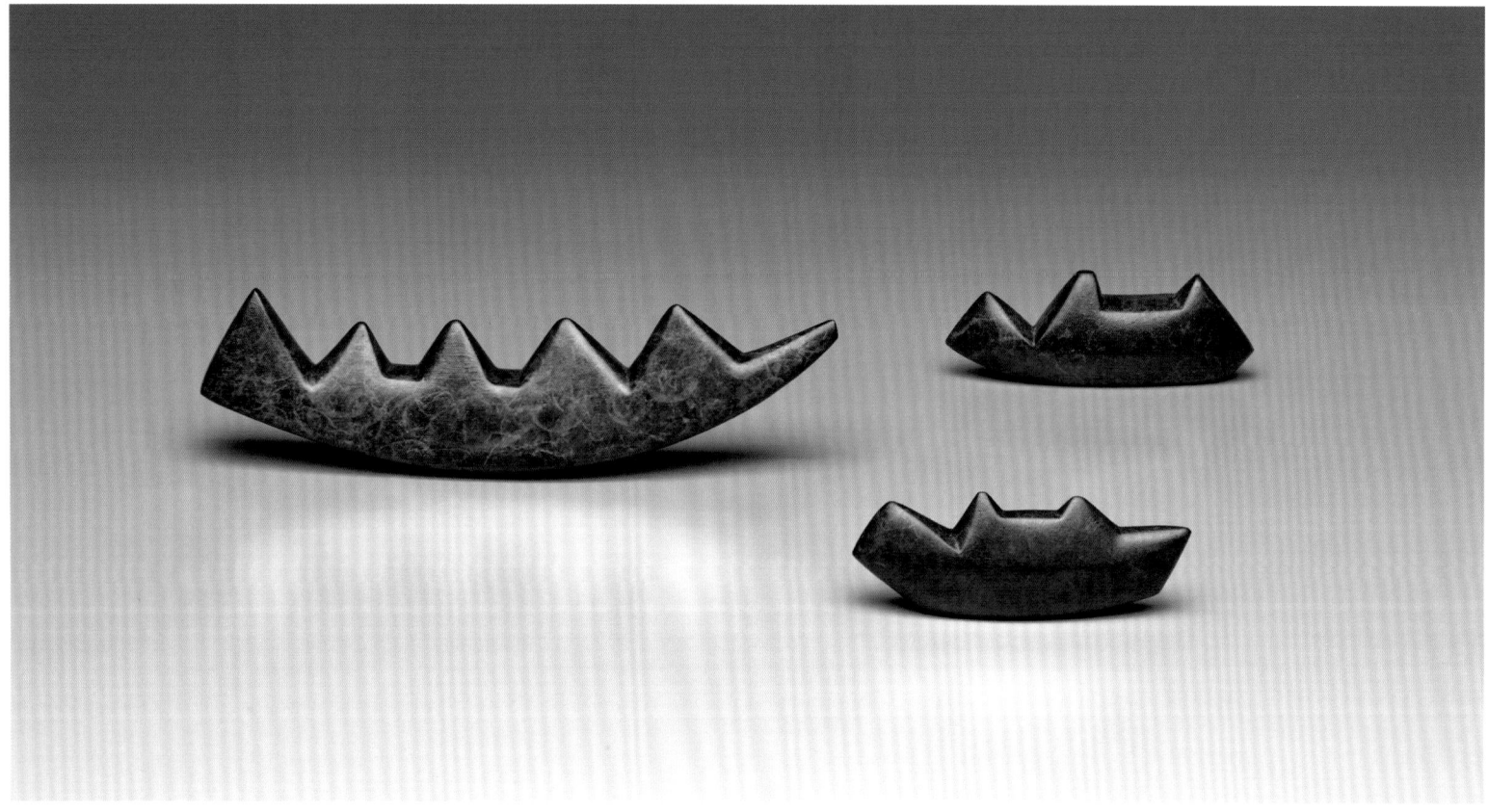

PLATE 42

Brothers, 2009
Bronze
15⁄16 x 3½ x ⅝ in. (3.3 x 8.9 x 1.5 cm)
Collection of the artist

PLATE 43

Asylum Seekers, 2021
Bronze
Largest: 15⁄16 x 5³⁄16 x 8 in. (3.3 x 13.2 x 20.3 cm)
Collection of the artist

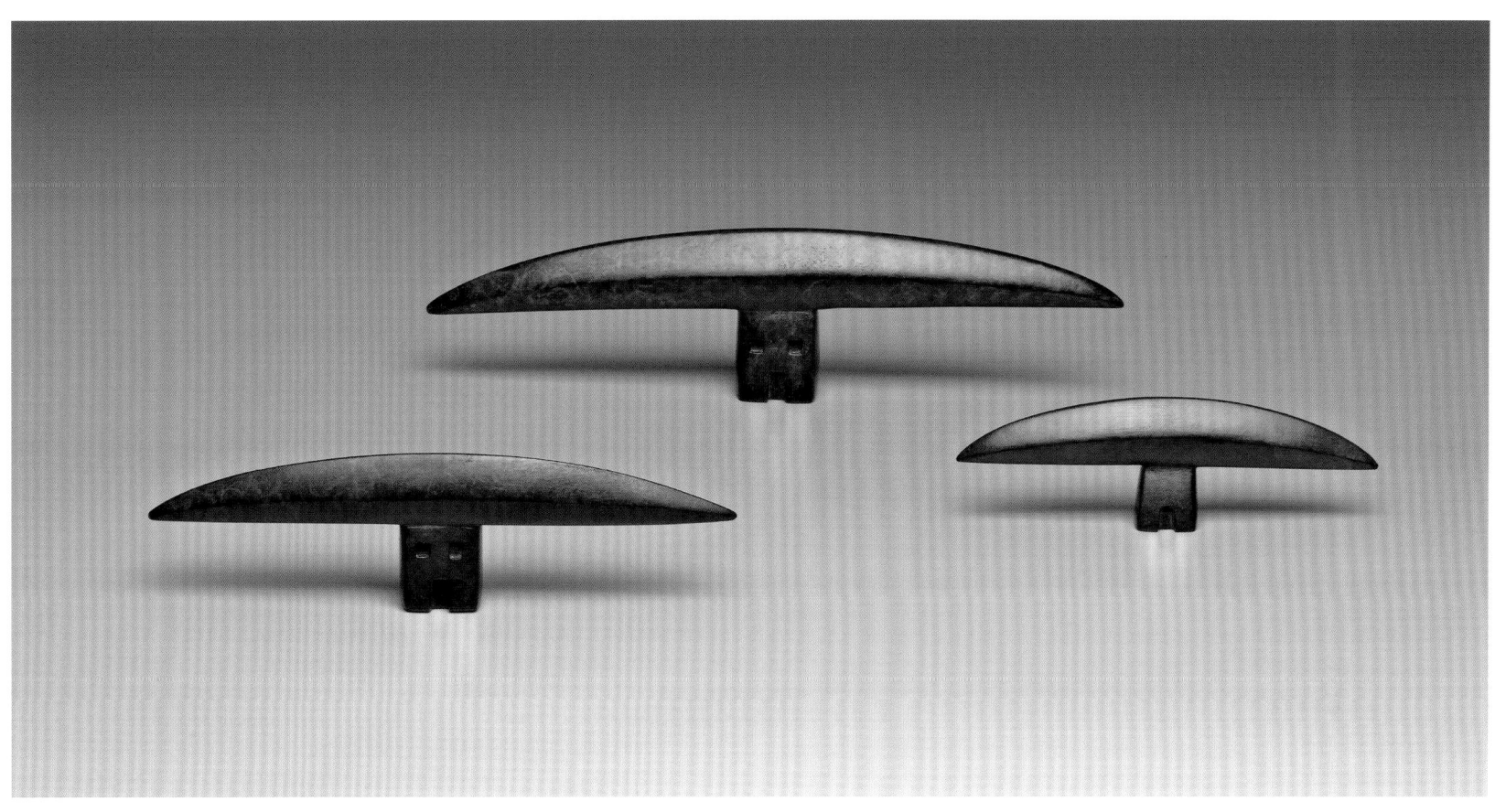

PLATE 44

Settlement, 2021
Bronze
Largest: 2⁵⁄₁₆ x 9½ x 1⅛ in. (5.8 x 24.1 x 2.8 cm)
Collection of the artist

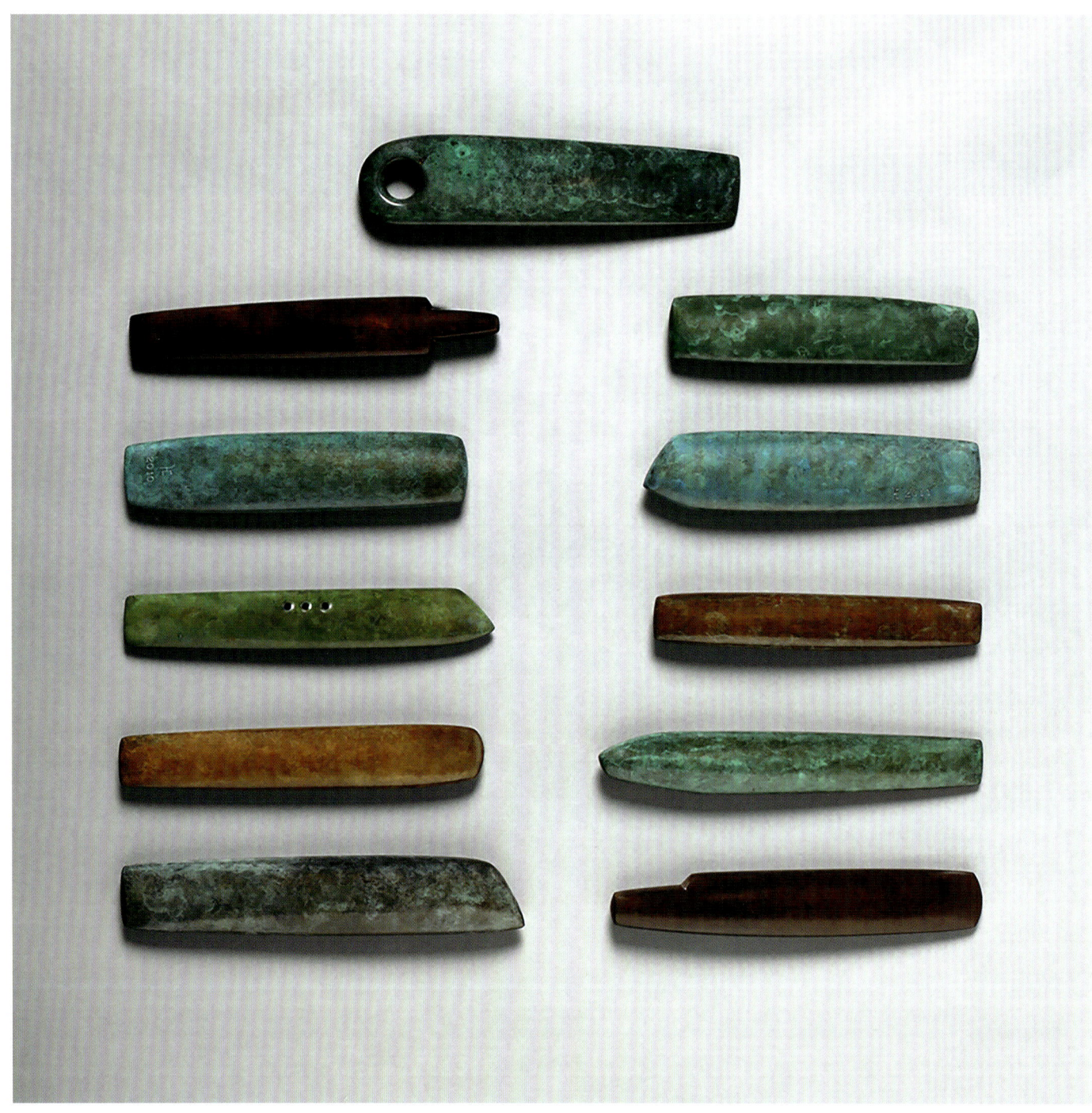

PLATE 45

Celts Cashe, 2010–2011
Bronze
6 in. longest (15.2 cm)
Collection of the artist

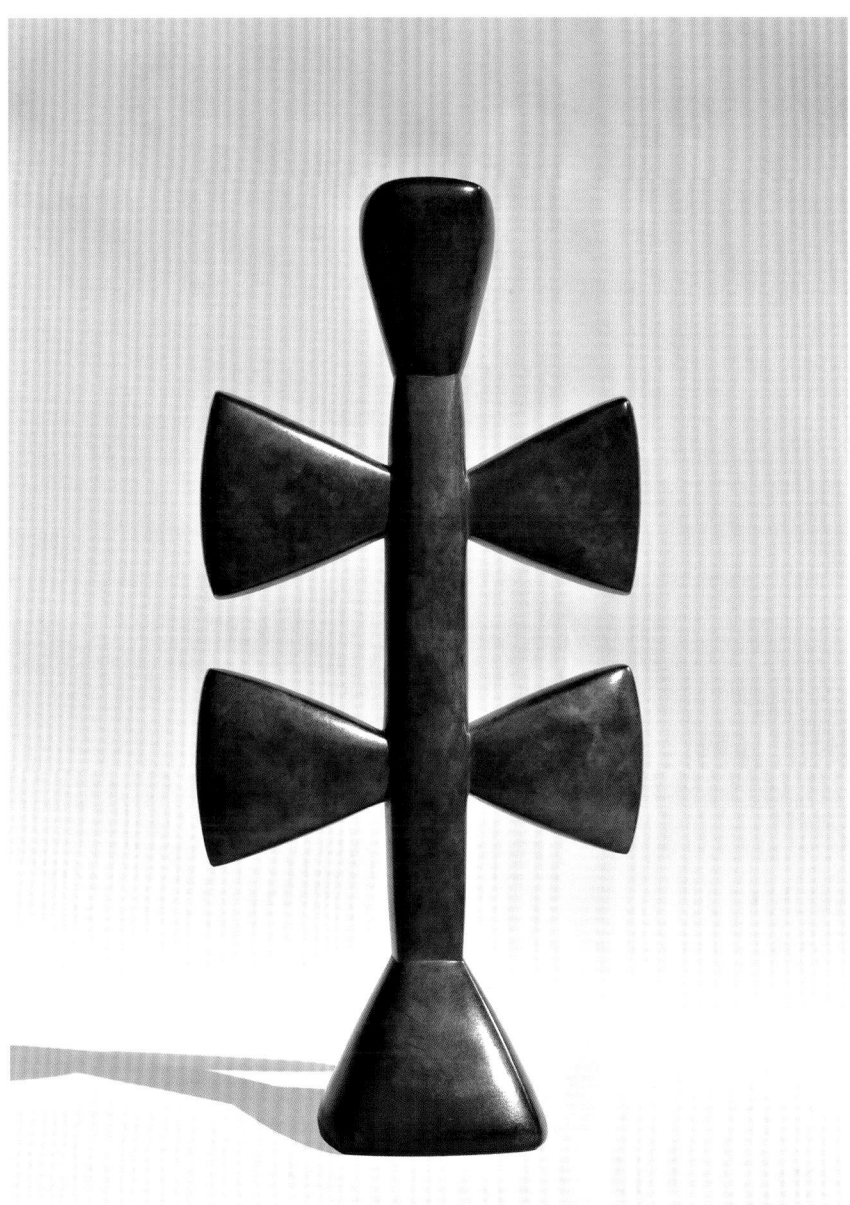

PLATE 46

Butterfly Man, 2010
Bronze
10 x 5 x 2⁵⁄₁₆ in. (25.4 x 12.7 x 5.8 cm)
Collection of the artist

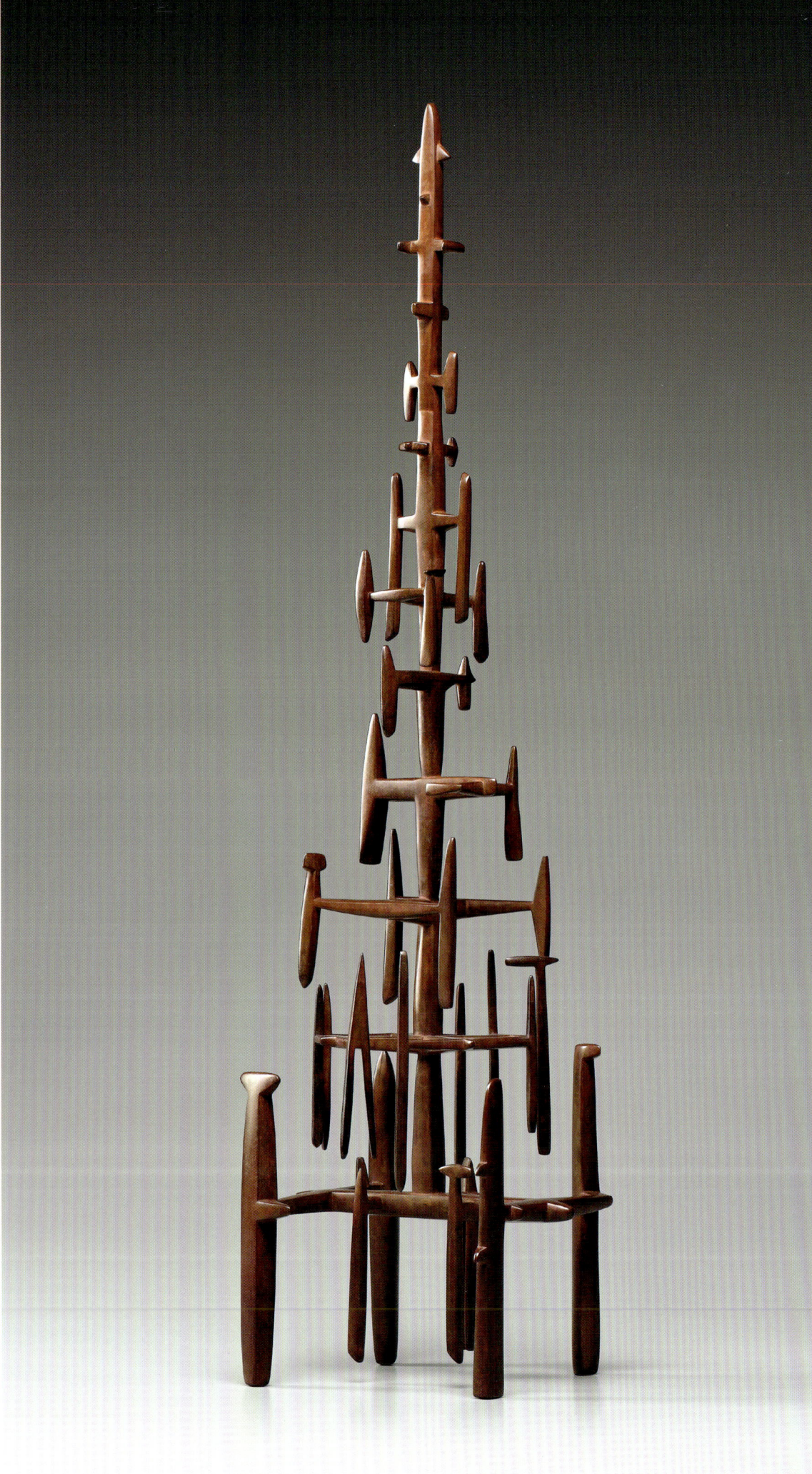

PLATE 47

Off the Grid, 2011
Bronze
29¹³⁄₁₆ x 6¹¹⁄₁₆ x 6⁵⁄₈ in. (75.7 x 17 x 16.8 cm)
Private collection

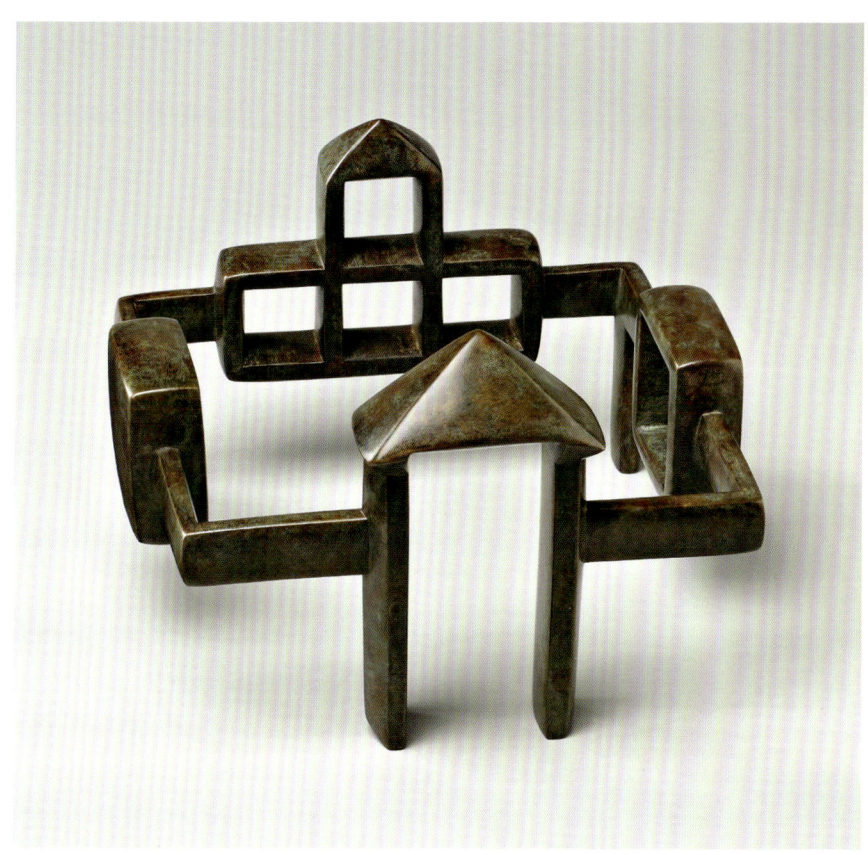

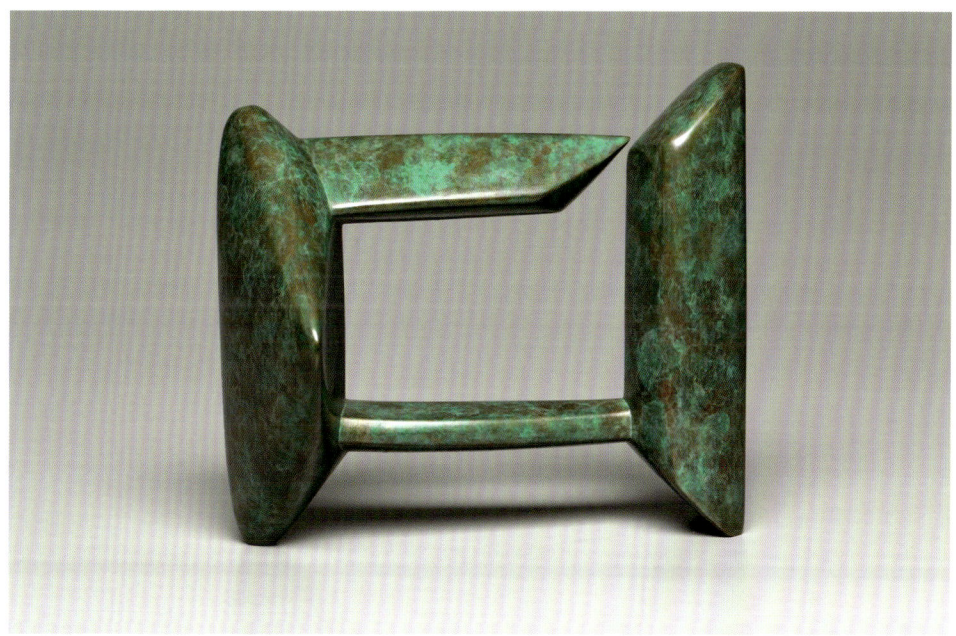

PLATE 48

Peristylium, 2011
Bronze
5⁵⁄₁₆ x 7¹³⁄₁₆ x 8⅛ in. (13.5 x 19.8 x 20.6 cm)
Private collection

PLATE 49

Open Window, 2011
Bronze
6⅛ x 6⅞ x 5⅝ in. (15.5 x 17.5 x 14.2 cm)
Private collection

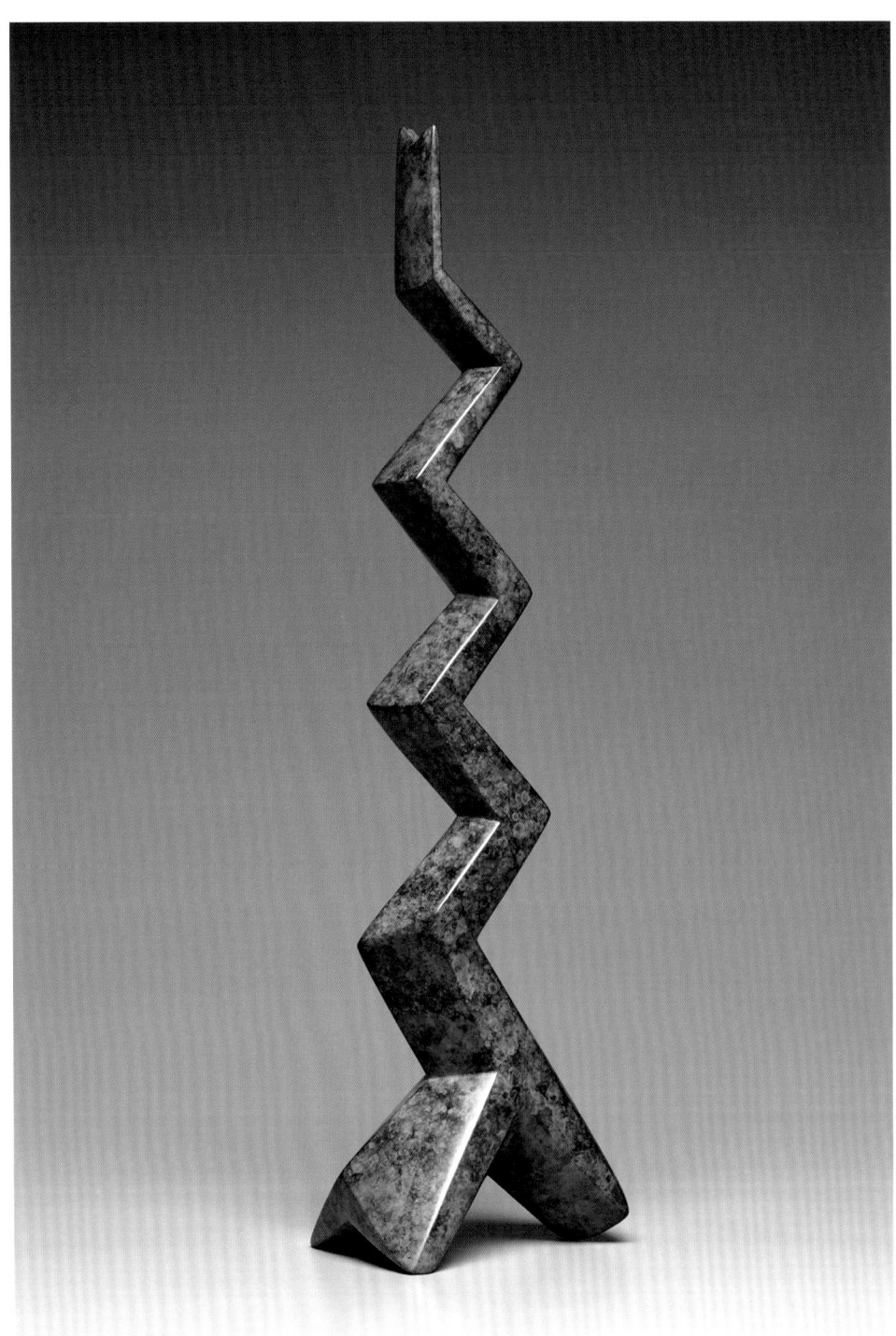

PLATE 50

Lightning Snake, 2011
Bronze
21$\frac{11}{16}$ x 5$\frac{11}{16}$ x 4$\frac{5}{16}$ in. (55.1 x 14.5 x 10.9 cm)
Collection of the artist

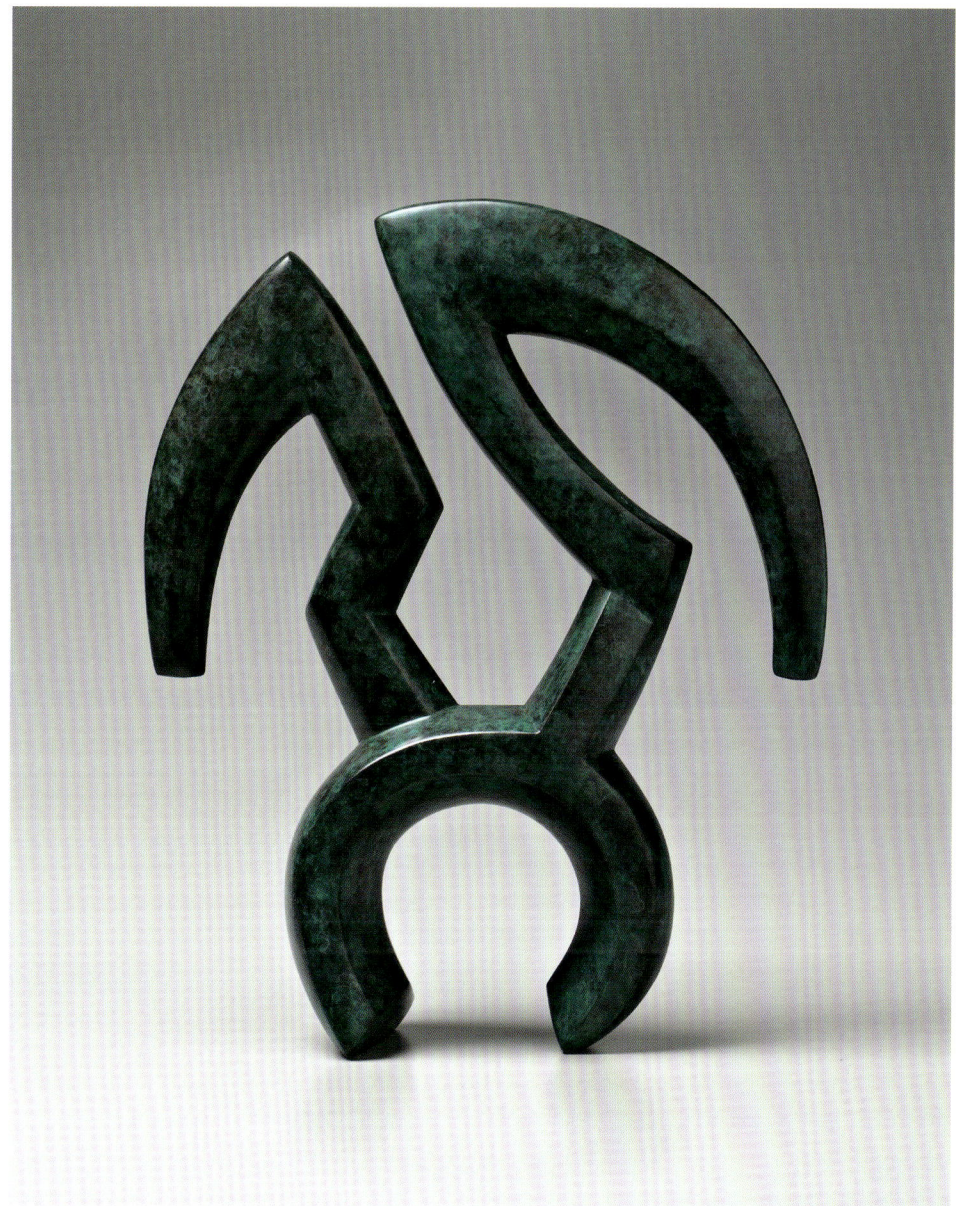

PLATE 51

Anzu, 2011
Bronze
14⅝⁄₁₆ x 11½ x 3½ in. (36.3 x 29.2 x 8.9 cm)
Collection of the artist

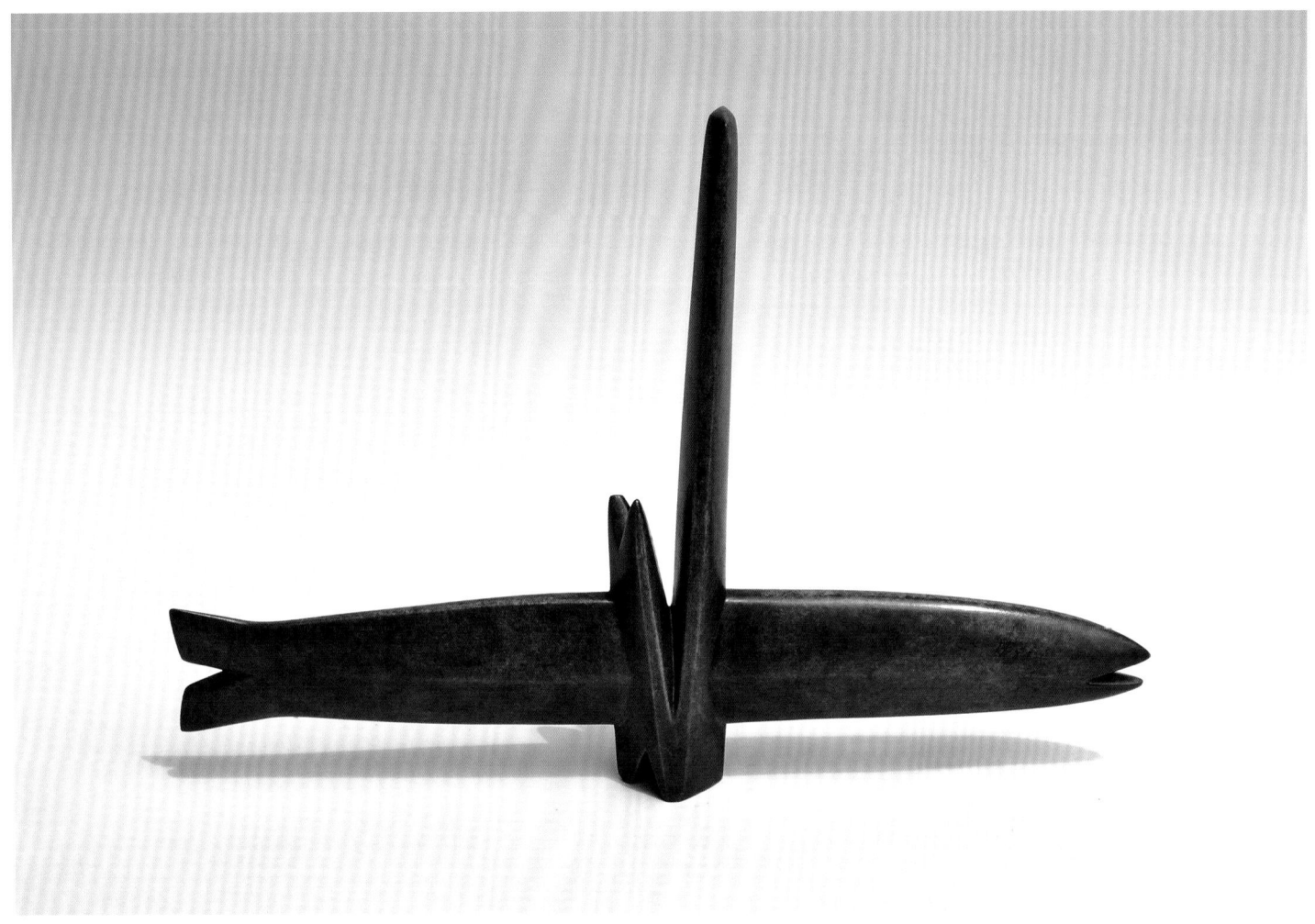

PLATE 52

Fish in the Reeds, 2017
Bronze
9 x 13 x 1.2 in
Private Collection

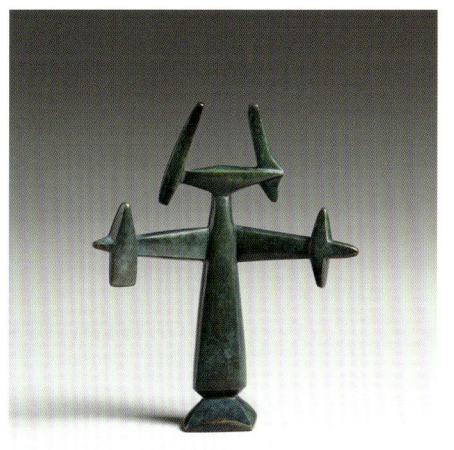

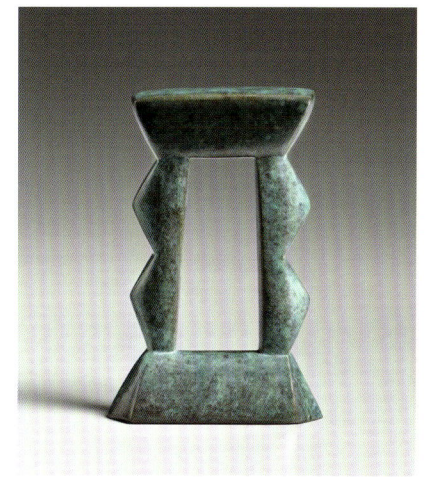

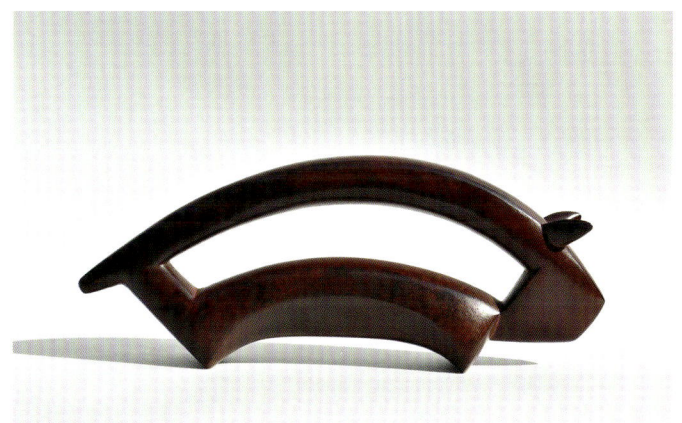

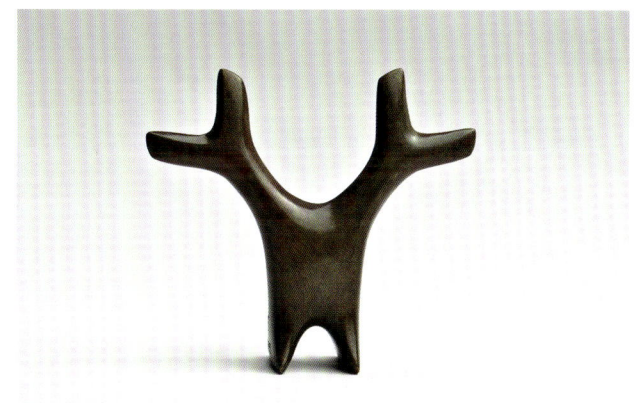

PLATE 53

Shaman, 2011
Bronze
3½ x 2¹³⁄₁₆ x ¹³⁄₁₆ in. (8.9 x 7.1 x 3.0 cm)
Collection of the artist

PLATE 54

Empty Pig, 2018
Bronze
2½ x 6½ x 1 in. (6.3 x 16.5 x 1 cm)
Collection of the artist

PLATE 55

Portal III, 2012
Bronze
3½ x 2½ x ¹³⁄₁₆ in. (8.9 x 6.3 x 2 cm)
Collection of the artist

PLATE 56

Tree Shaman, 2015
Bronze
2¹¹⁄₁₆ x 3¹⁵⁄₁₆ x ¹⁵⁄₁₆ in. (6.8 x 7.8 x 2.3 cm)
Private collection

PLATE 57

Vulpine Standard, 2012
Bronze
88 x 16⅚₁₆ x 11½ in. (223.5 x 41.4 x 29.2 cm)
Collection of the artist

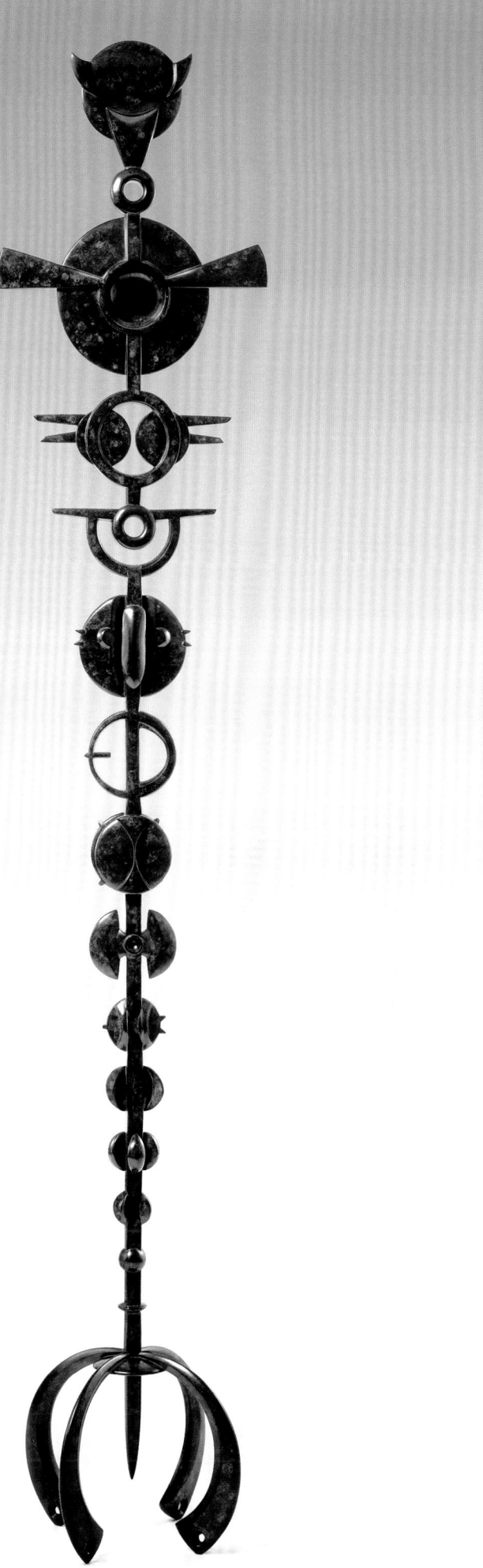

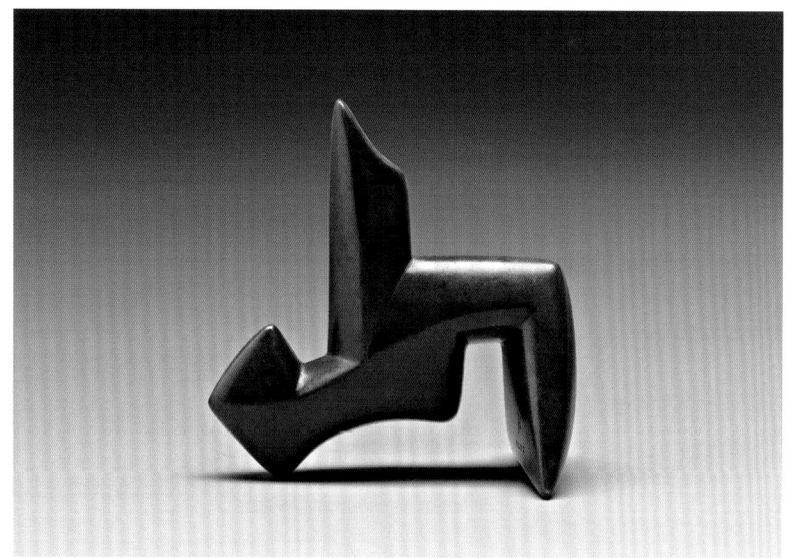

PLATE 58

Which Way from Here, 2012
Bronze
4⁵⁄₁₆ x 4³⁄₁₆ x 2⁵⁄₈ in. (10.9 x 10.7 x 6.6 cm)
Private collection

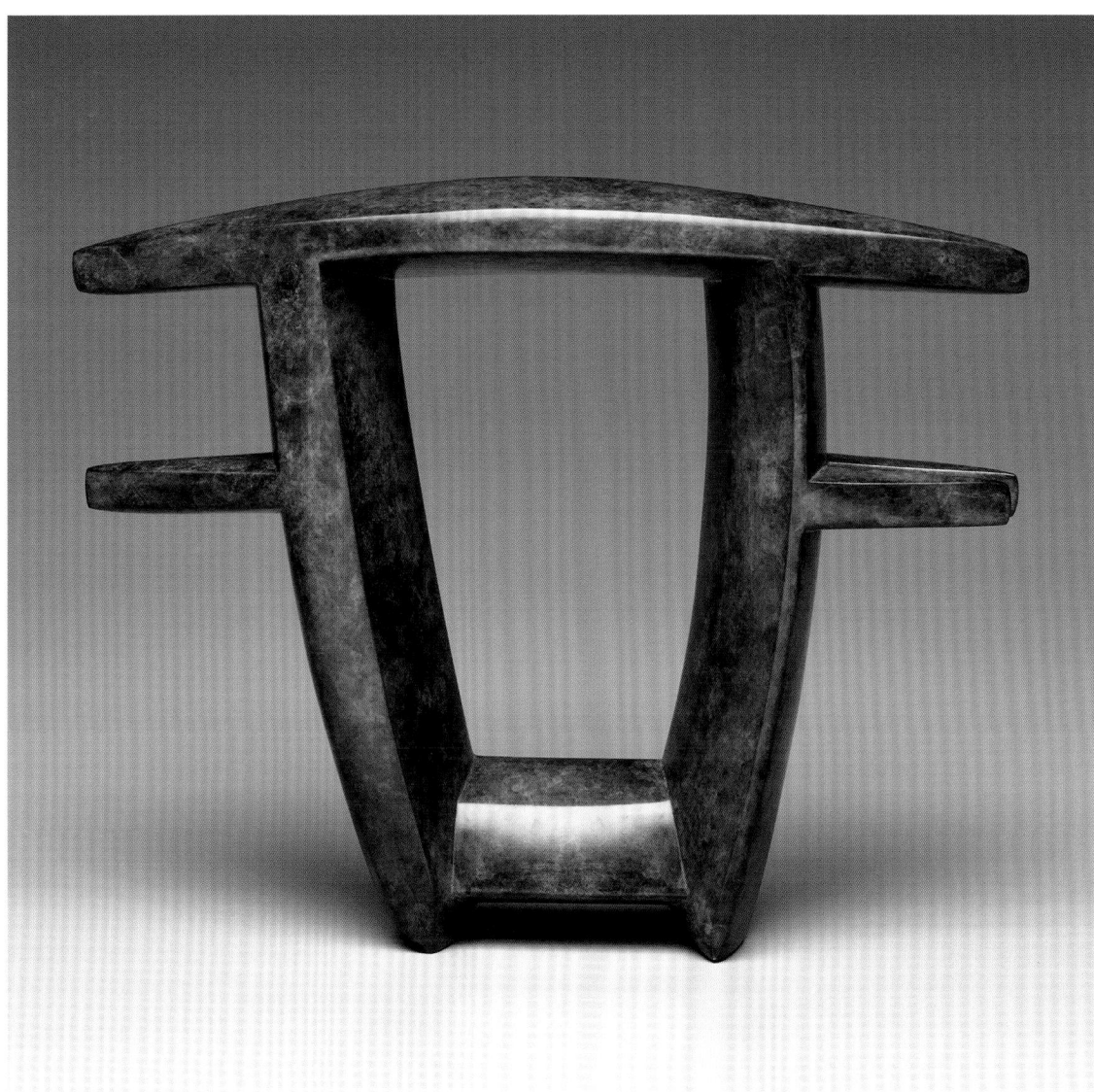

PLATE 59

Visage, 2013
Bronze
9¹⁵⁄₁₆ x 12³⁄₈ x 2¹¹⁄₁₆ in. (25.1 x 31.5 x 6.8 cm)
Collection of the artist

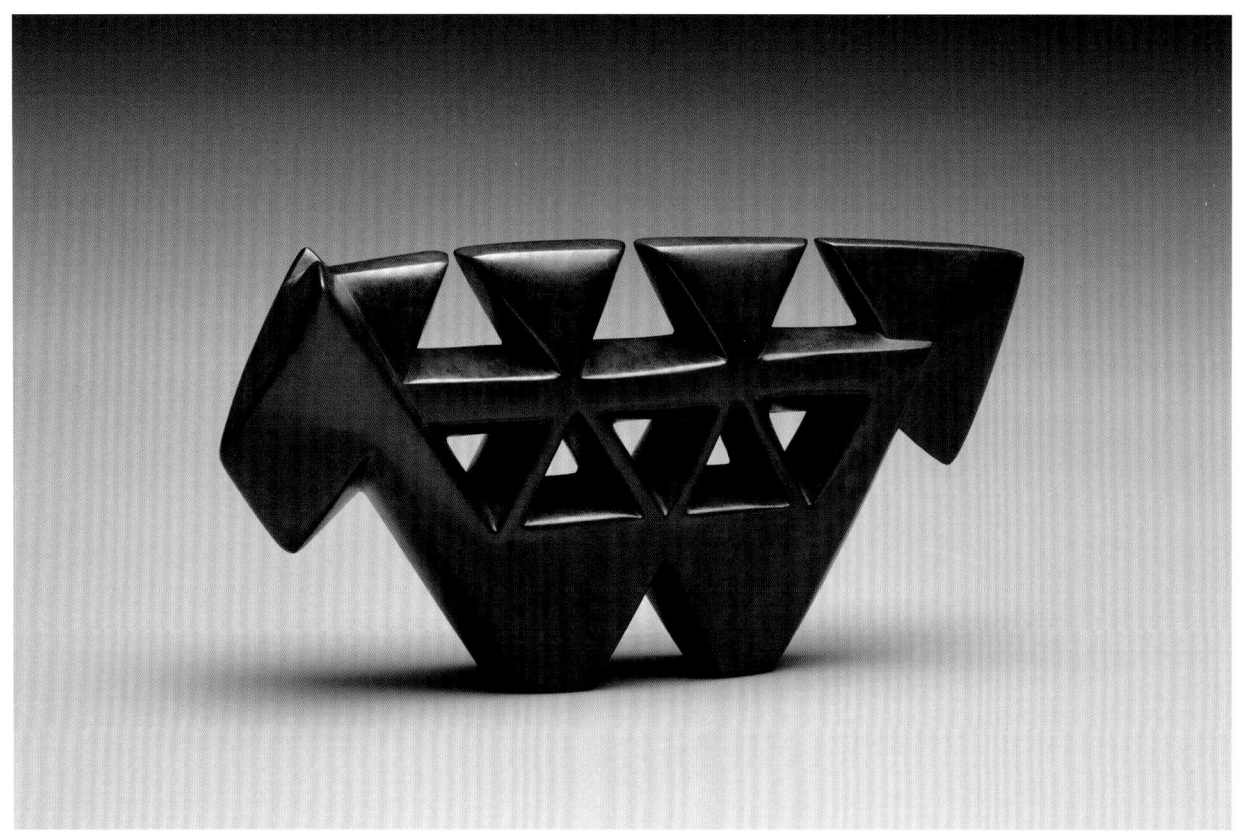

PLATE 60

Lattice Mammal, 2013
Bronze
5 3/16 x 10 x 2 in. (13.2 x 25.4 x 5.1 cm)
Collection of the artist

PLATE 61

Griffon Arabesque, 2013
Bronze
19 3/16 x 18 x 4 3/16 in. (48.8 x 45.7 x 10.7 cm)
Collection of the artist

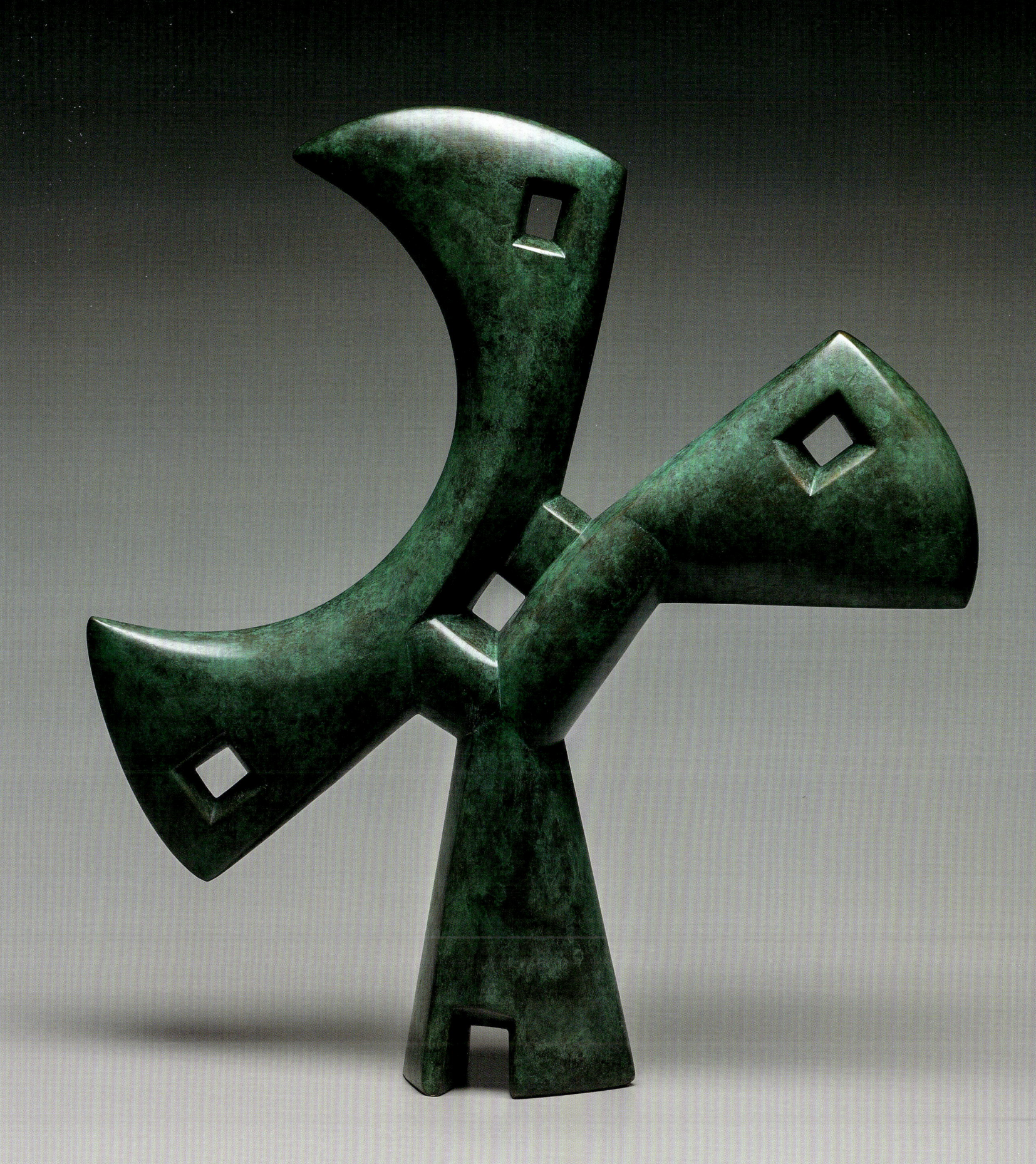

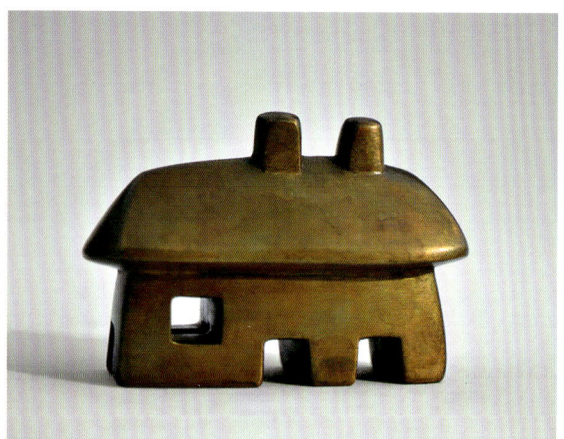

PLATE 62

Bronze House, 2013
Bronze
1⅝ x 2½ x ¹³⁄₁₆ in. (4.1 x 6.3 x 2.8 cm)
Private collection

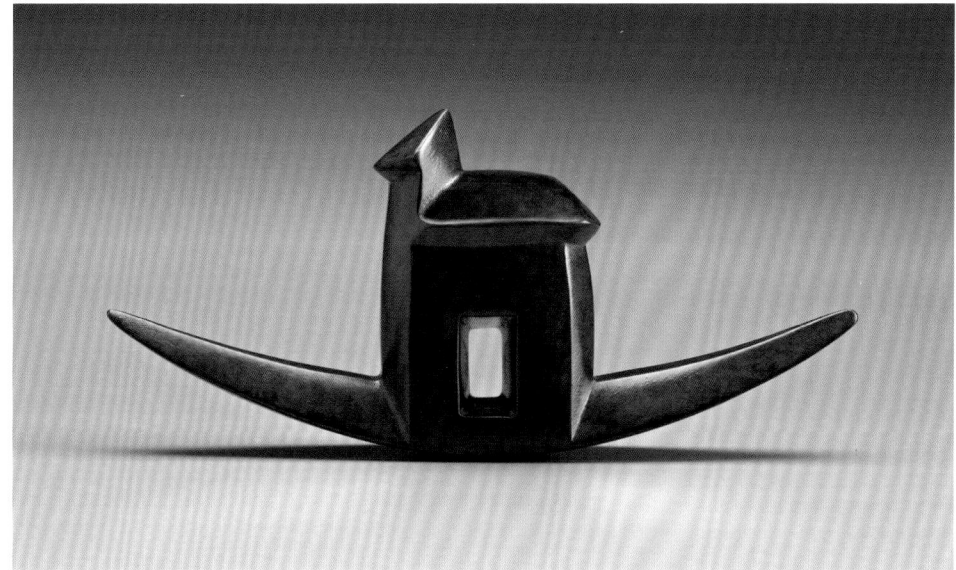

PLATE 63

Rocking House, 2013
Bronze
2³⁄₁₆ x 5 x 1 in. (5.6 x 12.7 x 2.5 cm)
Private collection

NEXT SPREAD:
PLATE 64

Teddy Bears' Picnic, 2013
Bronze
Tallest: 5 in. (12.7 cm)
Collection of the artist and private collection

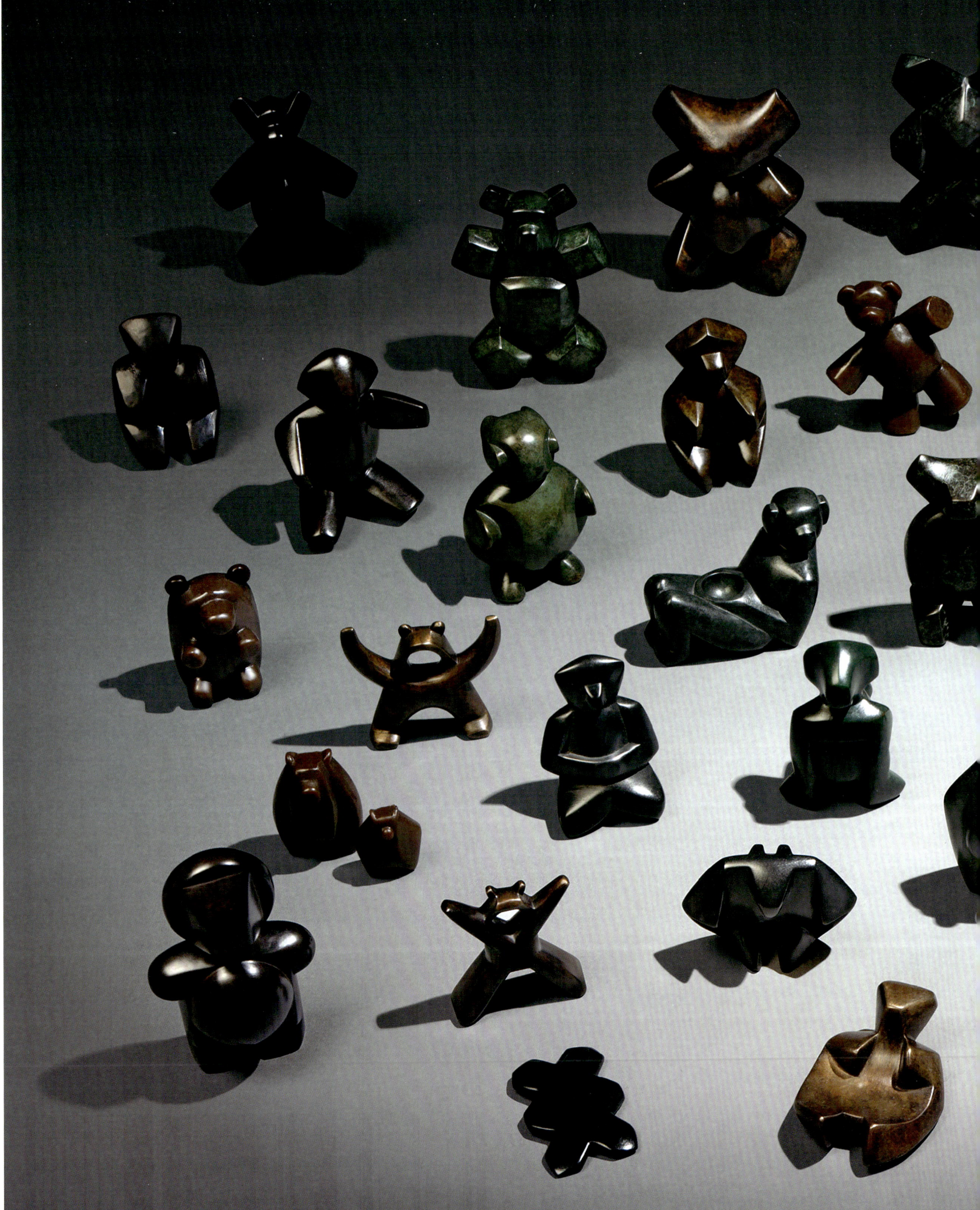

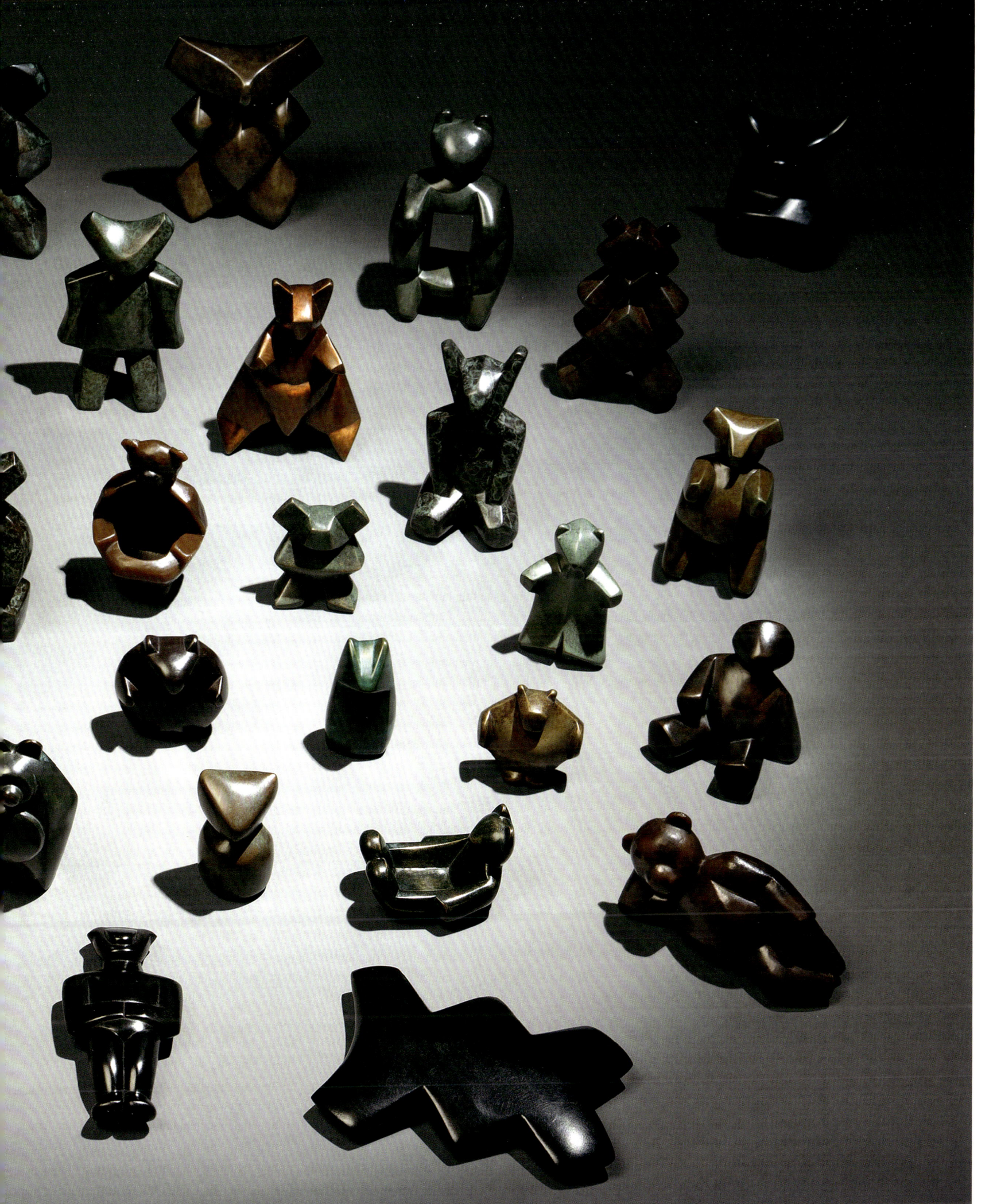

This series of 36 bronzes was inspired by the theme song "Teddy Bears' Picnic" used by the radio show "Big John and Sparky," a half-hour Saturday morning program which I routinely listened to as a child. Now, more than 60 years later, the impressions made by that strangest of children's songs have bubbled up into a narrative artwork. My seven-year-old self could not comprehend the contradictions in the song. The somber beginning is fairy-tale frightening: *"If you go out in the woods tonight, you'd better not go alone."* The music then becomes exuberant: *"for every bear that ever there was...tonight's the night the Teddy Bears have their picnic."* My use of the teddy bear image is not intended to be kitch or ironic, but rather a sculptural exploration of these befriended childhood daemons.

Peter DeCamp Haines

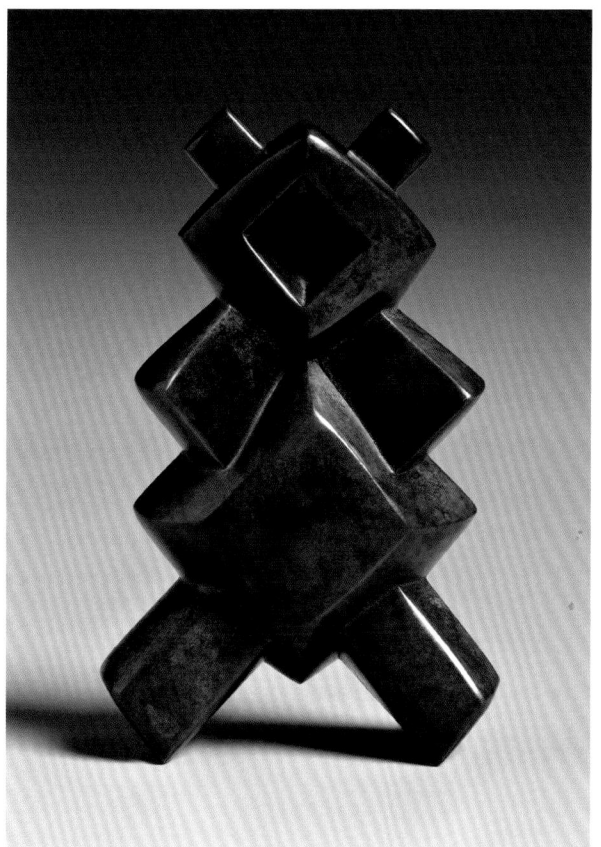

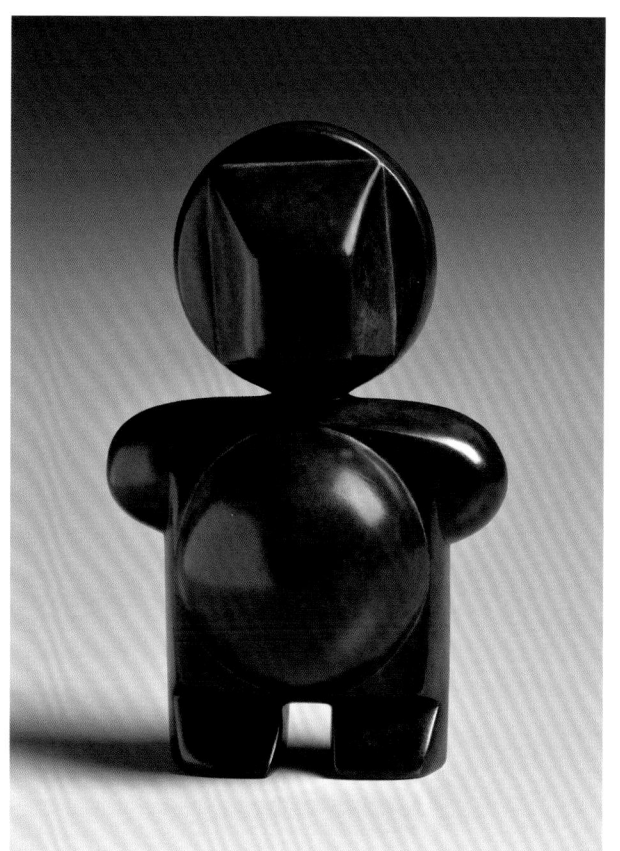

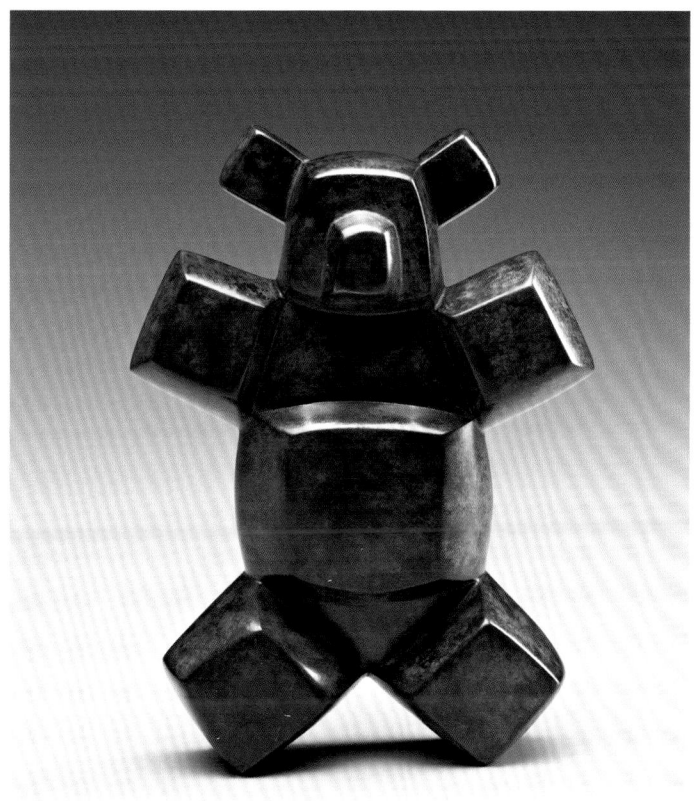

PLATE 65

TOP LEFT
Armored Bear, 2013
Bronze
4³⁄₁₆ x 2¹³⁄₁₆ x 2⁵⁄₁₆ in. (10.7 x 7.1 x 5.8 cm)
Private collection

PLATE 66

TOP RIGHT
Mandala Bear, 2014
Bronze
4³⁄₁₆ x 2⁵⁄₈ x 1½ in. (10.7 x 6.6 x 3.8 cm)
Private collection

BOTTOM LEFT
PLATE 67

Squares Bear, 2014
Bronze
4¹¹⁄₁₆ x 3⁷⁄₁₆ x 1⁵⁄₁₆ in. (11.9 x 8.6 x 3.3 cm)
Private collection

PLATE 68

Two-Sided Head, 2014
Fiberglass with epoxy paint
90 x 82 x 40 in.; base: 15 in. (228.6 x 208.3 x 101.6 cm; base: 38.1 cm)
Collection of the artist

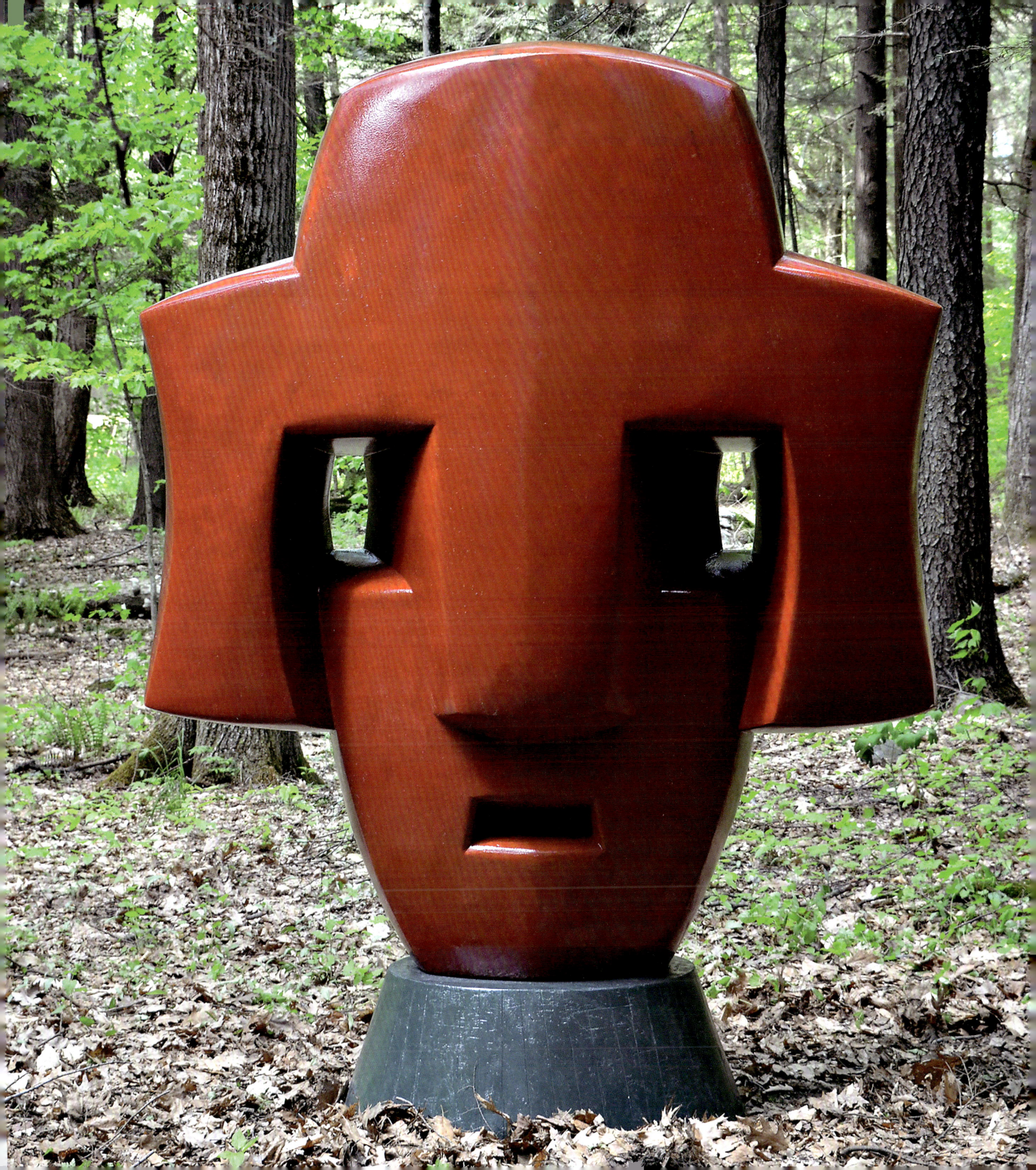

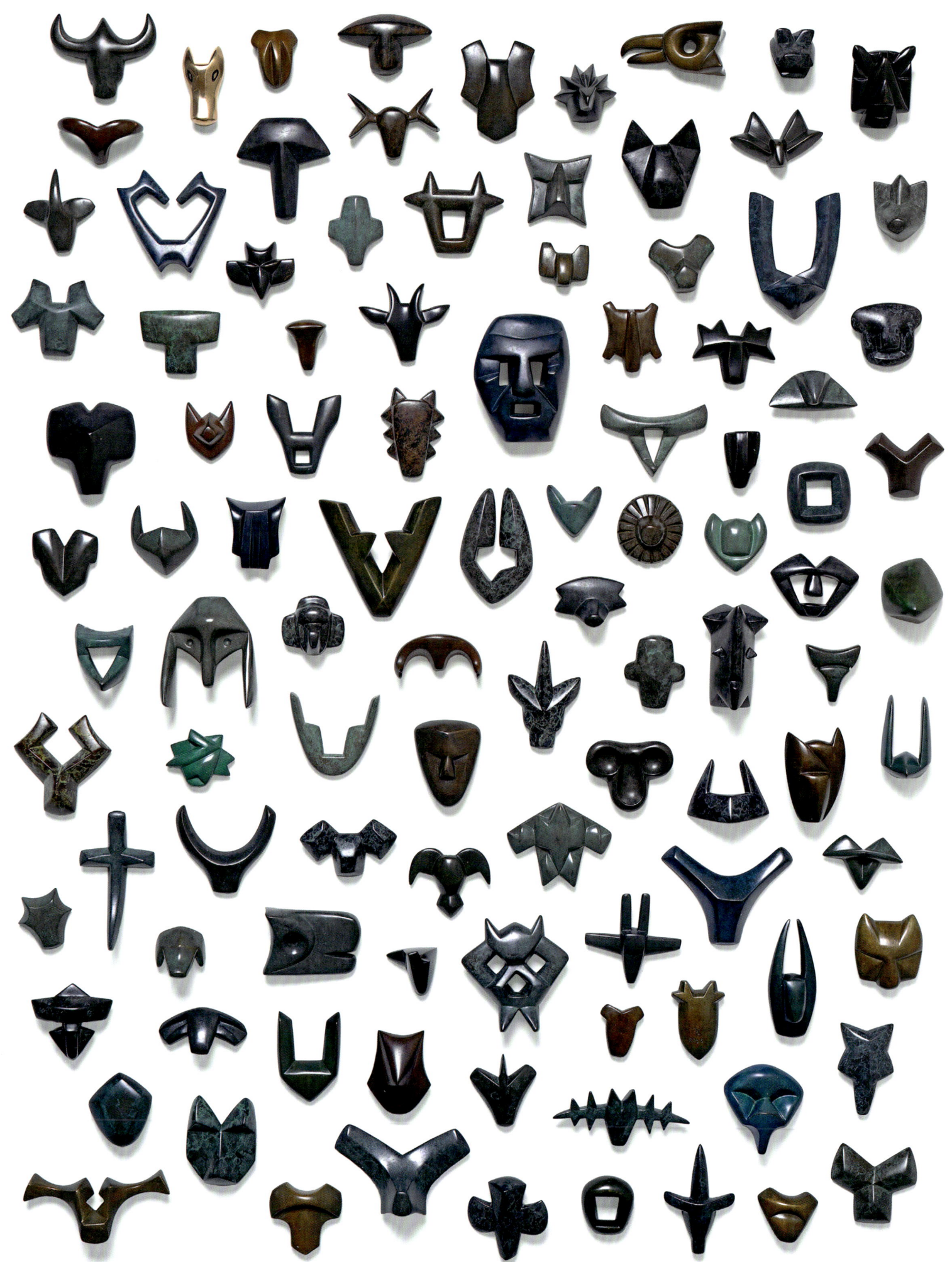

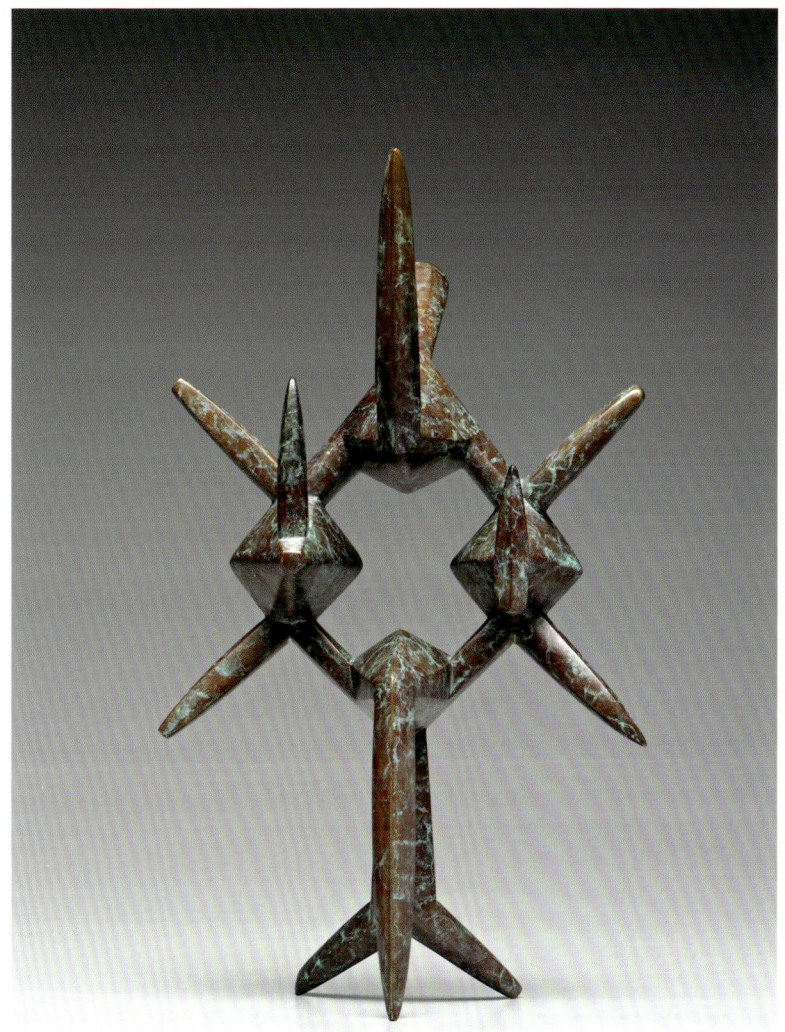

PLATE 69

100 Heads, 2015–2022
Bronze
2 in. average (5.1 cm)
Collection of the artist and private collection

PLATE 70

Head Stand, 2016
Bronze
10⅜ x 6³⁄₁₆ x 4¹³⁄₁₆ in. (26.4 x 15.7 x 12.2 cm)
Private collection

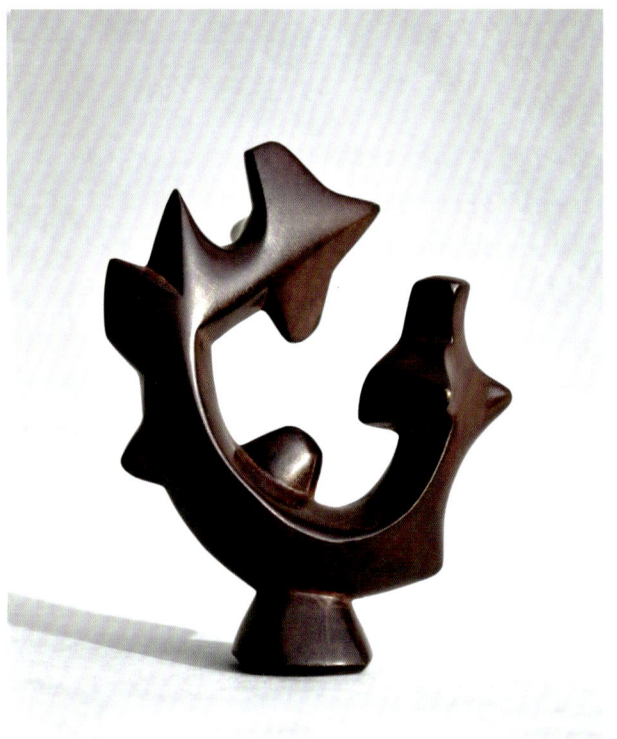

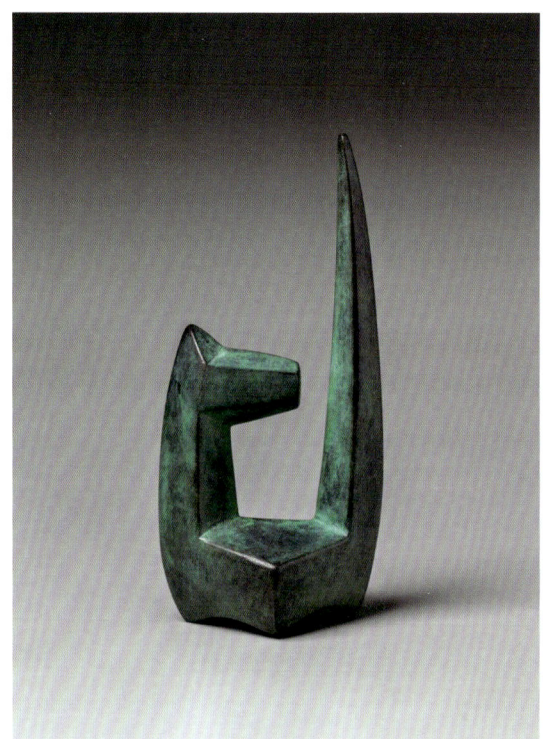

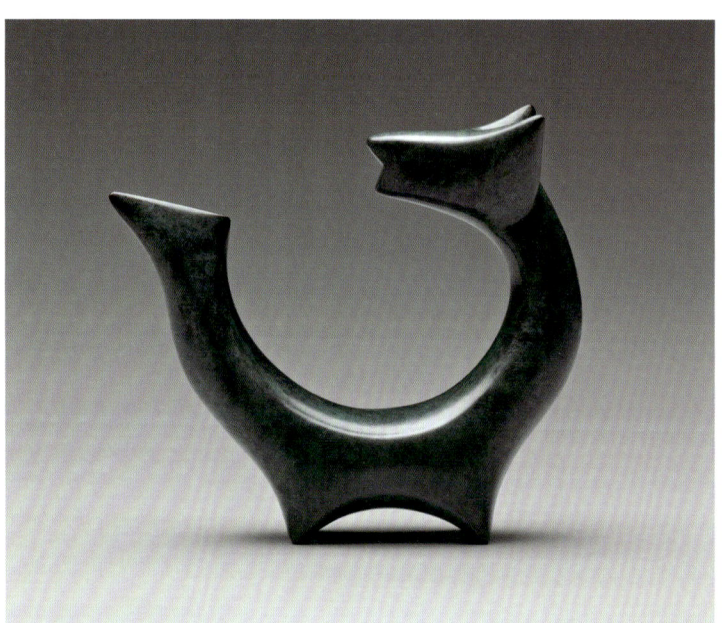

PLATE 71

Dragon Love, 2016
Bronze
4⅛ x 3⁷⁄₁₆ x 2⅛ in. (10.4 x 8.6 x 5.3 cm)
Private collection

PLATE 72

Dragon with Long Tail, 2019
Bronze
3³⁄₁₆ x 1³⁄₁₆ x 1⅝ in. (8.1 x 3 x 4.1 cm)
Collection of the artist

PLATE 73

Dragon Looking Back, 2020
Bronze
3 x 3⁵⁄₁₆ x 2¹⁵⁄₁₆ in. (7.6 x 8.4 x 7.4 cm)
Collection of the artist

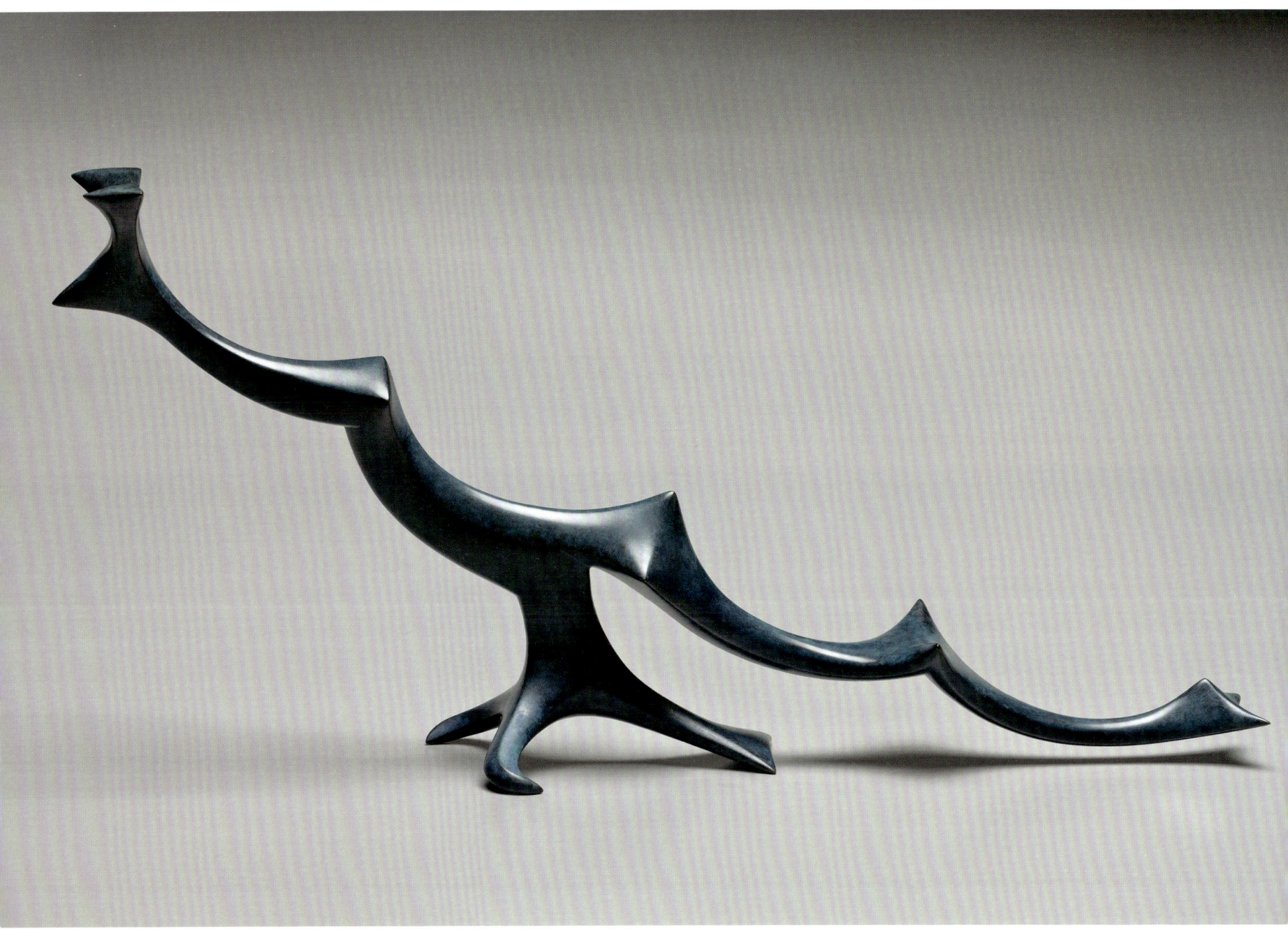

PLATE 74

Dragon, 2020
Bronze
11⅛ x 23½ x 4⅝ in. (28.2 x 59.7 x 11.7 cm)
Private collection

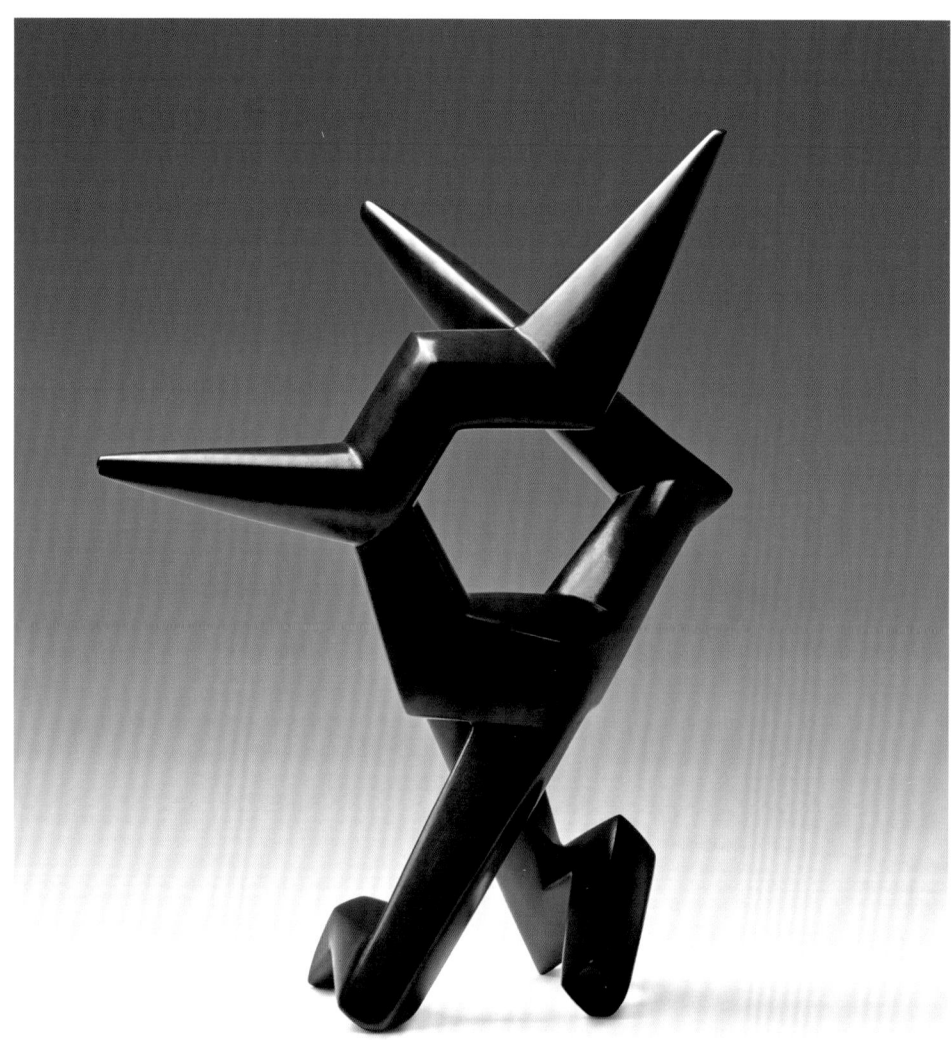

PLATE 75

Dark Star, 2018
Bronze
11⅝ x 9⅝ x 6⅝ in. (29.5 x 24.4 x 16.8 cm)
Collection of the artist

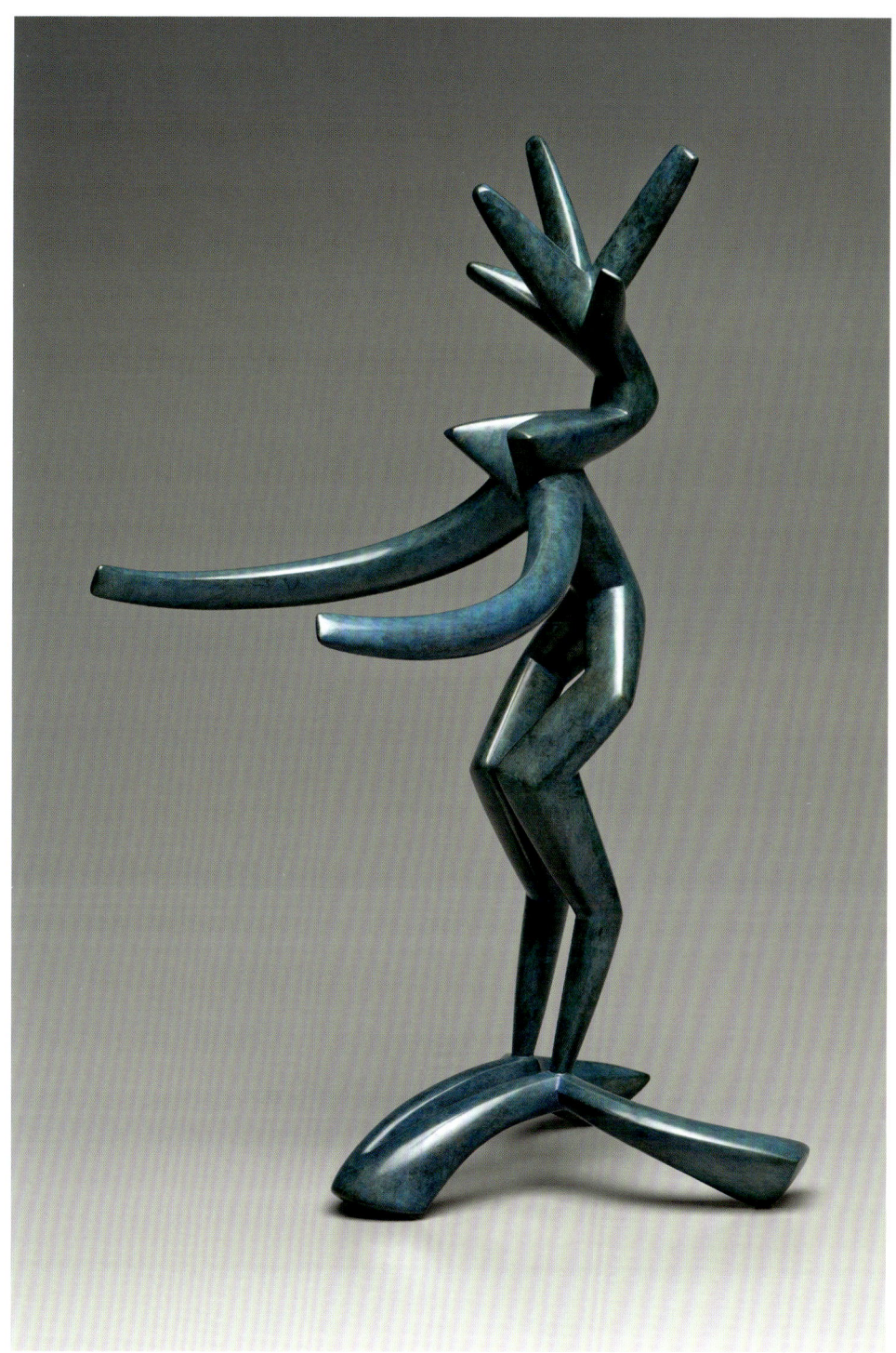

PLATE 76

Greeter, 2021
Bronze
17⅜ x 7½ x 10¾ in. (44.1 x 19 x 27.3 cm)
Private collection

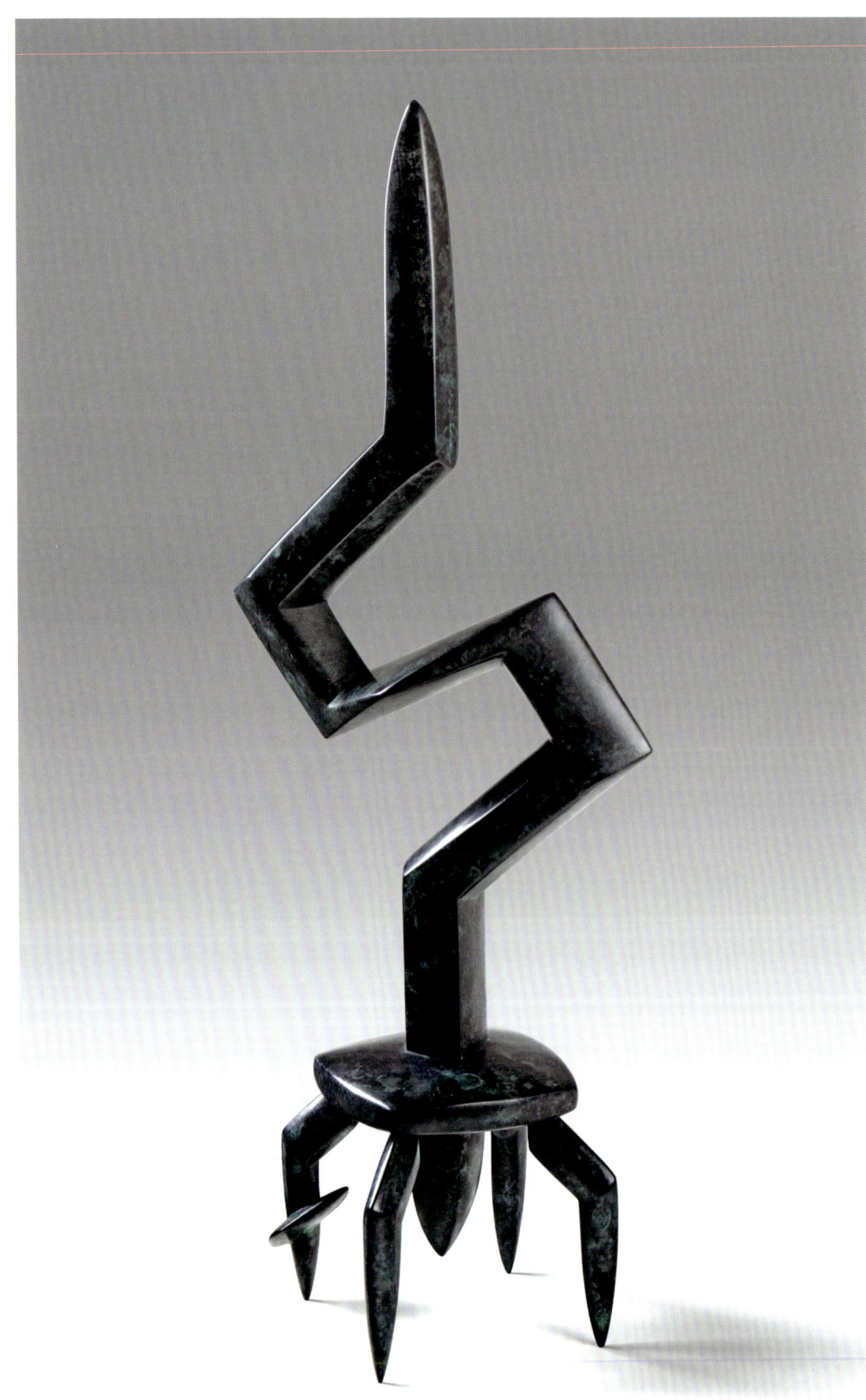

PLATE 77

Thorn, 2015
Bronze
18¾ x 6 x 6 in. (47.8 x 15.2 x 17.8 cm)
Collection of the artist

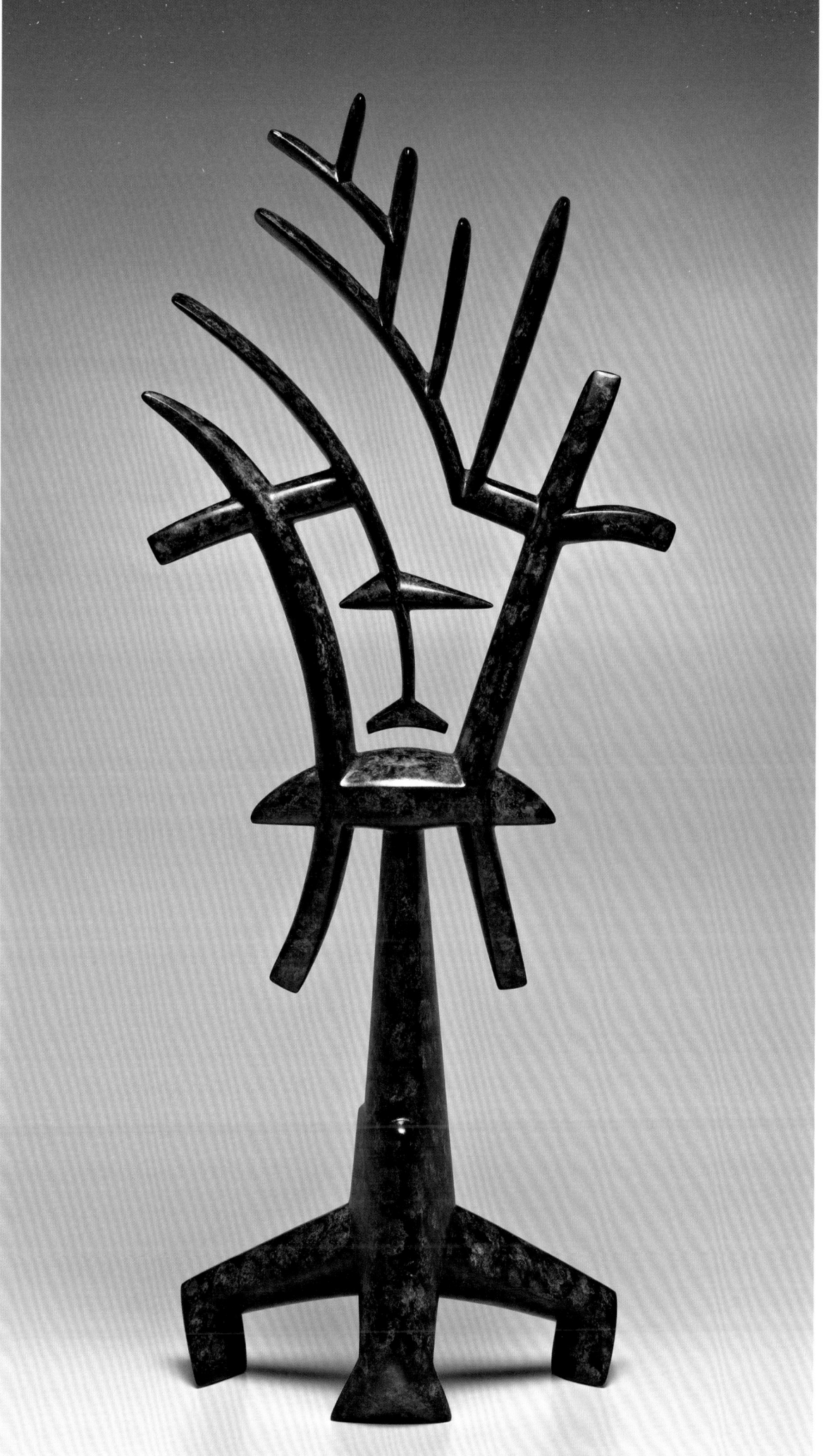

PLATE 78

Night Walker, 2020
Bronze
22¹¹⁄₁₆ x 9⁵⁄₁₆ x 4⅝ in. (57.6 x 23.6 x 11.7 cm)
Collection of the artist

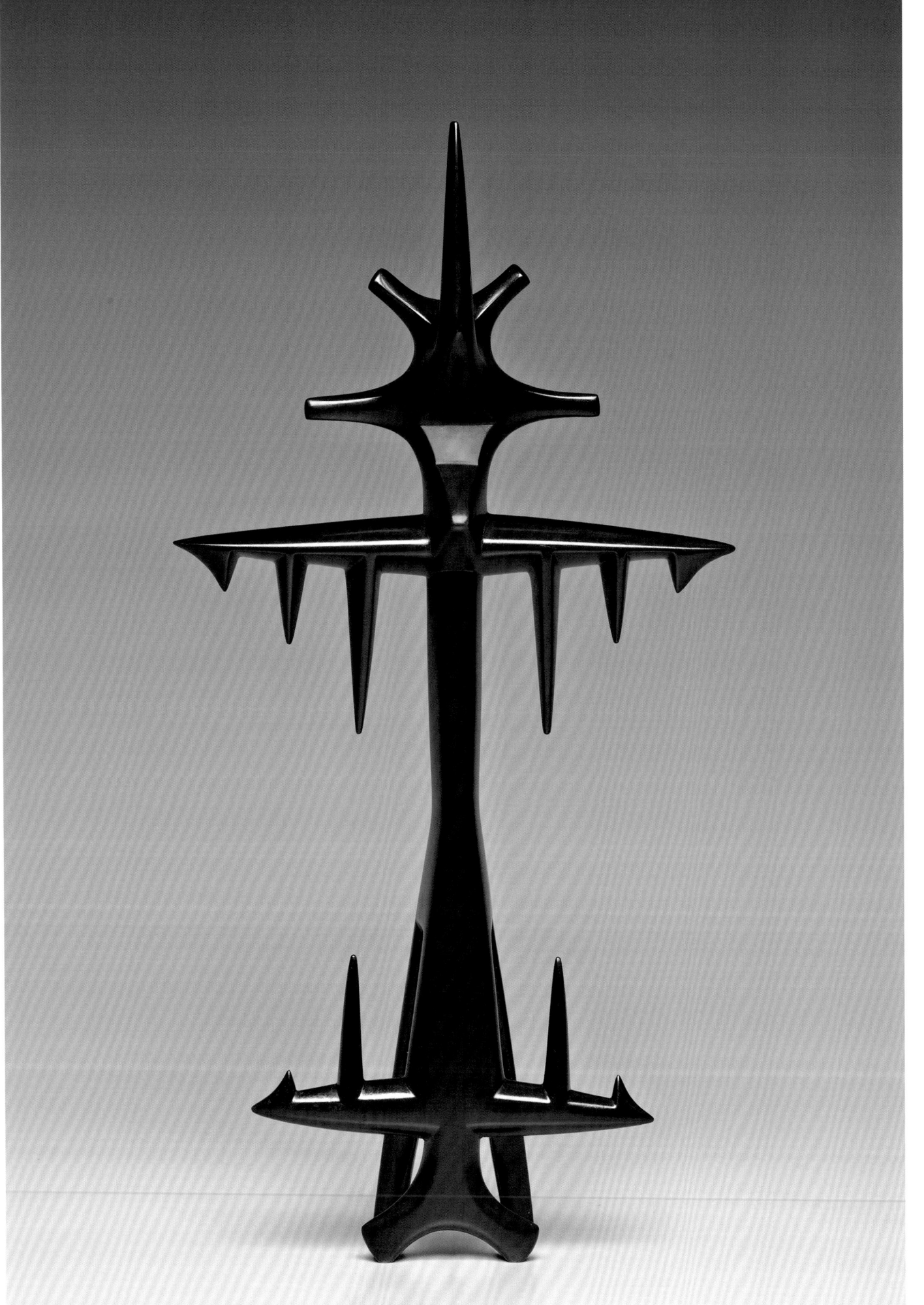

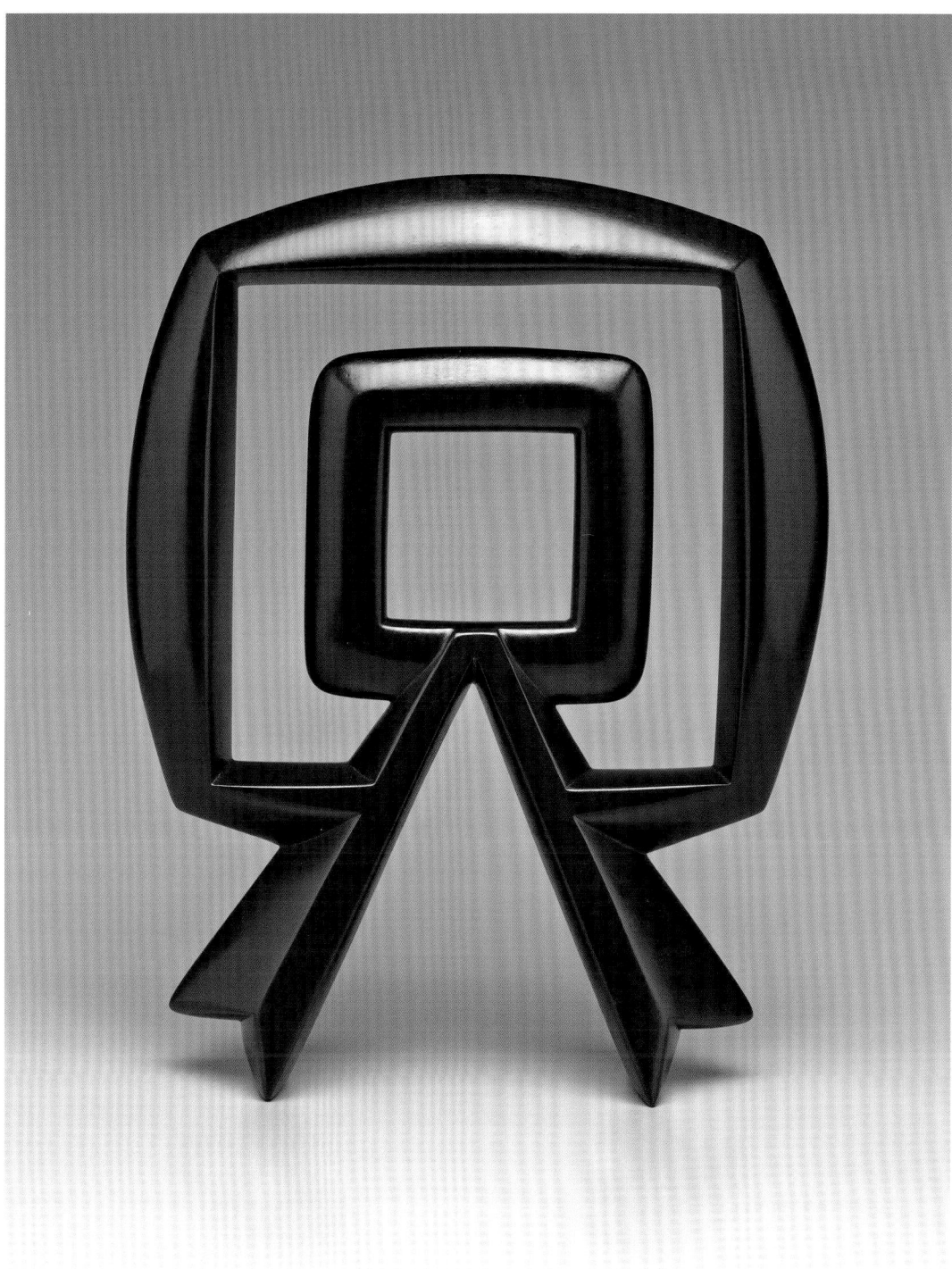

PLATE 79

Fight or Flight, 2021
Bronze
20½ x 10⅜ x 4 in. (52.1 x 26.4 x 10.2 cm)
Collection of the artist

PLATE 80

Viewfinder, 2021
Bronze
14½ x 11 x 4 in. (36.8 x 27.9 x 10.2 cm)
Collection of the artist

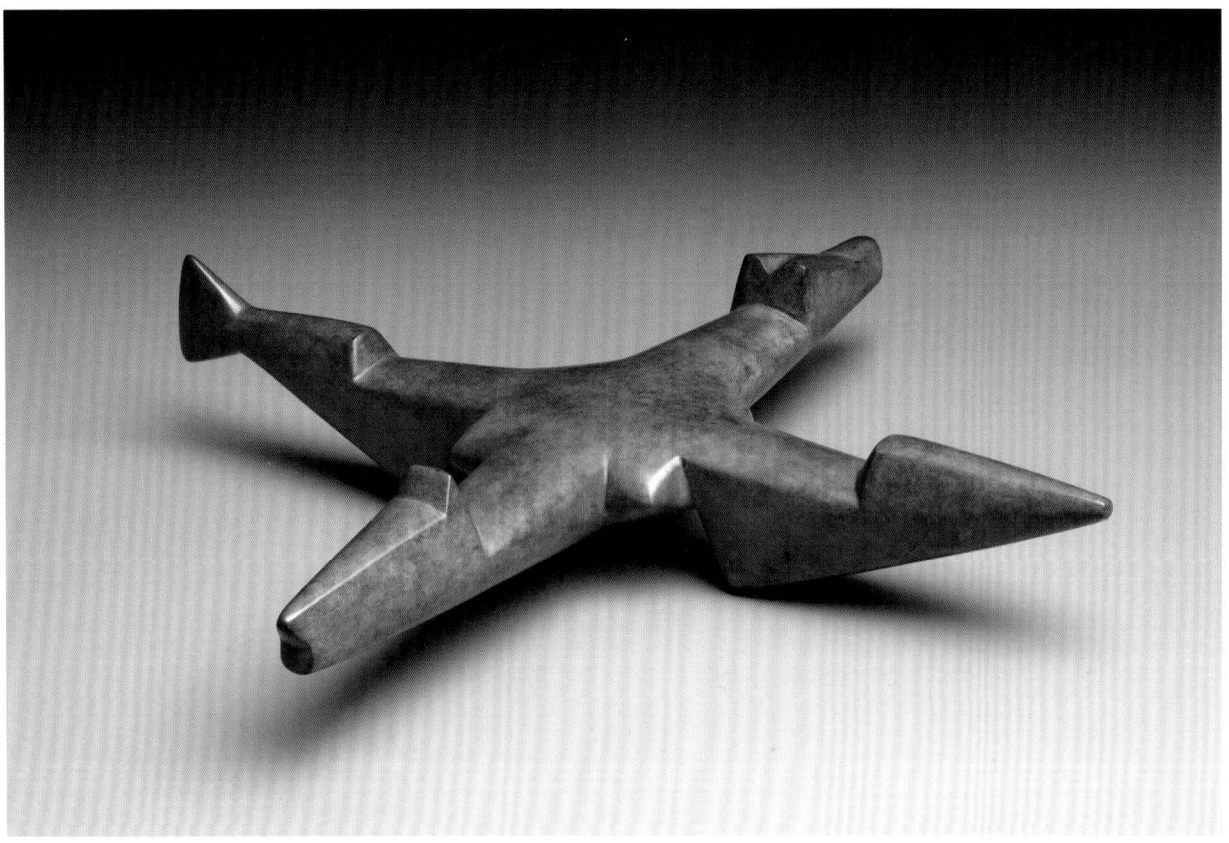

PLATE 81

Moral Compass, 2021
Bronze
2⅝ x 12¹¹⁄₁₆ x 12⅝ in. (6.6 x 32.2 x 32 cm)
Private collection

PLATE 82

Satyr, 2021
Bronze
33¹³⁄₁₆ x 22⁵⁄₁₆ x 16 in. (85.8 x 56.6 x 40.6 cm)
Collection of the artist

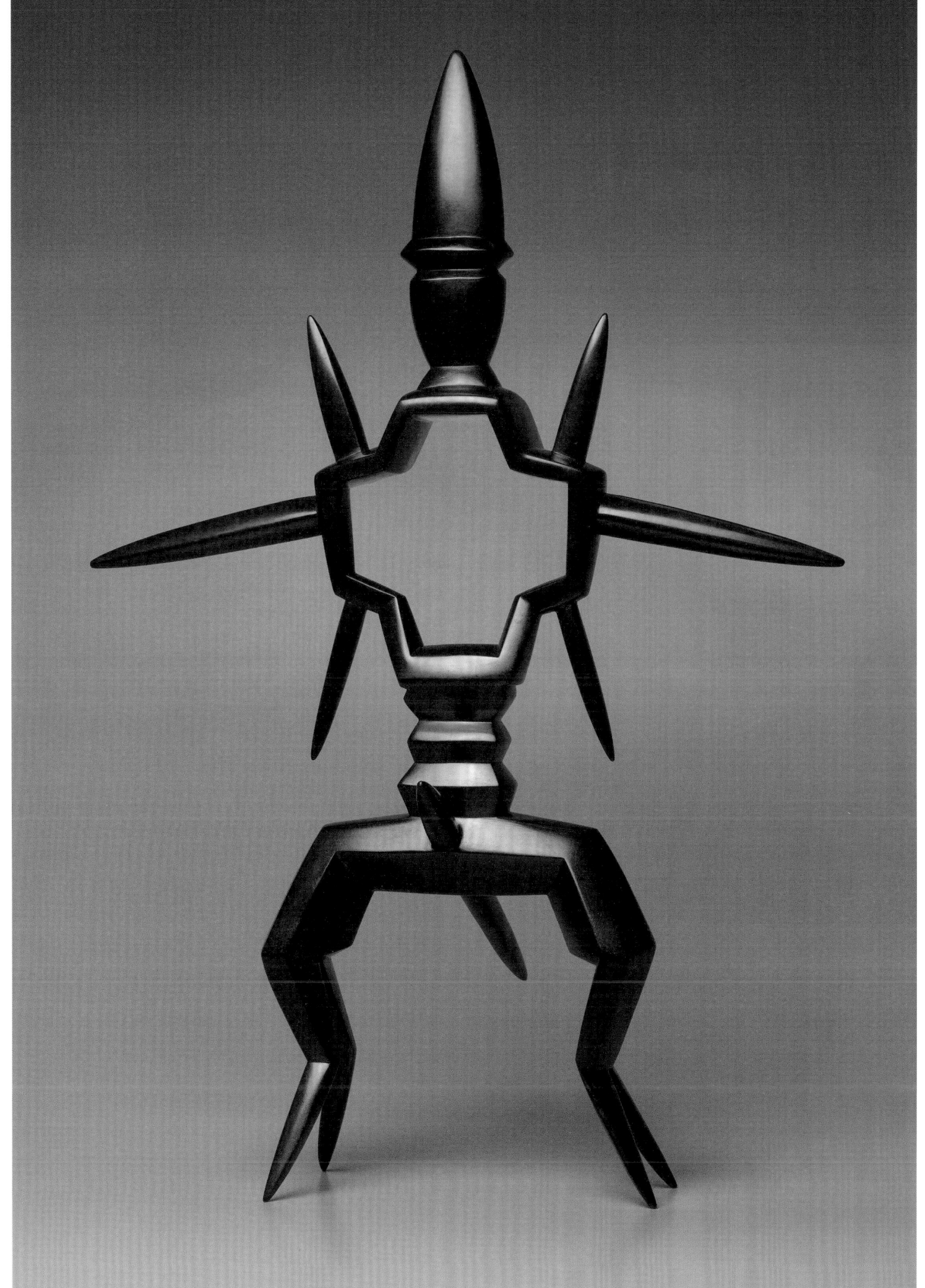

PLATE 83

Palace Pet, 2021
Bronze
8 5/8 x 19 5/16 x 3 5/8 in. (21.8 x 49 x 9.1 cm)
Collection of the artist

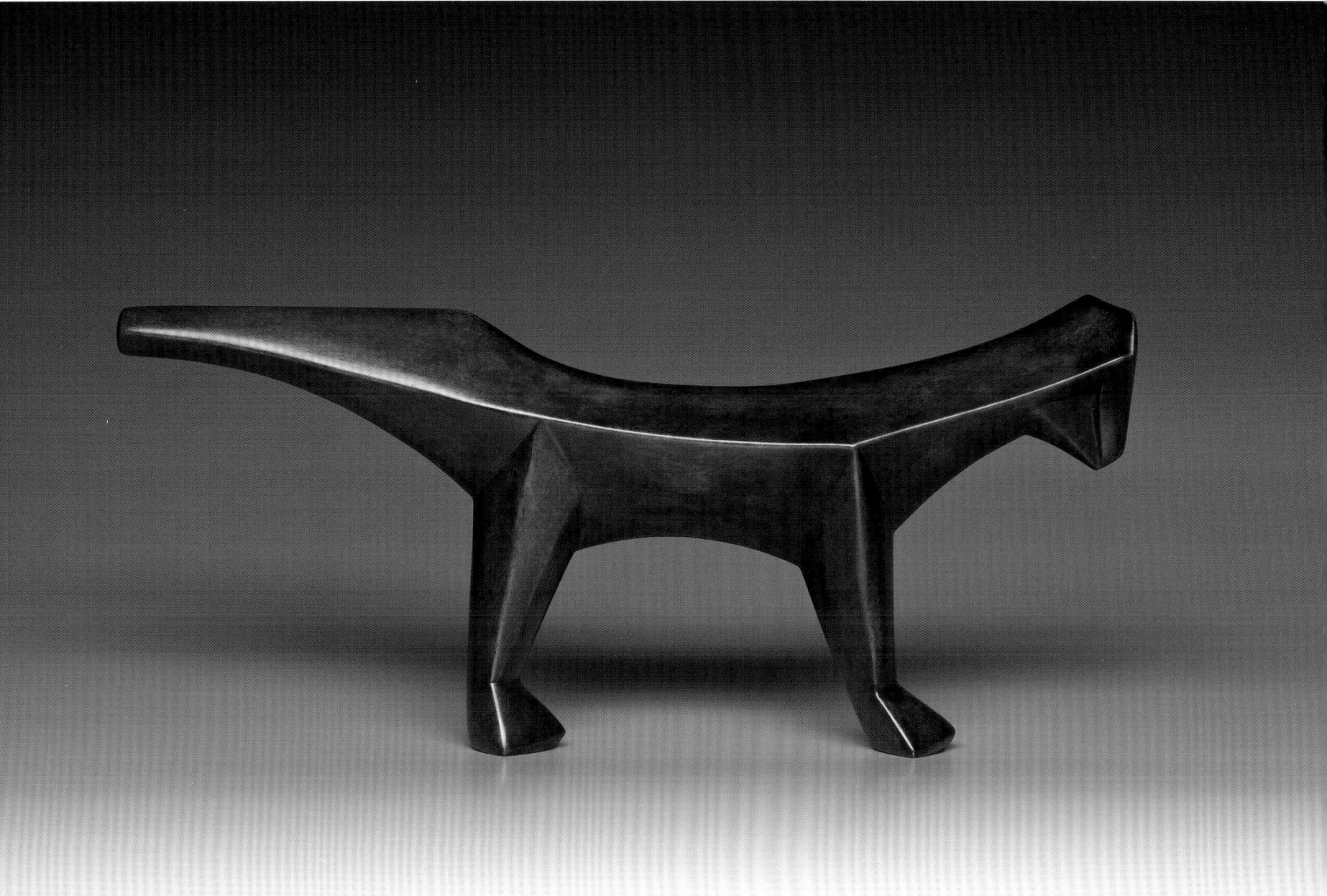

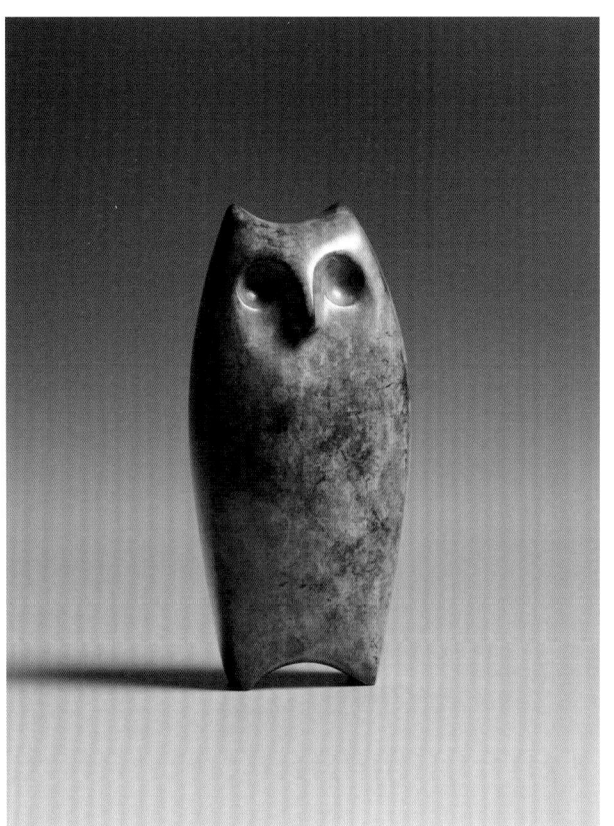

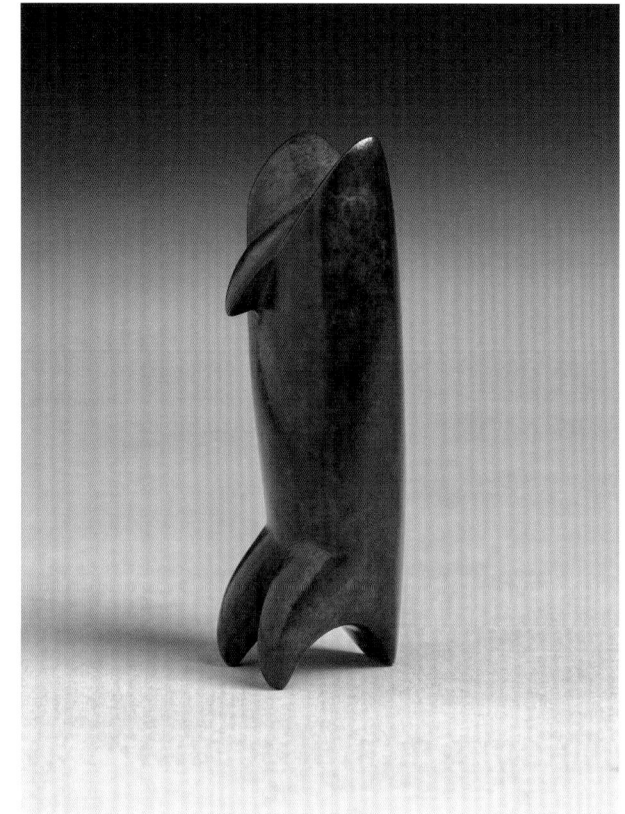

PLATE 84

Owl, 2021
Bronze
2⅝ x 1³⁄₁₆ x ⅞ in. (6.6 x 3 x 2.3 cm)
Collection of the artist

PLATE 85

Raptor, 2021
Bronze
3⅛ x 1 x 1⅛ in. (7.9 x 2.5 x 2.8 cm)
Collection of the artist

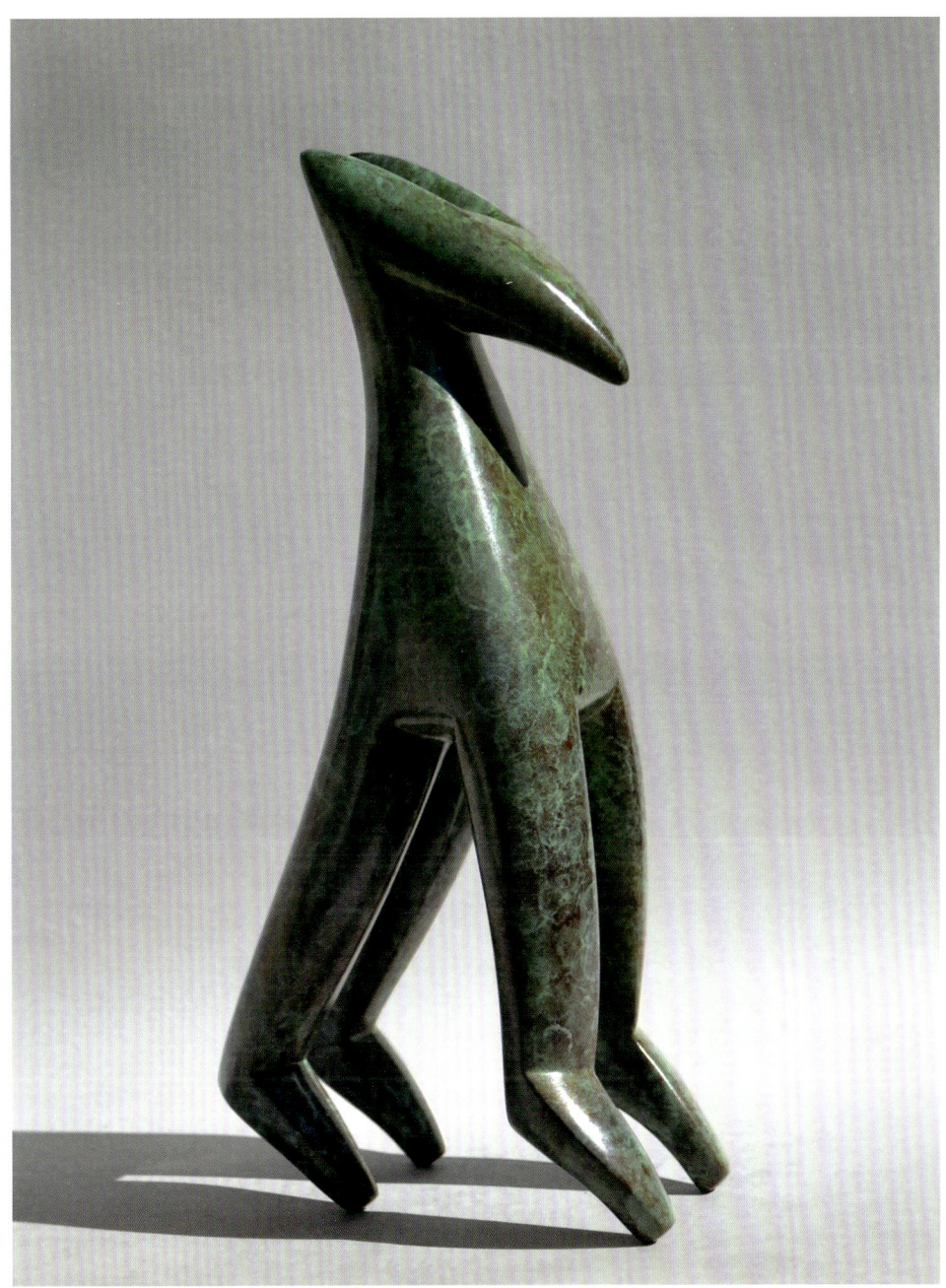

PLATE 86

Pet en Point, 2019
Bronze
9½ x 46 x 2⅜ in. (24.1 x 116.8 x 6.1 cm)
Collection of the artist

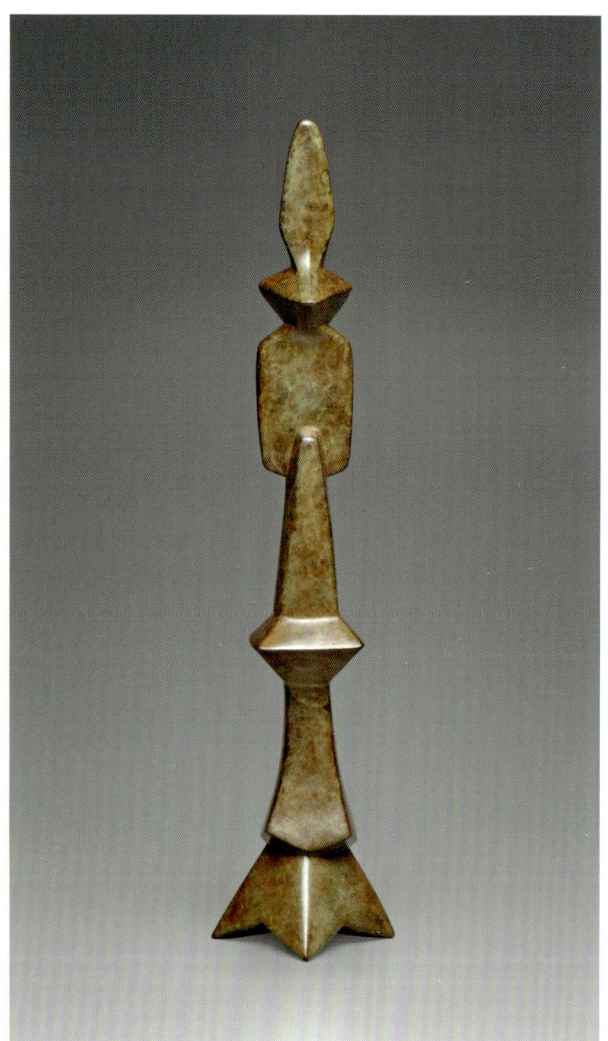

PLATE 87

Participation Award, 2021
Bronze
10 x 2⁵⁄₁₆ x 2⁵⁄₁₆ in. (25.4 x 5.8 x 5.8 cm)
Private collection

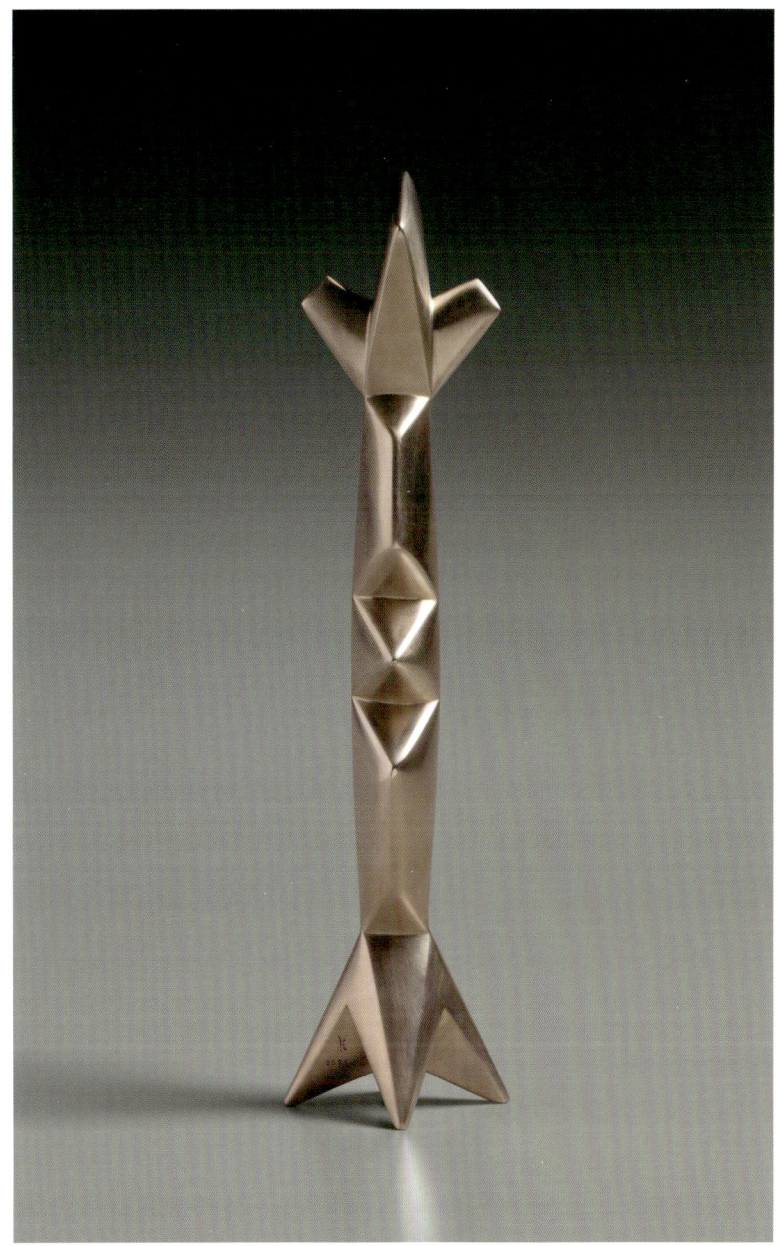

PLATE 88

Chief Impact Officer, 2021
Bronze
13½ x 3⁵⁄₁₆ x 2⅝ in. (34.3 x 8.4 x 6.6 cm)
Collection of the artist

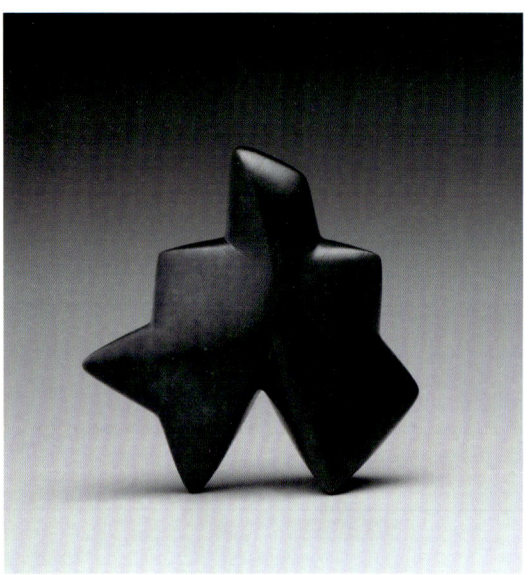

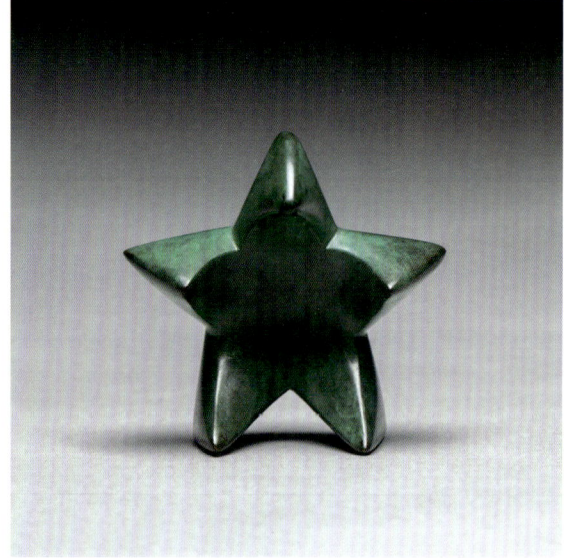

PLATE 89

Walking Star 2, 2021
Bronze
2¹³⁄₁₆ x 2¹³⁄₁₆ x ¹³⁄₁₆ in. (7.1 x 7.1 x 2 cm)
Private collection

PLATE 90

Star Boy, 2022
Bronze
2³⁄₁₆ x 2³⁄₈ x ¹³⁄₁₆ in. (5.6 x 6.1 x 3 cm)
Private collection

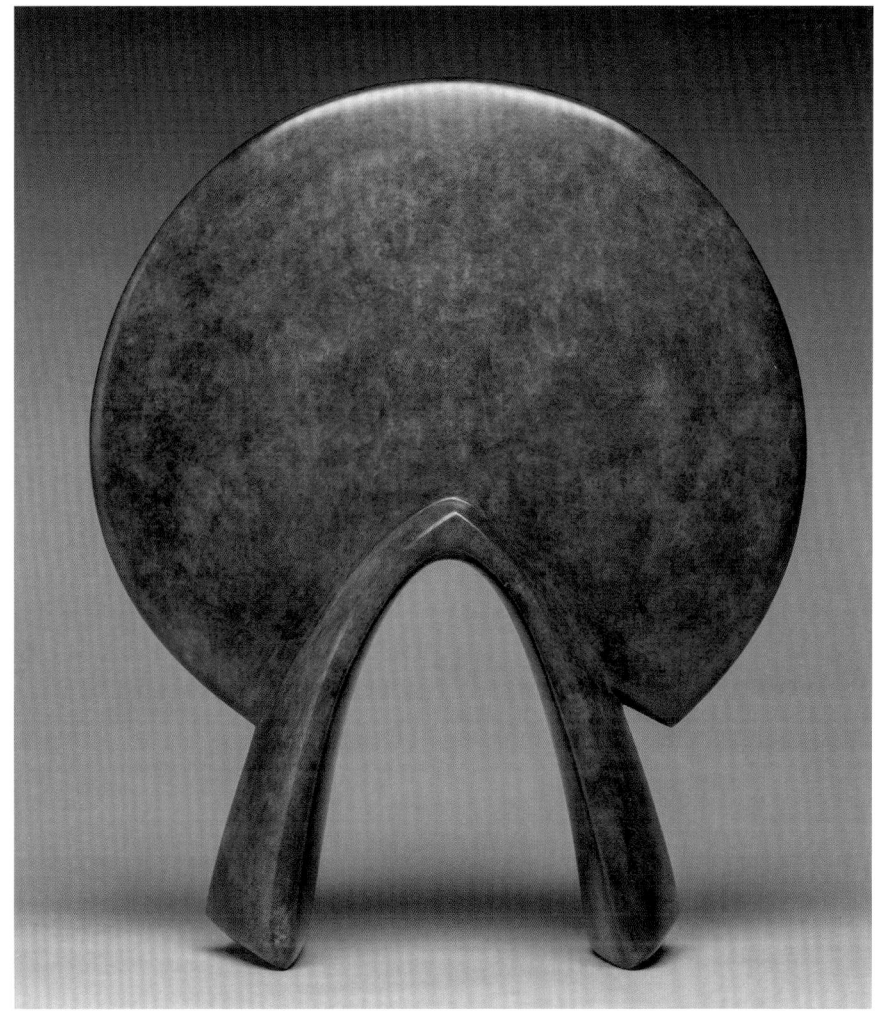

PLATE 91

Moon Over Mt. Analog, 2022
Bronze
10 ⁵⁄₁₆ x 8 ½ x 3 ⅛ in. (26.2 x 21.6 x 7.9 cm)
Collection of the artist

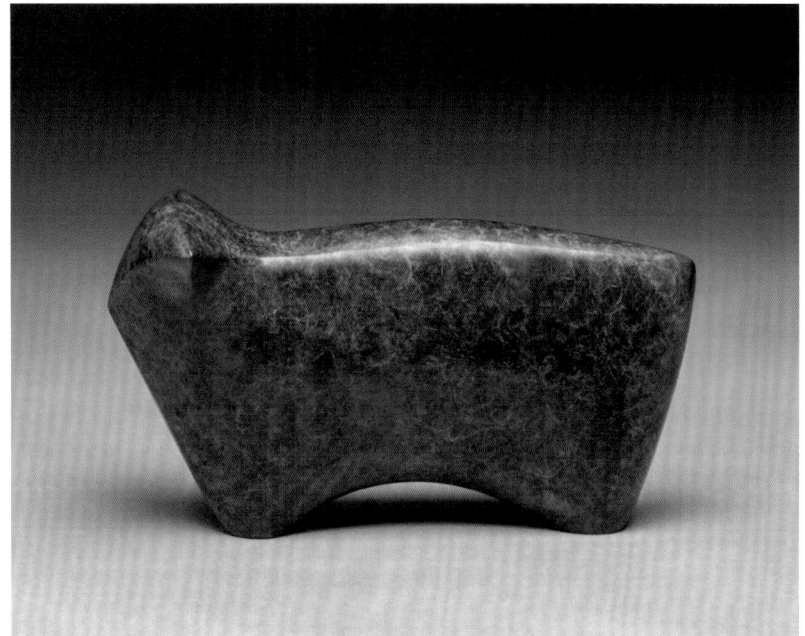

PLATE 92

Steer, 2022
Bronze
4⅛ x 7⅜ x 3½ in. (10.5 x 18.7 x 9 cm)
Private collection

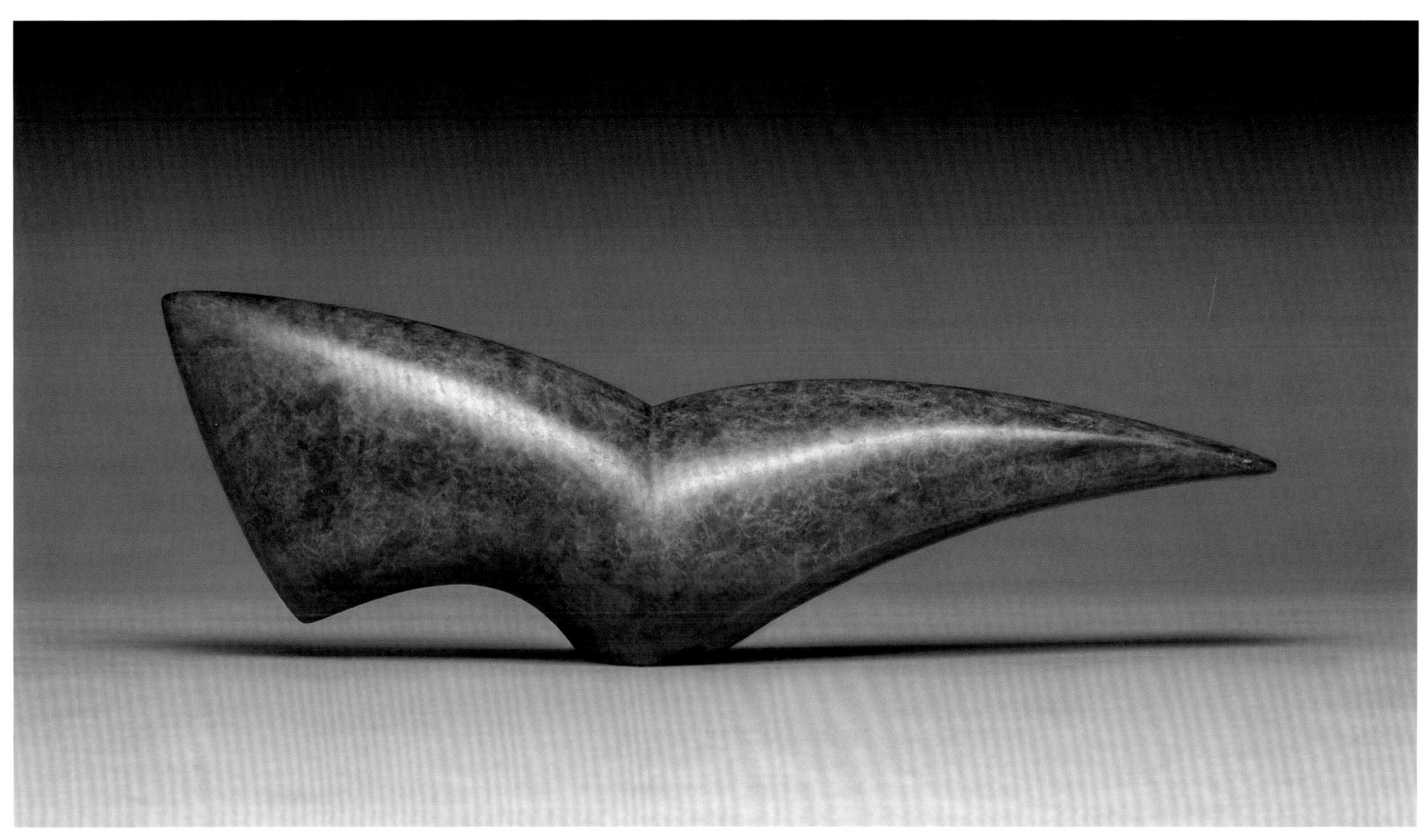

PLATE 93

Liftoff, 2023
Bronze
4½ x 14⁵⁄₁₆ x 2½ in. (11.4 x 36.3 x 6.3 cm)
Private collection

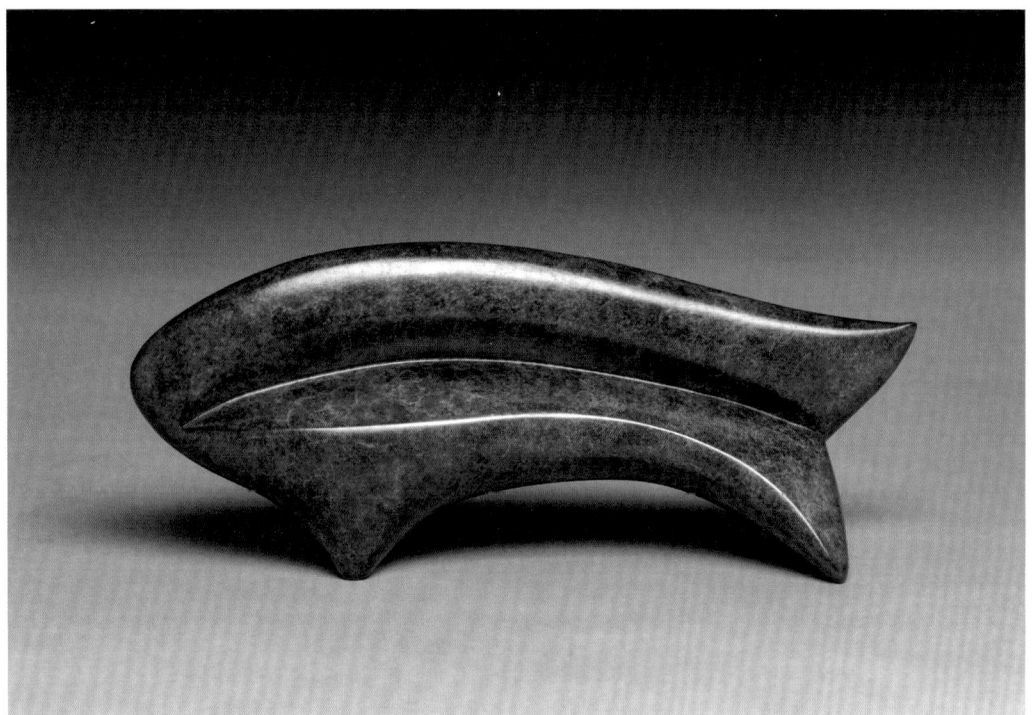

PLATE 94

Tetrapod, 2023
Bronze
3¹³⁄₁₆ x 9⅛ x 2 in. (9.6 x 23.1 x 5.1 cm)
Private collection

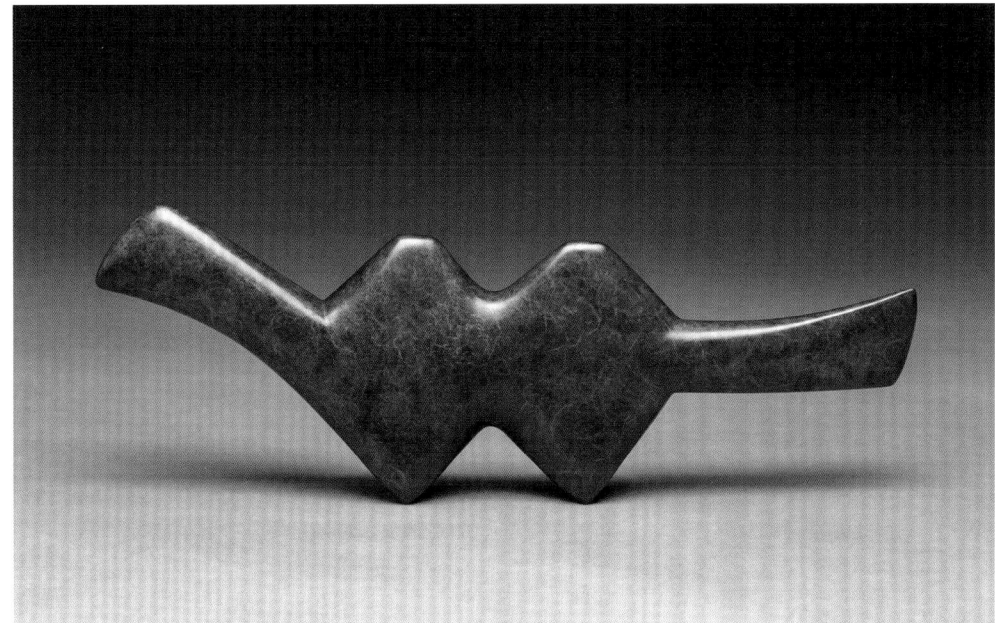

PLATE 95

Dino, 2023
Bronze
4 x 9 x 1¹¹⁄₁₆ in. (10.2 x 22.9 x 4.3 cm)
Private collection

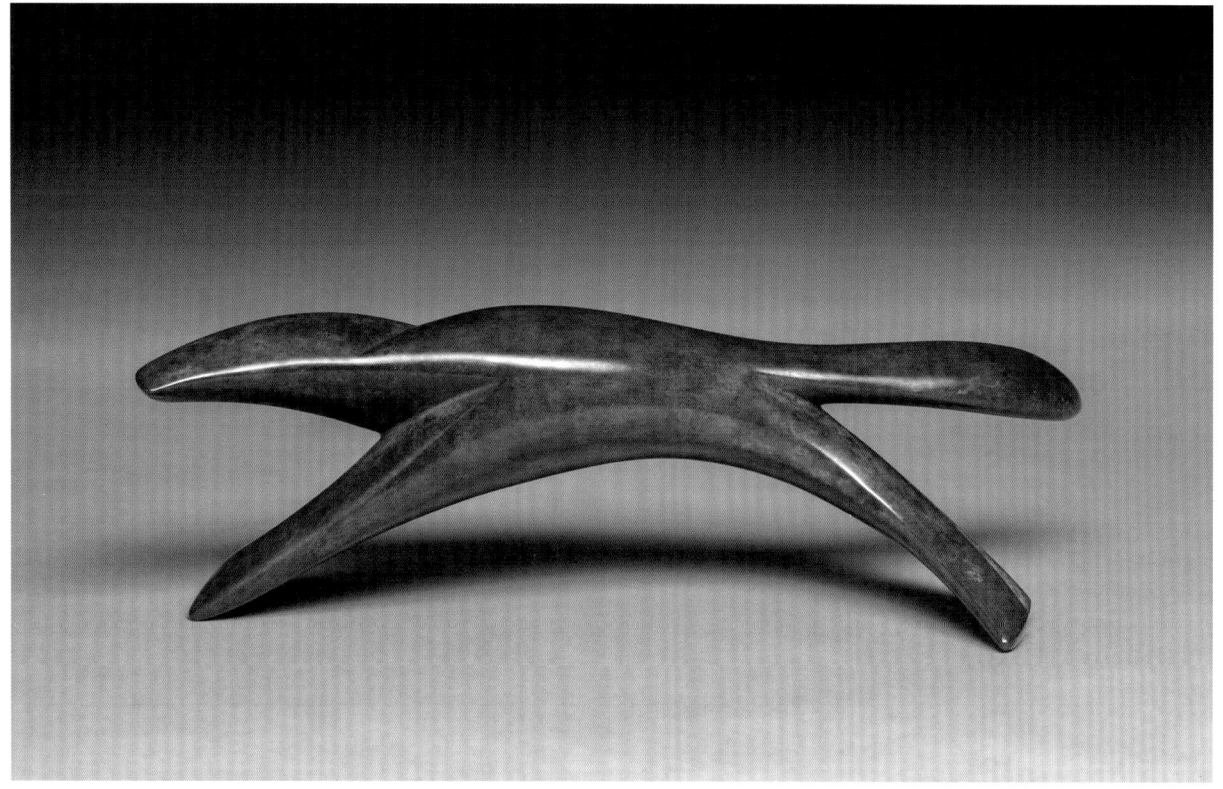

PLATE 96

Trickster, 2023
Bronze
3½ x 11⅛ x 3¹³⁄₁₆ in. (8.9 x 28.2 x 9.6 cm)
Collection of the artist

PLATE 97

Neptune's Pet, 2023
Bronze
17 x 8 x 10 in. (43.2 x 20.3 x 25.4 cm)
Collection of the artist

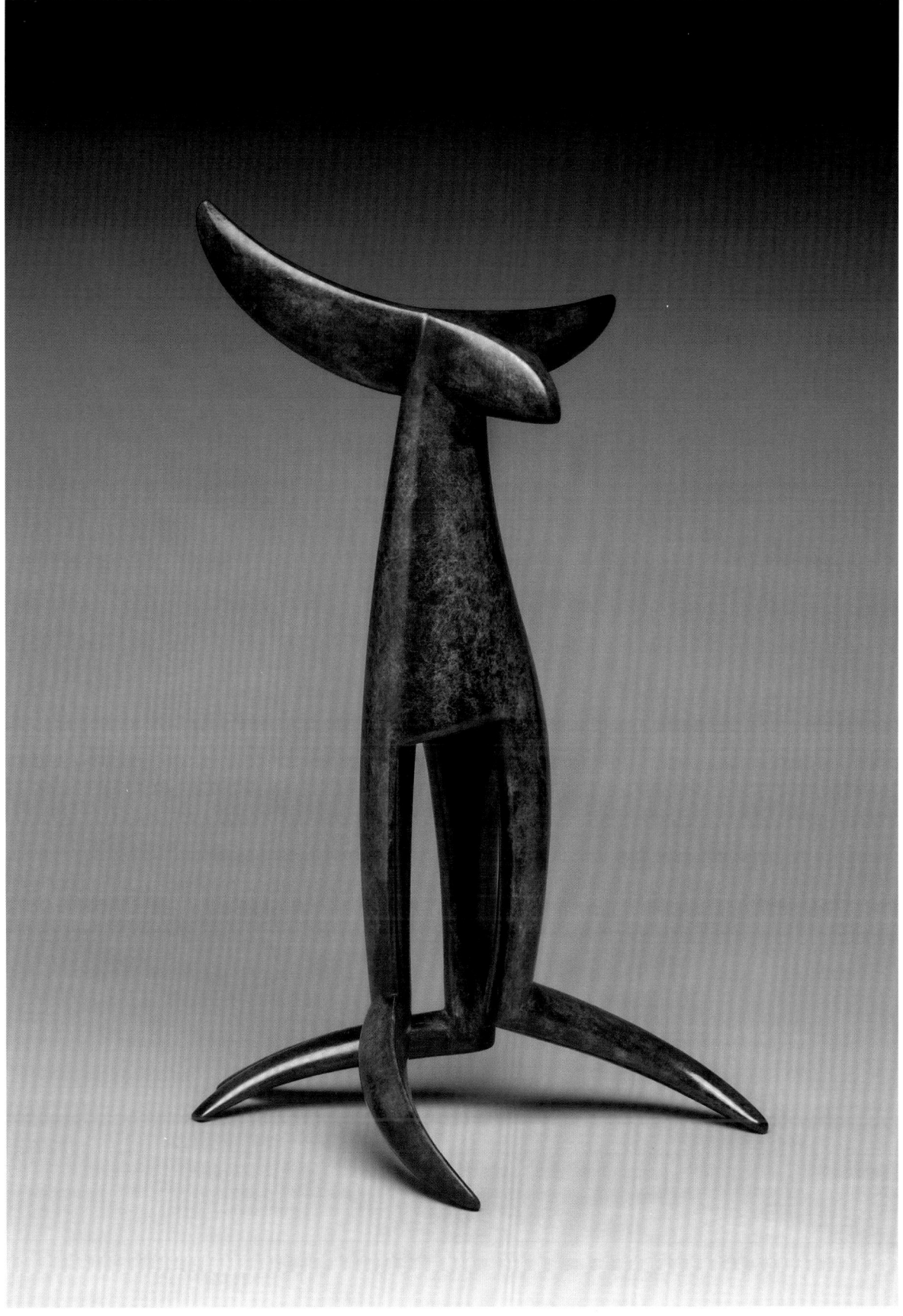

PLATE 98

Bird Salad, 1978, 2024
Inkjet print, digitally reworked from a silkscreen print
17 x 15 in. (43.2 x 38.1 cm)
Collection of the artist

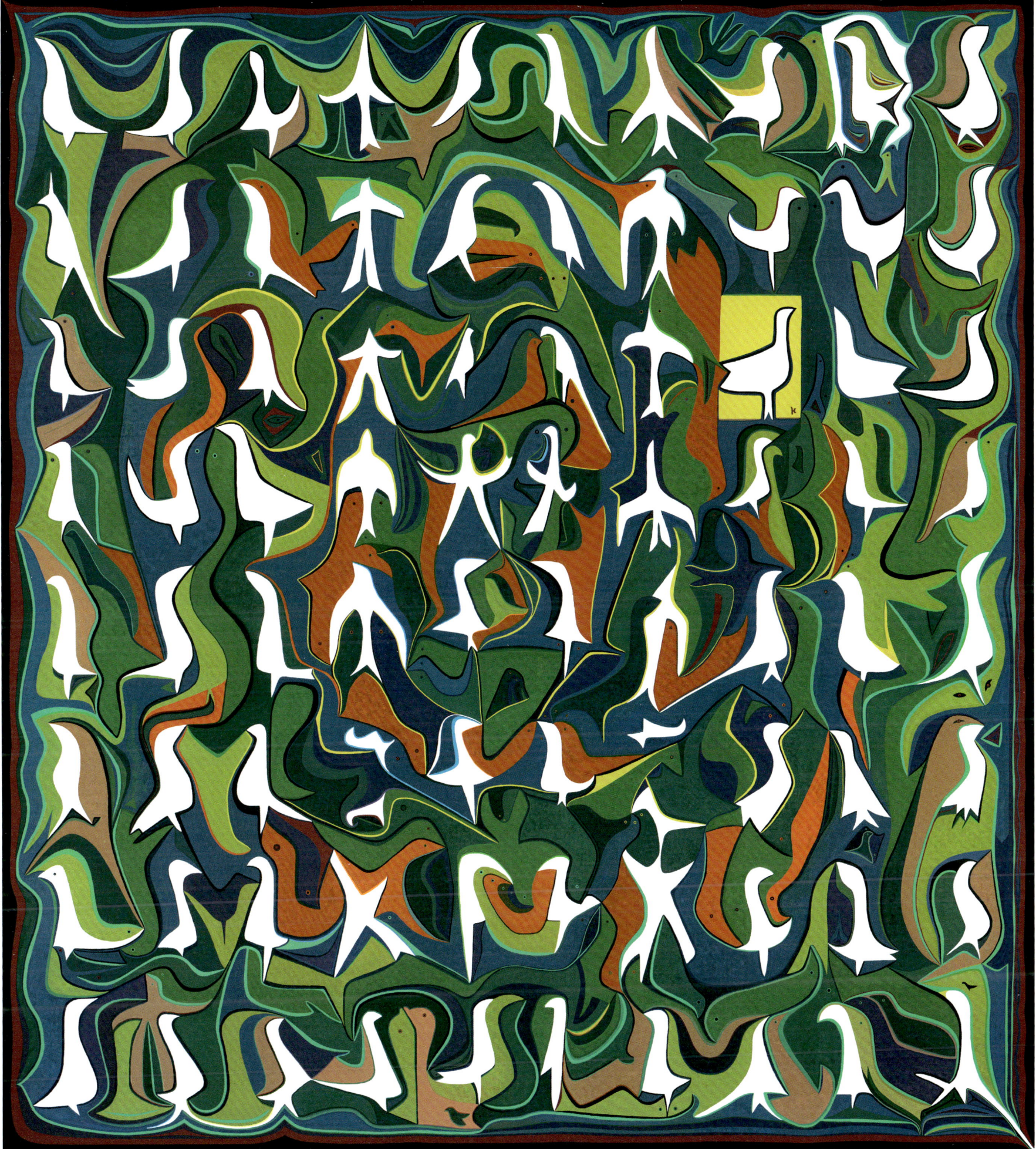

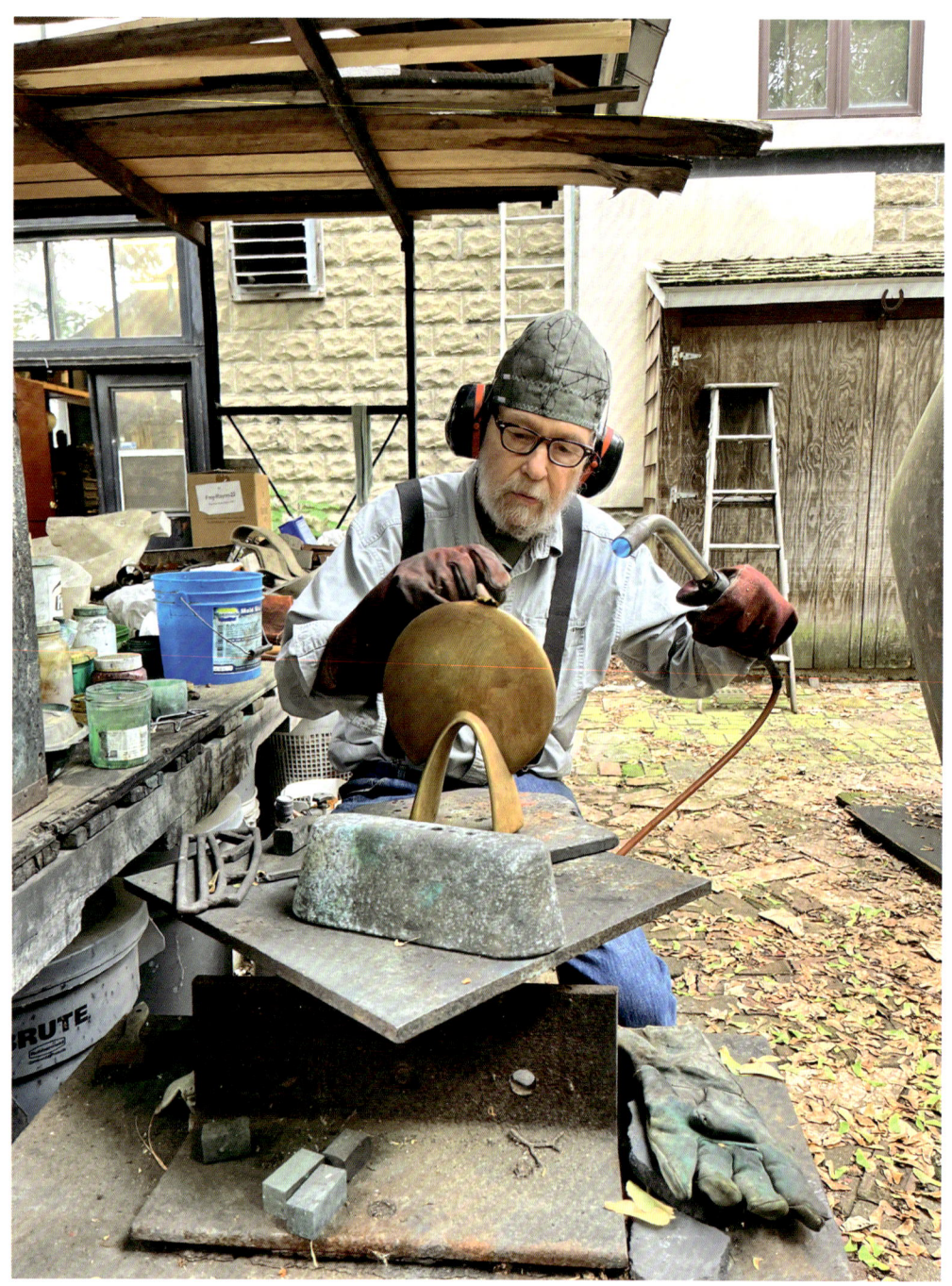

Peter in his studio yard doing a patina

ACKNOWLEDGMENTS

My family and friends have supported and encouraged my pursuit of art throughout the years, and this book is no exception. My friend, Rob Perkins, first suggested the idea of a book. Belinda Rathbone began as my biographer, but took on the important role of project manager, as I was in the most need of wrangling. Thank you to Murray Whyte for his humbling critical essay, and to my wonderful photographers—Bruce Rogovin, Stewart Clements, and Will Howcroft. This book would not have been completed without the tremendous efforts of my daughters, Pendry and Julia, and my former assistant Cathy Sherwood combed through old photos, tracked down missing data, and organized files.

This book is the final legacy project of my career. I have had many talented assistants over the years, including Danny Kessler, Matt Callahan, Bayne Peterson, Jeff Jorge, Aki Bates, and Pedro Alexander, and I appreciate all the time and labor they put in at the shop.

I am grateful to the current and former members of the Boston Sculptors Gallery, especially Mac Dewart, Robert Schelling, Larry Pollans, and the late Joe Wheelwright for their many years of friendship and collaboration.

Thank you to my hundreds of collectors. My brothers, Perry and Chris Haines; Chris whose first purchase was a $100 painting in 1972, which took him a year to pay off and Perry who bought my first significant bronzes. My dear friend Steve Pond, who was never an art collector but a believer in me who purchased at least one bronze every year for over 50 years.

I would like to acknowledge my kindred spirits and interlocutors, including those from the following walks of life: Columbus Academy, Seekers, Marine Corps, Jung Book Club, Harvard Business School, Breakfast Group, Tavern Club, Haines and Nam family.

Finally, thank you to my wife Sekyo, my fiercest critic and biggest supporter.

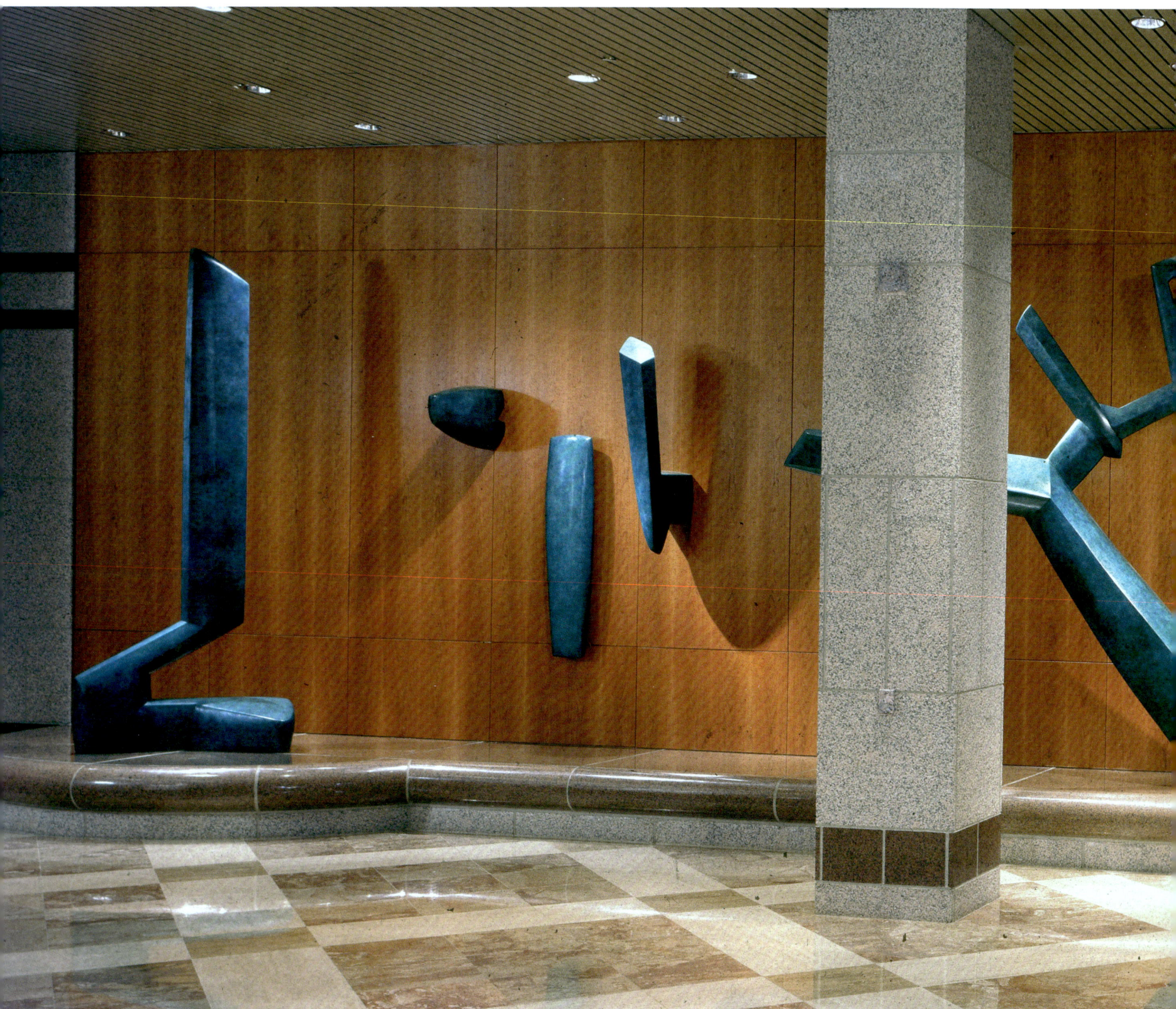

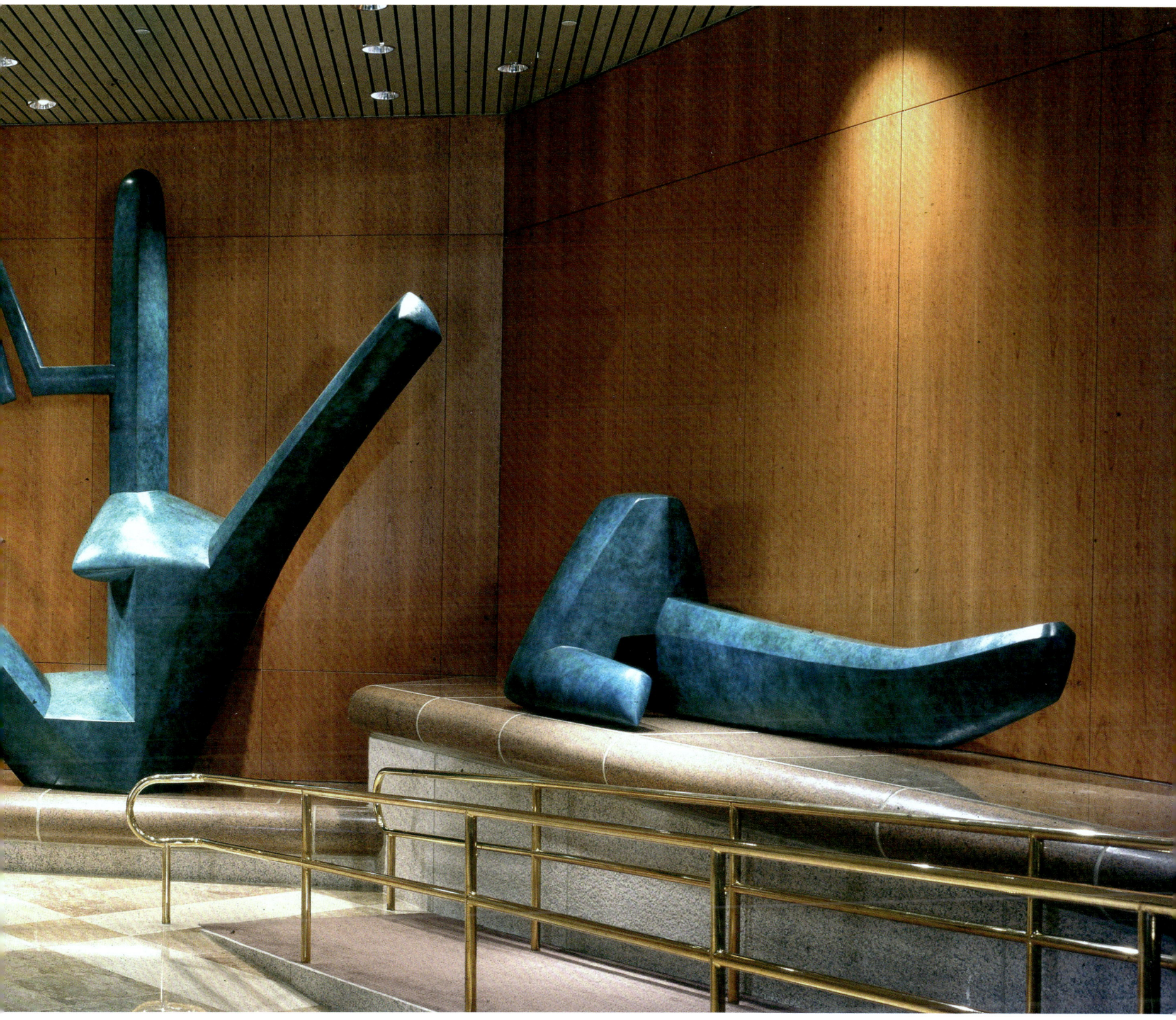

The Landmark Suite installed at 150 Federal Street

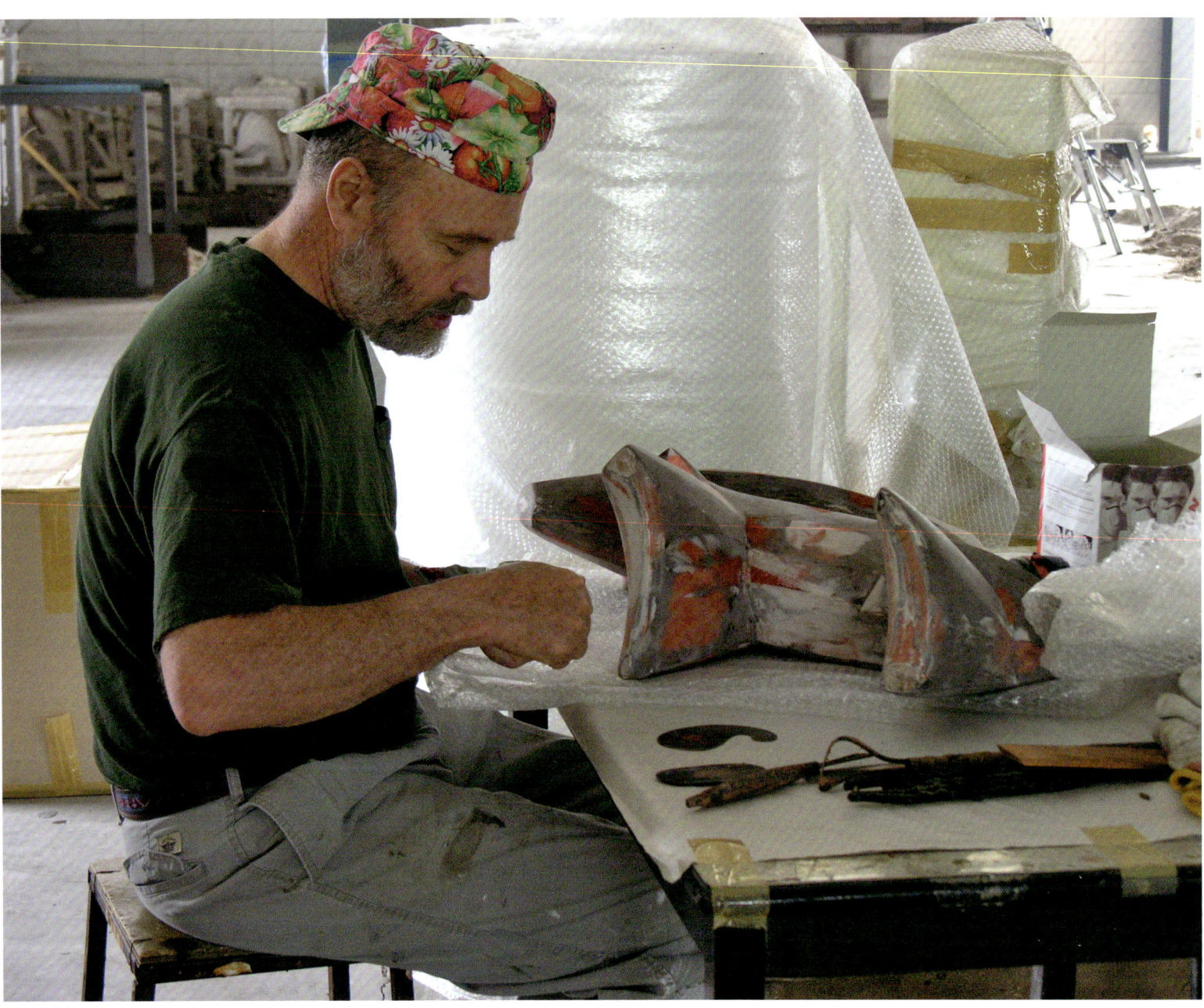

Peter working at a foundry in Thailand

CHRONOLOGY

1942   Born in Quantico, VA, to John Percy Haines and Pendery Spear Haines.

1947   Attends kindergarten where his father was stationed at the Naval Air
Facility on Midway Island.

1949   Moves to Columbus, OH, when his father becomes commander of the
Naval Air Station there.

1953   Wins a citywide children's drawing contest and is awarded attendance at
Saturday morning art class at the Columbus College of Art and Design.

1960   Graduates high school from the Columbus Academy.

Enters University of Colorado on a ROTC scholarship.

1965   Graduates from the university with BA in anthropology and psychology;
commissioned 2nd lieutenant in Marine Corps.

1967– Completes a 13-month tour in Vietnam and is awarded the Bronze Star
1968   after a Tet Offensive battle.

1971   Father, John Percy Haines, dies.

Graduates Harvard Business School with an MBA degree.

1974   Graduates from the School of the Museum of Fine Arts, Boston, MA,
with an MFA degree.

1975   Purchases a small factory building on Sidney Street in Cambridge and
converts into his home and art studio.

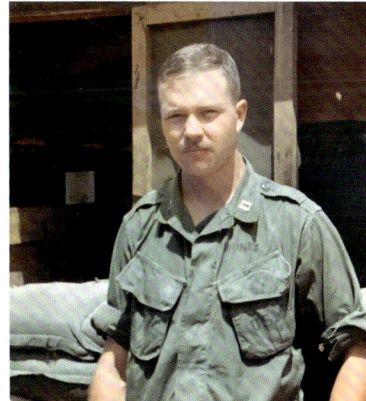

Peter in the Marine Corps

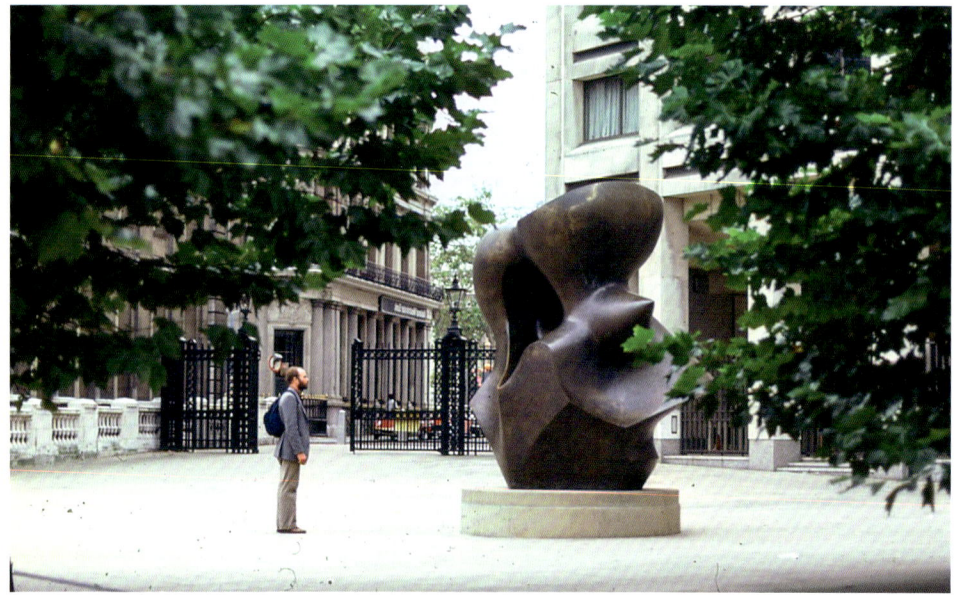

Peter with Henry Moore's *Spindle Piece*
in London, 1982

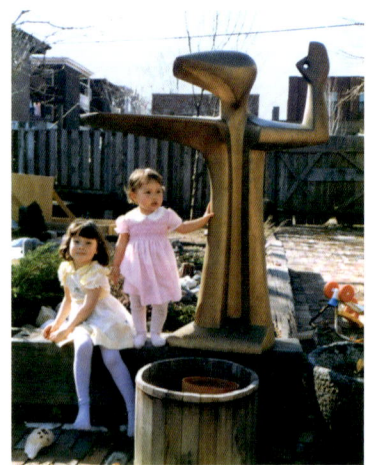

Pendry and Julia Haines in their
backyard with *St. Francis Preaching to
the Birds*, ca. 1987

1979 First solo show, *Artifacts*, at Impressions Gallery, Boston, MA.

1980–
1981 Awarded a Traveling Fellowship from The School of the Museum of Fine
Arts, Boston; travels to Egypt, Rome, Florence, Paris, Stonehenge, London,
and Henry Moore's studio in Hertfordshire, England.

1982 Marries Sekyo Nam in Cambridge, MA; spends honeymoon traveling around
Ireland looking at neolithic monuments.

1983 Daughter Pendry Ming Haines born.

1985 Daughter Julia Jong Haines born.

1988 First major commission, *The Landmark Suite*, enlarges 7 original bronzes;
installed at 150 Federal Street, Boston, MA.

1992 Boston Sculptors Gallery opens; Peter is a founding member with 19 others.

1993 Mother, Pendery Haines Reese, dies.

1994 Brother, Perry Vansant Haines, dies.

1995 Major renovations to the building on Sidney Street in Cambridge transform
the Haines household and give Peter a new three-story studio space.

1996 Co-founds the Vermont Gentlemen's Foundry in East Corinth, VT, with
Robert Schelling, Joe Wheelwright, and Larry Pollans.

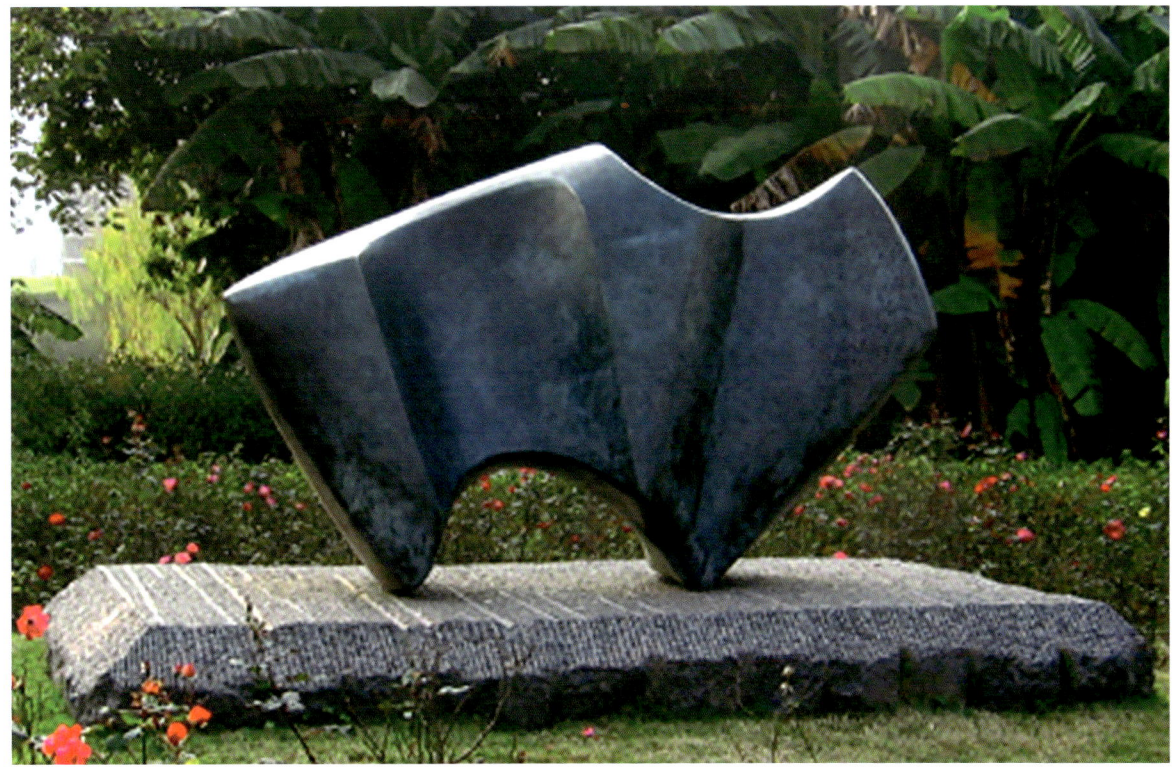

Bison Mountain, 2003
Bronze
4 x 7 x 3 ft. (1.2 x 2.1 x .9 m)
International Sculpture
Symposium, Fuzhou, China

2000   Travels to Arctic Circle for a rafting trip and witnesses the migration of thousands of caribou. This inspires his installation *Migration*, a collection of over 700 small abstract animals.

2001   Visits Korea for the first time with Sekyo and his daughters. He is inspired to make *Sprue Tower* after visiting Buddhist temples where he saw stacks of stones (doltaps) made by visitors.

2003   Selected to make *Bison Mountain* as part of the International Sculpture Symposium in Fuzhou, China.

2005   Travels to Thailand to work with a foundry there; casts enlargements of *Inner Eagle* and *Updated Goat*.

2008   Selected to make *Bear* as part of the Goyang Sculpture Symposium in Ilsan, South Korea.

2011   Returns to Vietnam for a vacation and visits Khe San, where he was stationed.

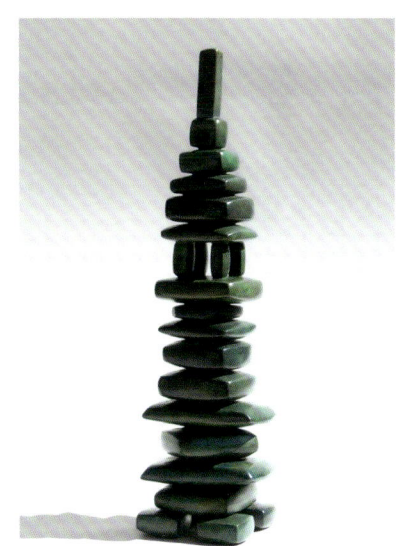

Sprue Tower, 2005
Bronze
17 3/16 x 4 5/8 x 4 3/16 in. (43.7 x 11.7 x 10.7 cm)
Collection of the artist

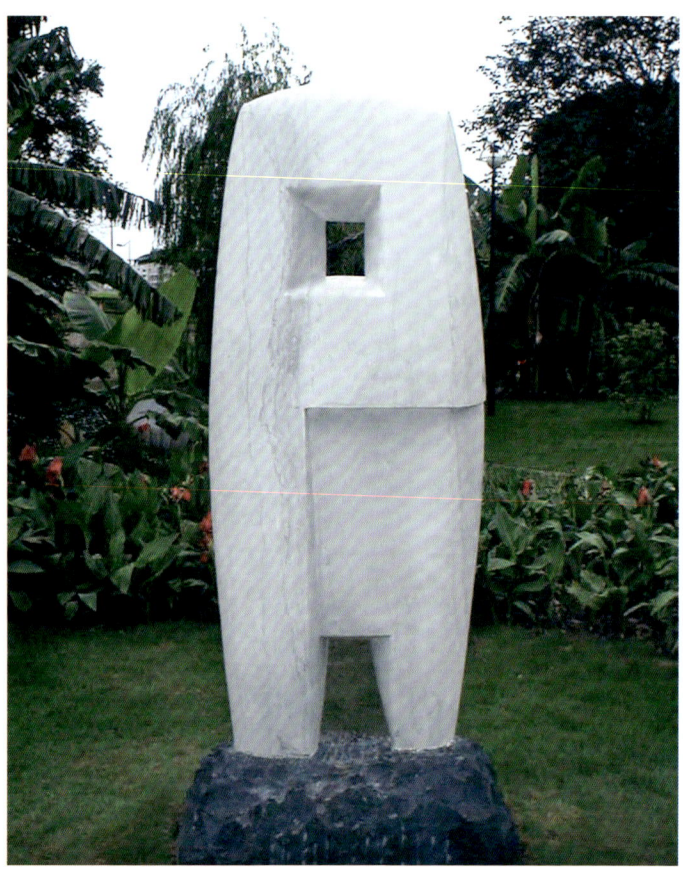

Ancestor, 2013
Marble
5 x 2 x 1 ft. (1.5 x .6 x .3 m)
Qingdao/Seoul Sculpture
Symposium, Shandong, China

2013 Selected to make a sculpture as part of Qingdao/Seoul Sculpture Symposium in Jimo City, Shandong, China.

Participates in *Convergence*, a group sculpture exhibition on the Christian Science Plaza in Boston, MA.

Designs *Bearskin Rug*, a carpet woven in Afghanistan by local weavers, a project coordinated through his daughter Pendry Haines who worked with women artisans

2021 Grandson Forrest Arlo Costa-Haines born to Pendry and Jay Costa.

2023 Diagnosed with Stage 4 stomach cancer.

Solo exhibition in October at the Boston Sculptors Gallery; he displays a table of 1000+ artifacts representing 45 years of work.

2024 October: dies peacefully at home in Cambridge.

2025 Publication of Peter's first major monograph.

Peter drawing with his grandson Forrest

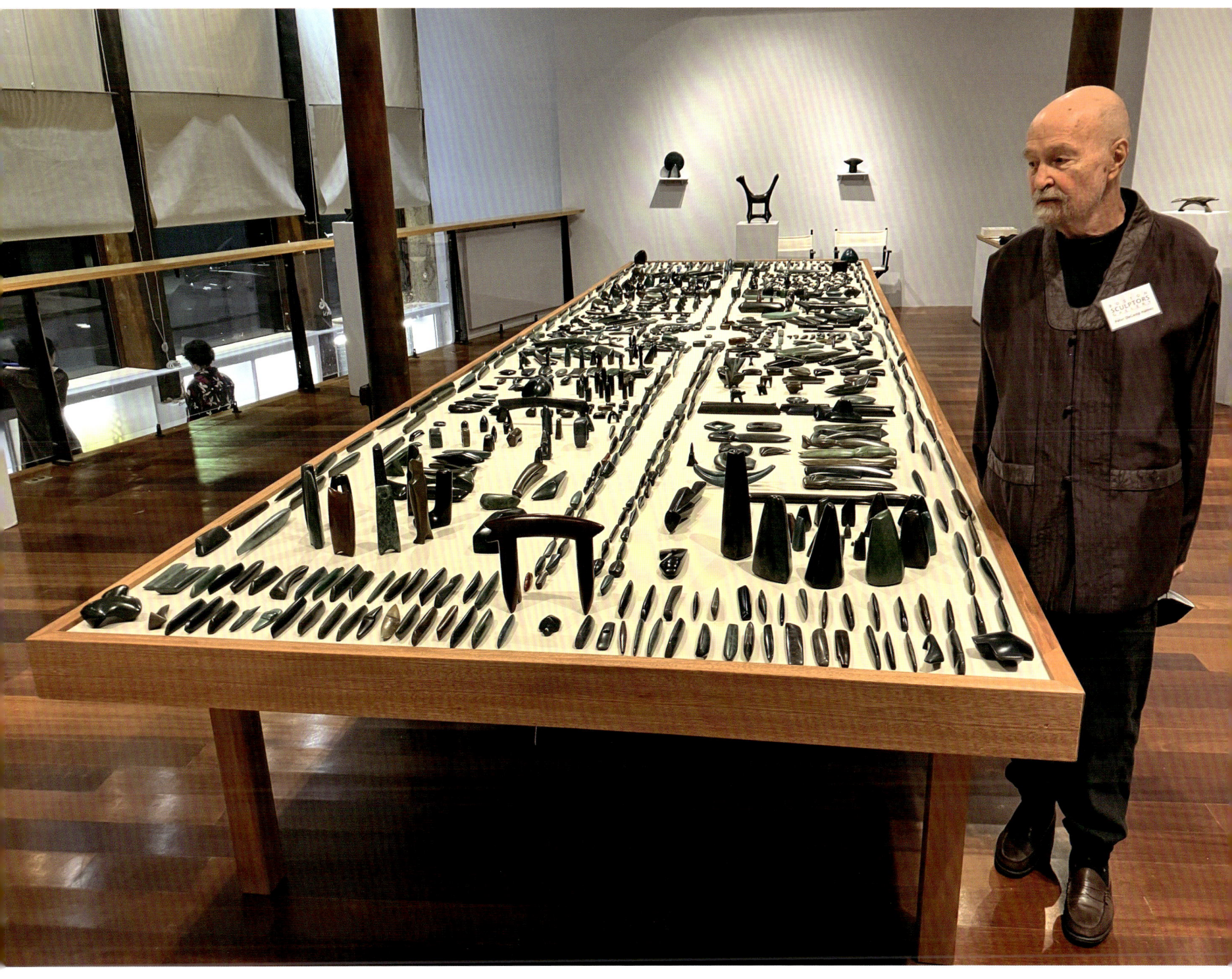

Peter at his final show, Boston Sculptors Gallery 2023

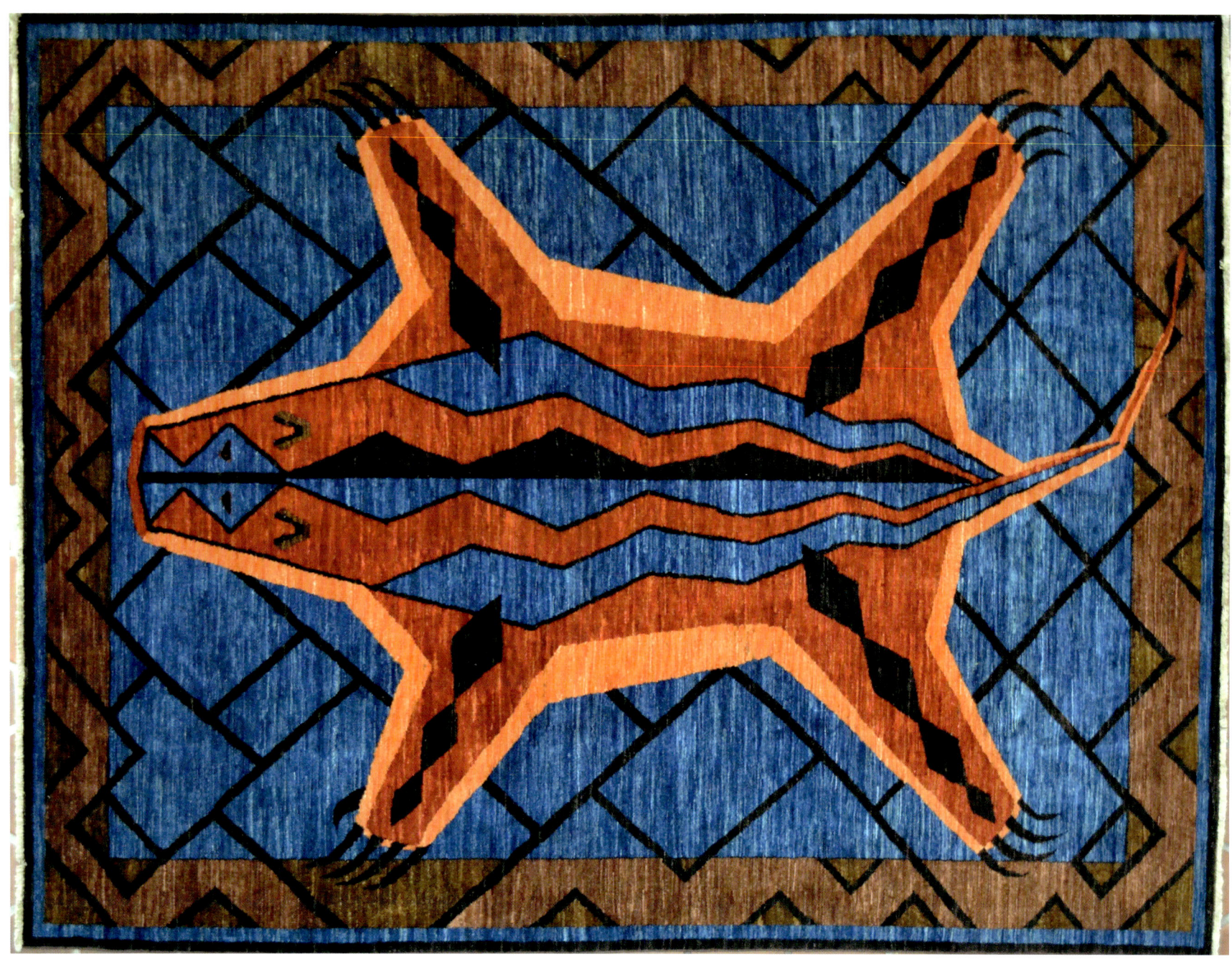

Bearskin Rug 1019, 2014
Wool on cotton warp
99 x 76 in. (251.5 x 193 cm)
Collection of the artist

BIBLIOGRAPHY

"Sculptors Haines and Veevers-Carter at Harbor Square Gallery." *The Free Press* (Camden, ME), September 4, 2014.

Hall, Jacqueline. "Bronze forms are deceptively simple." *Columbia (OH) Dispatch*, October 22, 1989.

———. "Windels bids adieu with Haines' works." *Columbus (OH) Dispatch*, May 16, 1993.

Masheck, Joseph. Brochure for *The Landmark Suite*, 150 Federal St., Boston, 1988.

———. *Smart Art: Point 1 Art Visuals/Visual Arts*. New York: Willis Locker & Owens Publishing, 1984.

Smee, Sebastian. "A convergence of Boston sculpture." *Boston Globe*, June 27, 2013.

Temin, Christine. "Going for the Bronze." *Boston Globe*, May 9, 2001.

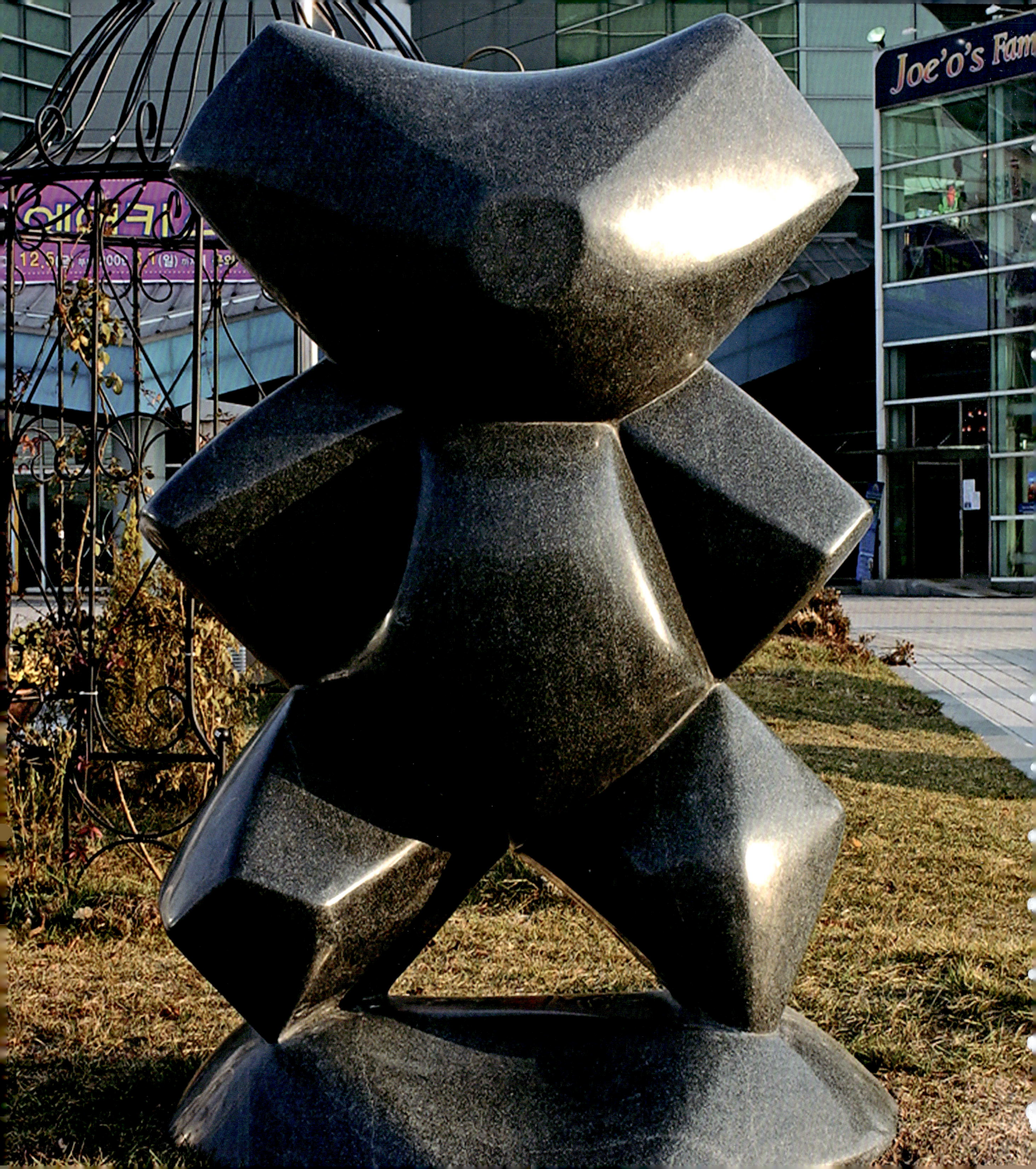

SELECTED GROUP AND SOLO EXHIBITIONS

GROUP EXHIBITIONS

2020   *Ring*, Boston Sculptors Gallery, Boston, MA

2019   *Opposites Attract*, Boston Sculptors Gallery, Boston, MA

2018   *Breath and Matter*, Boston Sculptors Gallery, Boston, MA

   Heart, Boston Sculptors Gallery, Boston, MA

2017   *Love/Lust*, Boston Sculptors Gallery, Boston, MA

2015   *Twice As Good*, Boston Sculptors Gallery, Boston, MA

2014   *Gallery Show*, Harbor View Gallery, Rockland, ME

   Sketchy Sculptors: Sculptors' Drawings in Different Materials, Boston Sculptors Gallery,
      Boston, MA

   Twelve Nights, Boston Sculptors Gallery, Boston, MA

   Visions y Visiones, Museo Qorikancha, Cuzco, Peru

2013   *Convergence*, The Christian Science Plaza, Boston, MA

   Summer Show, Jonathan Frost Gallery, Rockland, ME

2012   *Stirring the Waters/Between Two Bodies*, The Sculpture Center, Cleveland, OH

   Summer Show, Jonathan Frost Gallery, Rockland, ME

2011   *Big Art 2*, Emerson Umbrella, Concord, MA

   Contemporary Sculpture, Chesterwood, Stockbridge, MA

   Grounds for Sculpture, Trenton, NJ (through 2014)

   Strand, Boston Sculptors Gallery, Boston, MA

   Summer Show, Jonathan Frost Gallery, Rockland, ME

   Summer Show, Mill Brook Gallery, Concord, NH

2010   *On/Of/Like/AboutPaper*, Boston Sculptors Gallery, Boston, MA

   Sculpture Scoop, Boston Sculptors Gallery, Boston, MA

   Show, Mill Brook Gallery, Concord, NH

Gom (Bear), 2008
Granite
39⅜ x 27⅝ x 71 in. (100 x 70.2 x 180.3 cm)
Ilsan, South Korea

2009   *Personal Icons*, Capital University, Columbus, OH

        Summer Show, Mill Brook Gallery, Concord, NH

2007   *Recent Acquisitions*, The DeCordova Museum and Sculpture Park, Lincoln, MA

2006   *Celebrating 25 Years*, Keny Galleries, Columbus, OH

        DeCordova Sculpture Park, Lincoln, MA (through 2010)

        Figuratively Speaking, Art in Public Places, Stamford, CT

        Recent Print Acquisitions, The DeCordova Museum and Sculpture Park, Lincoln, MA

2005   *Bronze*, Vermont Gentlemen's Foundry, Concord Art Association, Concord, MA

2004   *Collection*, Connection Art Complex Museum: Duxbury, MA

        Summer Show, Hammond Harkin Gallery, Edgartown, MA

        Summer Show, Nan Mulford Gallery, Rockport, ME

2003   *Lifeforce*, The Schumacher Gallery, Columbus, OH

        Summer Show, Nan Mulford Gallery, Rockport, ME

2002   *Carin Croft Gardens Sculpture Show*, Carin Croft Gardens, Dover, MA

        Summer Show, Nan Mulford Gallery, Rockport, ME

2001   *Carin Croft Gardens Sculpture Show*, Carin Croft Gardens, Dover, MA

        Summer Show, Nan Mulford Gallery, Rockport, ME

2000   *Cambridgeport in 3D*, Stebbins Gallery, Cambridge, MA

        Sculpture Works, The Society of Arts and Crafts, Boston, MA

        Summer Show, Nan Mulford Gallery, Rockport, ME

1998   *October Show*, Acacia Gallery, Gloucester, MA

1997   *Spring Sculpture Show*, The Happy White Gallery, Barrington, RI

1996   *Sculpture '96*, Virginia Lynch Gallery, Tiverton, RI

1994   *Sculptures in the Landscape*, Four Corners, Tiverton, RI

1992   *Art and Context: Successful Integration*, The Boston Society of Architects, Boston, MA

1991   *Fourth International Shoebox Exhibition*, University of Hawaii, Honolulu, HI

1990   *Contemporary Sculpture*, Chesterwood, Stockbridge, MA

1989   *Tools, Instruments, Implements, Utensils*, San Francisco Airports Exhibition, CA

        Creative Collaborations-Artists/Architects, Cambridge Art Association, Cambridge, MA

1988   *This Is Your Garden*, Federal Reserve Bank of Boston, Boston, MA

1987   *Modern Forms/ Archaic Echoes*, Victoria Munroe Gallery, New York, NY

1985   *Sculpture the Language of Scale*, Bruce Museum, Greenwich, CT

        Smart Art, Carpenter Center Harvard University, Cambridge, MA

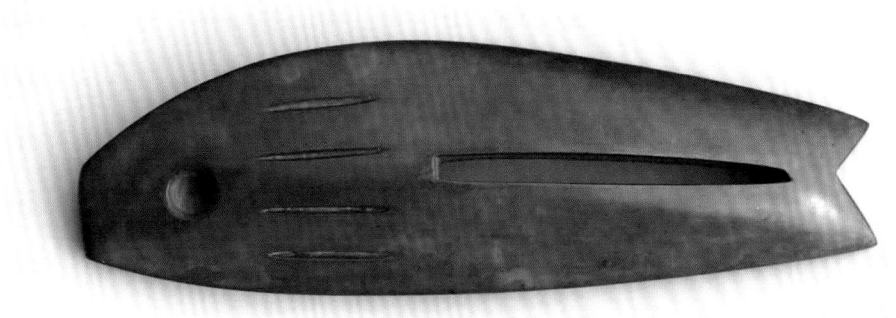

1984	*Do Touch, Society of Arts and Crafts*, Boston, MA
	The Human Form Explored in Sculpture, Fitchburg Art Museum, Fitchburg, MA
	Sculpture Trends, Lopoukhine Gallery, Boston, MA
1983	*Interim 1*, Chesterwood Studio, Stockbridge, MA
1981	*Summer Show*, Clark Gallery, Lincoln, MA
1980	*Fellowship Exhibition*, Museum of Fine Arts, Boston, MA
1979	*Summer Show*, Ehrlich Gallery, New York, NY
1978	*100 Years of the Museum School*, Museum of Fine Arts, Boston, MA

Fish Man, 1979
Bronze, 6$\frac{13}{16}$ x 2$\frac{3}{16}$ x $\frac{13}{16}$ in.
(17.30 x 5.6 x 3 cm)
Collection of the artist

Fish Man was one of the bronzes exhibited at Haines's first solo show, *Artifacts*

SOLO EXHIBITIONS

2023	*Archaic Echos*, Boston Sculptors Gallery, Boston, MA
2021	*Visitors*, Boston Sculptors Gallery, Boston, MA
2018	*More Fish Than Usual*, Boston Sculptors Gallery, Boston, MA
2016	*Mostly Heads*, Boston Sculptors Gallery, Boston, MA
2014	*Teddy Bears' Picnic*, Boston Sculptors Gallery, Boston, MA
2012	*Elements and Compounds*, Boston Sculptors Gallery, Boston, MA
2009	*Elements Converging*, Boston Sculptors Gallery, Boston, MA
2007	*Abstraction*, Boston Sculptors Gallery, Boston, MA
2005	*New Work*, Boston Sculptors Gallery, Boston, MA
2002	*Collections*, Columbus College of Art & Design, Columbus, OH
	Recent Sculpture, Keny Galleries, Columbus, OH

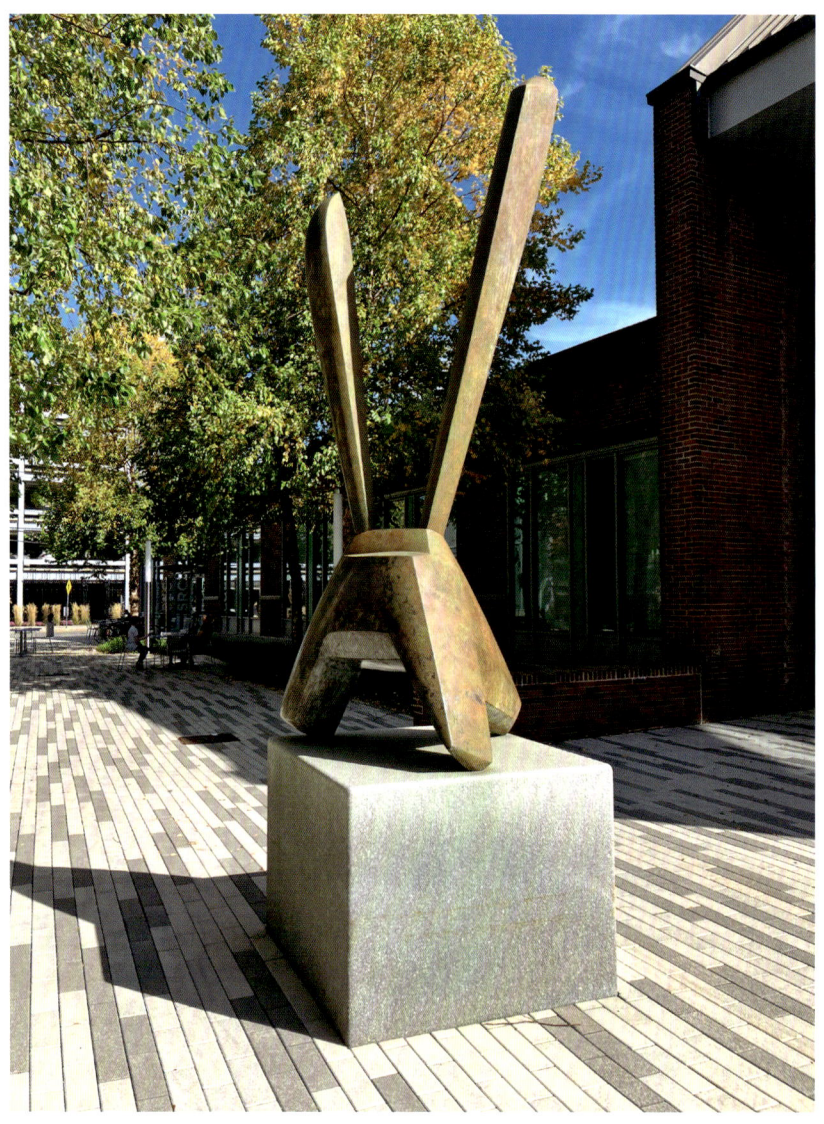

Rabbit Has Landed
Bronze
9½ x 4 x 4 ft. (289.5 x 122 x 122 cm)
Sidney Research Campus,
200 Sidney Street

2001	*Peter DeCamp Haines*, Boston Sculptors at Chapel Gallery, Newton, MA
1999	*Peter DeCamp Haines*, Boston Sculptors at Chapel Gallery, Newton, MA
1998	*Recent Sculpture*, Keny Galleries, Columbus, OH
1997	*New Bronzes*, Boston Sculptors at Chapel Gallery, Newton, MA
1996	*Peter Haines Bronze Sculpture*, Keny Galleries, Columbus, OH
1995	*Objects and Narratives*, Boston Sculptors at Chapel Gallery, Newton, MA
1994	*Peter Haines Bronzes*, Glen Street Gallery, Yellow Springs, OH
1993	*Bronze*, Boston Sculptors at Chapel Gallery, Newton, MA

1992   *Peter Haines*, Episcopal Divinity School, Cambridge, MA

1991   *Peter Haines New Bronzes*, Gallery on the Green, Lexington, MA

1989   *Peter DeCamp Haines*, Victoria Munroe Gallery, New York, NY

1990   *Bronzes*, Sally Windels Gallery, Columbus, OH

1986   *An Archaeology*, Laumeier Sculpture Park, St. Louis, MO

1982   *Bronze*, Sculpture Society of Arts and Crafts, Boston, MA

1979   *Artifacts*, Impressions Gallery, Boston, MA

LARGE COMMISSIONS

2013   *Qingdao/Seoul Sculpture Symposium*, Jimo City, Shandong, China

2008   *Goyang Sculpture Symposium*, Ilsan, South Korea

2003   *International Sculpture Symposium*, Fuzhou, China
            Long-Eared Unicorn, The Columbus School for Girls, Columbus, OH

2000   *Rabbit from Another Planet*, Lyme Properties LLC, Cambridge, Cambridge, MA

1995   *The Dow-Winslow Award Bronze*, The Rotary of Cambridge, Cambridge, MA

1991   *The Presidential Award Bronze*, Arthur D. Little, Cambridge, Cambridge, MA
            The Viking Award Bronze, The Columbus Academy, Columbus, OH

1988   *The Landmark Suite*, The Stubbins Associates, Cambridge, Cambridge, MA

1982   *Antelope on a Bridge*, The Piney Woods School, Jackson, MS

COLLECTIONS

Chemical Bank, New York, NY

Cheng Yunxian Museum, Nanchang, China

Dana Farber Cancer Institute, Boston, MA

Danforth Museum, Framingham, MA

DeCordova Museum and Sculpture Park, Lincoln, MA

E.F. Hutton, New York, NY

Fidelity Investments, Boston, MA

Fuller Craft Museum, Brocton, MA

Huntington National Bank, Columbus, OH

Marriott Hotel, Boston, MA

Raytheon Co. Lexington, MA

Vero Beach Art Center, Vero Beach, FL

First Edition

© 2025 The Artist Book Foundation

Published in the United States by The Artist Book Foundation
1327 MASS MoCA Way, North Adams, MA 01247

Distributed in the United States, its territories and possessions, and Canada by National Book Network, Inc.

Distributed outside North America by National Book Network, Inc.

Publisher and Executive Director: L. Pell van Breen
Art and Production Director: David Skolkin
Design: Irene Cole
Editor: Deborah Thompson
Proofreader: Nicole Barone
Printed in Italy

Library of Congress Cataloging in Publication Control Number: 2025007187

Library of Congress Cataloging-in-Publication Data

Names: Rathbone, Belinda, author.
Title: Peter DeCamp Haines : sculpture, 1975-2024 / foreword by Murray
   Whyte ; essay by Belinda Rathbone.
Description: First edition. | North Adams, Massachusetts : The Artist Book
   Foundation, [2025] | Includes bibliographical references.
Identifiers: LCCN 2025007187 (print) | LCCN 2025007188 (ebook) | ISBN
9798987228289 (hardback) | ISBN 9798992169409 (ebook)
Subjects: LCSH: Haines, Peter, 1942---Criticism and interpretation.
Classification: LCC NB237.H233 R38 2025 (print) | LCC NB237.H233 (ebook)
   | DDC 730.92--dc23/eng/20250228
LC record available at https://lccn.loc.gov/2025007187
LC ebook record available at https://lccn.loc.gov/2025007188

ISBN: 979-8-9872282-8-9
eISBN: 979-8-9921694-0-9

COVER
Fish Riff, 2018
Bronze
15 x 6 3/16 x 2 5/16 in. (38.1 x 15.7 x 5.8 cm)
Private collection

PP. 4–5
The artist's studio

P. 7
Bird Man, 2009
Bronze
34 5/16 x 14 5/16 x 11 in. (87.1 x 36.3 x 27.9 cm)
Collection of the artist

P. 8
Doggie Dragon, 2016
Bronze
8 5/16 x 8 x 4 3/8 in. (21.1 x 20.3 x 11.2 cm)
Collection of the artist

PHOTOGRAPHERS
Bruce Rogovin, Stewart Clements, and Will Howcroft Photography

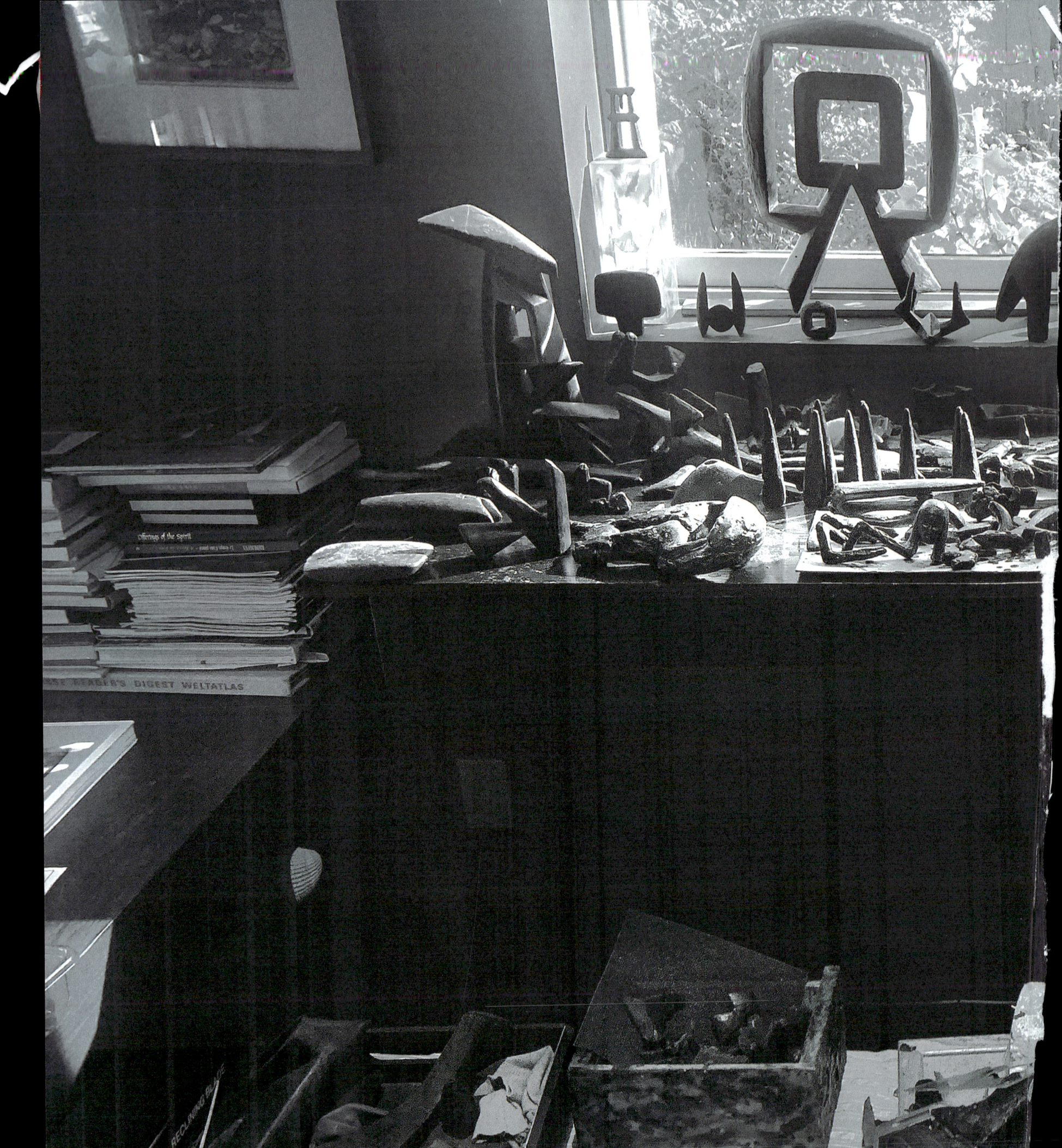